WHAT THEY DON'T TEACH YOU
IN SALES SCHOOL

WHAT THEY DON'T TEACH YOU
IN SALES SCHOOL
SALES 101

TONY REA

iUniverse LLC
Bloomington

WHAT THEY DON'T TEACH YOU IN SALES SCHOOL
Sales 101

iUniverse books may be ordered through booksellers or by contacting:

iUniverse LLC
1663 Liberty Drive
Bloomington, IN 47403
www.iuniverse.com
1-800-Authors (1-800-288-4677)

Because of the dynamic nature of the Internet, any web addresses or links contained in this book may have changed since publication and may no longer be valid. The views expressed in this work are solely those of the author and do not necessarily reflect the views of the publisher, and the publisher hereby disclaims any responsibility for them.

Any people depicted in stock imagery provided by Thinkstock are models, and such images are being used for illustrative purposes only.
Certain stock imagery © Thinkstock.

ISBN: 978-1-4759-9375-2 (sc)
ISBN: 978-1-4759-9376-9 (ebk)

Library of Congress Control Number: 2013910218

Printed in the United States of America

iUniverse rev. date: 07/11/2013

To my father, Tony, who deeply inspired me
to appreciate what it takes to be a true salesperson.

CONTENTS

PREFACE

We are all salespeople, whether we know it or not. If you talk to people, you sell. If you ask for something, inquire how someone is doing, or try to influence someone to make a decision, you are selling yourself, your wishes, or your opinions. We do this every day of our lives but are mostly unaware of it as a distinct process.

Some people do it better than others. Others learn how to do it over time. People who have good personal skills can sell. Developing sales skills can make you more comfortable around people and, in doing so, help you become a better person. Even if you don't think you understand what selling is, you really do know how to sell. You're just not consciously aware there is a process to follow.

Why don't high schools and colleges teach sales? Some have curricula on sales, but there is a glaring lack of these studies in most educational institutions. Most people who get into sales have a background in something else—business, psychology, sociology, teaching. They all have one thing in common: good interpersonal skills.

But don't think you can't be a good salesperson if you haven't studied it. One of the greatest things about a career in sales is that it's truly based on performance. It's one of the few careers where politics is important, but producing results is tops. If you can produce results, that's 99 percent of the game.

What you need the most is practical advice, the kind you can only get on the job. I wrote this book because I didn't think there was any compendium of business and sales topics that offered simple guidance and explanations. Looking back, it would have been valuable to me to have a book like this when I started my first job as a salesperson.

This book is a go-to reference for advice on situations, business taxonomy, politics, and basic rules of the sales life. Consult it to get creative ideas, seek advice on a dilemma, or discover something you didn't know before. Much of this stuff will be handy to the person who is learning about sales and the sales environment. Some people will find the information to be useful in life as well as sales. This is no coincidence. Sales have taught me many great lessons about life. I consider the two inseparable.

I want to mention that this subject is limitless in its depth. I could write forever about sales. Maybe I will. I make no claims that this book is definitive on all sales subjects. I tried to cover as many topics as I could, but in reality, I think about more to add every day. So if you have ideas, let me know what they are. Send feedback to my website at salestony.com.

Almost all of the examples are from actual situations I personally experienced. I left out names of people and companies intentionally, just because some of the situations are not very flattering. The point of illustrating these things is to help you understand something better. Mentioning names only adds needless distraction.

In the text, I refer to "customers" and "factory people." Factory people are the ones you deal with in your company. Customers are the people you do business with outside of your company. The word "factory" may give the impression of a big company, but in the context of this book, it means any size company, public or private, small or large.

One of the most important skills of a good salesperson is the ability to understand how people will behave. This comes in handy when you need to understand how someone will react to a given situation. Knowing how the customer will respond helps you to fine-tune your persuasion. Chances are, if you're in sales now or are thinking about it, you have an innate ability already.

The idea that every person has two personalities—conscious and unconscious—is something that most salespeople do not understand. I've added an introduction just for the purpose of presenting this concept. Though it may be controversial, my real-life experience has shown me that there is something to it. Understanding this duality helps you see more deeply into motivations and behavior.

The introduction is a mixture of my personal experience and education in psychology. It does not represent the current thinking in psychology, only my opinion of what works for me and what I think will work for you. If you can improve your ability to understand people, why not do it?

There are great salespeople and there are salespeople who have the potential to be great. This book is for both.

THE CONSCIOUS AND UNCONSCIOUS PERSON

Every person you deal with—customer, friend, relative, lover, wife, whoever—has two distinct personalities. They are two people. We can call these two beings the *conscious person* and the *unconscious person*.

The conscious person is easy to read. You can see and hear the conscious person directly. This is what you, as a person, are conscious of, what you perceive as reality. What you are thinking right now is the conscious you. The conscious person can articulate why he or she does most things. Conscious persons have the perception they are in touch with what and why they do things. This is true most of the time.

However, there are times when people can't tell you why they did something. More interestingly, they may not even be aware they are doing something in the first place. The unconscious person is someone who you, as a person, are not aware of, but it is contained within your personality.

There is linkage between the conscious and unconscious person. Feelings are one of those links. There are indicators, but most are transparent to the conscious person because he or she doesn't know how to read them. You can't see what the unconscious you is thinking. The unconscious influences the conscious by making us do things or feel things for reasons we may not realize. Just as you are aware of what you're thinking, the unconscious is also thinking things, but these things are hidden from conscious thought.

Sometimes the unconscious drives conscious behavior without the conscious person knowing. If you are conscious of something you do, you can explain why you did it and what you did. When the unconscious takes over, you may not be conscious of why you are doing something or even what you are physically doing. It can be that powerful.

The unconscious person drives behavior because it has other, deeper reasons for behaving the way it does. It can seize control because it is threatened and perceives the need to survive. Usually the reasons are related to strong internal conflicts that haven't been resolved and the frustration and the strong desire to protect oneself at any cost.

Interactions with people that trigger fear, jealousy, loathing, or a perceived threat can make us do things to protect ourselves that our conscious mind isn't aware of. Chances are good these issues are related to family or things that have deeply affected us in some way and are buried so far down that they're forgotten. Problems arise because painful issues like these can't be put away without consequences.

Not all unconscious behaviors are due to deep-seated issues. Sometimes they can be relatively superficial but still involve uncomfortable problems you decided to ignore. You can't make issues go away. You can choose to deny issues, but all that does is bury the problem and create an internal conflict—and then the unconscious will deal with it.

When that happens, the issue can surface as another problem seemingly completely unrelated to the one you are in denial of. You'll have no idea why you are having this problem. This can be very confusing for people. It's why they seek therapy—to discover why they are doing or feeling things for reasons they can't explain.

The unconscious person is immensely and clearly perceptive, maybe even more so than the conscious person. People who are not perceptive as conscious persons can have razor-sharp unconscious selves. No matter how unperceptive you think someone is, you can bet his or her unconscious is reading everything with crystal clarity. The unconscious will see through almost anything. Because of the separation between the two, the conscious person may never perceive something the unconscious person sees.

For example, if someone is trying to manipulate you or fool you, your unconscious will clearly see the strategy. If the person who is trying to manipulate you is very good at it, you may not be consciously aware of it—but your unconscious will be aware. If you are in touch with your unconscious, you will feel uncomfortable about what is happening and realize something is wrong, even if you can't put your finger on it. Your gut is a good unconscious indicator. If you are out of touch with your unconscious, you won't be able to connect the warning signals that something is wrong. This means people can do things they are completely unaware of. They can even pass a lie-detector test when asked if they did something their unconscious drove.

The unconscious can be an unfair judge of people and their motivations. It has its own way of interpreting the world, and it's out of a person's conscious control. An unconscious person can be vengeful and full of rage. Problems in childhood can shape how adult unconscious persons interpret the world around them.

When the unconscious person is out of balance with the conscious person, there are personality issues. A troubled unconscious person can be a problem. When you couple this type of unconscious personality with its ability to clearly perceive the outside world's intentions, you get paranoid thinking that can be extremely suspicious and judgmental. When the unconscious personality is in this state and interprets a threat, it can come out as intangible feelings of untrustworthiness or other types of distrust.

The unconscious is a master at protecting itself, so it is inherently distrustful. Protection and defense are paramount. The unconscious can affect the judgment of the conscious person without him or her knowing it. This influence on the conscious person will be subtle but powerful. That's why it's important to pay attention to the things the unconscious person looks for when you interact with a conscious person.

It's good to know when you deal with people if things they do are conscious or unconscious behaviors. Conscious behaviors can be dealt with easily; unconscious behaviors are difficult to deal with, as the person doesn't know why or what they're doing. If you bring it up, the individual won't know what you're talking about. Direct confrontation is a bad idea and can jeopardize your relationship with the person.

The best way to work around unconscious behavior is to avoid direct confrontation. If you confront a person about his or her unconscious behavior, you will cause the person to become defensive (not good), and you may run the risk of becoming a target of his or her unconscious. So a good rule to follow is, if you are going to address someone about a particular behavior, make sure you know whether it's conscious or unconscious.

Understanding the concept of the unconscious person is vitally important to how you relate to people; if you're in sales, it gives you an edge. You can influence, persuade, and have better relationships with people. If you don't understand the unconscious person, you will be selling with one eye closed. This can mean lost sales, superficial relationships, stagnation in deals, and even alienating someone without knowing what you did. You might not even know this is happening to you, and surprisingly, the person doing it to you might not know it either.

Carl Jung, the Swiss psychotherapist who, along with Sigmund Freud, established psychoanalysis as an institution, is quoted as saying, "The unconscious mind of man sees correctly even when conscious reason is blind and impotent." As a salesperson, everything you do with a customer is dependent on that individual's conscious and unconscious personality. The unconscious personality can be very black-and-white about issues, wildly opinionated, and quick to judge. The unconscious person can be completely different from the conscious one.

If you aren't careful about how you look, act, and perform, you can be blocked from reaching your goal by a ghostlike adversary you've unintentionally slighted. It could be as simple as dressing a little too different or being a little less professional or conservative than you could. The most subtle things you do can be a trigger. The rule is to be aware of the unconscious personality.

Everybody has the ability to be good at reading people. The problem is that many of us are disconnected from our unconscious, which communicates through feelings and other subtle messages to our conscious minds. Some people don't even know these messages are coming upward to their consciousness. Over two-thirds of our communication is nonverbal. Much of what we say isn't even said with words. It's the unconscious person who delivers the dialogue of nonverbal communication.

One way or the other, we are all students of psychology. People are social animals who behave in complex ways. Some people aren't very good at understanding this behavior and others are. As a salesperson, you probably have a natural understanding. You may be able to figure out why people say and do things. The better you are at this, the more effective you'll be. Your attempts to influence others will be more successful, and you will be a more versatile and competitive salesperson. You'll find both personal and professional advantages to this understanding.

The salesperson who has an eye for dealing with two personalities for every person can be more effective than the salesperson who is unaware of it. At times, the unconscious will communicate very clearly through nonverbal behavior. You communicate nonverbally too. The way you dress, use body language, comb your hair, maintain eye contact, shake hands, show up on time, behave dependably, return phone calls, complete action items, show your trustworthiness, and hundreds of other things is what you really say to the unconscious person.

The attention you pay to the little things is often more important than what you say. If you make an effort to communicate to both the conscious and unconscious person, you will be far more successful in what you do. That awareness is the basis of much of the sales advice you'll read in this book. It's something to always keep in mind.

CHAPTER ONE

GROOMING

The Basics of Personal Care

A salesperson has to jump into an immersive environment of people. Interacting with and influencing people is your specialty. How you look and the way you behave is one of the most important factors in how successful you can be. Before you take the role of a salesperson, you'd better look and behave like a normal human being. One of the most basic requirements for that is good grooming.

Hygiene

The rules are simple here. You want to minimize distractions to selling. If something about your appearance is distracting, it could derail your best efforts. Why chance it? Always remember: something that is trivial to you may be hugely significant to someone else. Hygiene is well within your control. Make sure it doesn't become the primary focus for your customer. You don't want to become the butt of jokes after you leave.

I know of salespeople who have various issues with hygiene, including bad breath; excessive nose, ear, and facial hair; brown teeth; or greasy hair that makes them look like they never shower. This may sound silly, but some people never got good training when they grew up. They might also be lazy or depressed.

Breath

Make sure you are aware of the state of your breath. Don't expect people to tell you if you have bad breath. There is something in our society that makes people very uncomfortable about doing that. I know some people who are unaware of their breath issues and nobody seems to be telling them about it. Personally, I only do that for people I am close with. (A friend is someone who tells you your breath is bad.)

Bad breath can be a detriment with customers. In an interview, it can kill an opportunity for you. I know of salespeople customers joke about because their breath is so bad. It's insensitive, but it happens. I am not a dentist, but I know there are several reasons for bad breath. These include lack of dental hygiene, infrequent dentist visits, plaque, and other mouth-related issues.

A problem with your breath can build up gradually, and you may not notice it right away. If you think you have bad breath, ask someone close to you to confirm it. Then go to the dentist and ask what is going on. If you are in denial about it, that's a bigger problem. The lesson is to take very good care of your teeth and visit the dentist regularly. This is very important not only for your job but for your overall health. There have been many scientific studies that show people with good dental hygiene are healthier and live longer.

Food is another source of bad breath. Vegetables like garlic and onions should be avoided at lunch. Use good judgment when you have to eat before you visit a customer. Use mints or something else to clean your breath. Parsley is a very good breath freshener.

Hair

Keep your hair well trimmed. Not too long. No long sideburns. I am sure there will be a time when everyone will be wearing longer hair. If that happens, okay, but be conservative.

Remove excessive hair from your face and ears. I'm not telling you to pluck your eyebrows, even though I am sure some salespeople do. But excessive nose and ear hair can be distracting to many people.

If you have dandruff, get rid of it. Dandruff can be very distracting when you're meeting with people. Beards can be prime sources of dandruff, even short beards. I have seen bearded salespeople—otherwise clean guys—walk around with dandruff spread all over their chests. Yuck! There are many off-the-shelf remedies for dandruff. They are not all the same.

One type may not work and another may. You might not find anything that works. If you need to, see your doctor or dermatologist about it. But get it fixed.

Body

Shower every day using a good shampoo and soap. Use a washrag to scrub yourself. Clean your ears out. It's gross to casually look into someone's ear and see a big glob of wax or flaking skin. (You can tell that I notice detail—do you?)

Don't wear cologne or fragrances. Some people are allergic to them. When I first started in sales, I called on a friend from engineering school who was now a prospect. I liked a particular cologne and wore it. After a few minutes, my friend asked me if I was wearing cologne. I replied yes. He laughed and said, "Why are you wearing cologne in a business situation? Are you trying to date me?" I promptly stopped using it.

Feet

Make sure your shoes don't smell. I know people who have a chronic odor problem with their feet. Their shoes become radiators of terrible smells. This is easily managed by special insoles you can buy over the counter. This can happen to anyone. Over time, shoes will pick up enough bacteria to begin to smell.

Change your socks and underwear every day. Reusing socks is another way to get smelly feet and athlete's foot. If you get recurrences of athlete's foot, it may be because you aren't drying between your toes after you shower or swim. Athlete's foot is contagious. You can pick it up off floors or pass it onto a floor. If you get athlete's foot, there are good over-the-counter treatments for it. If you have a more serious case, your doctor can prescribe something to get rid of it.

Health Concerns

If you have a cut on your finger, make sure you wear a bandage. Some people may think a cut on your finger will give them AIDS. Many people are scared of AIDS, though they don't understand it. Shaking hands with a customer who thinks you could be passing on AIDS because you have a cut on your finger isn't a good idea. I know of several senior managers who are scared to death of people with cuts on their fingers.

If you have a cold, don't feel obligated to shake hands when meeting or departing a meeting. Explain to the people that you would rather not pass your germs to them. While most people don't think of this, I know a CEO who obsesses over getting germs from handshaking. Most people will appreciate your concern for them if you pass on the handshake. Just explain why.

Cold sores on your mouth can be distracting. Get them treated. There are some new over-the-counter medications that seem to work very well to heal the sores quickly.

Diet

Some diets can make your body smell or give you bad breath. I know of people who went on the Atkins diet and began to have a whole body smell that was unpleasant. You notice it when you are in a small conference room with the door shut. Also, garlic can make your entire body smell terrible. One time I went to a big company dinner at a posh downtown restaurant and ordered a big steak smothered with garlic cloves. It was delicious. The next morning, I noticed I smelled like I had fell into a septic tank. It was really bad. I stayed home that day.

In interactive business situations, if you offend someone based on lack of hygiene, you will never be told about it. You may be avoided in the future, and you will never know why. Worse, you may be the butt of jokes by others. Don't take a chance and trust that people will accept a hygiene problem. Have healthy grooming habits, and then you don't have to worry about it.

Good hygiene is essential to your health and necessary for interacting with people. Taking care of yourself is something most normal, healthy people do. Now that you're squeaky clean, it's time to eliminate any bad habits you may or may not be aware of.

Bad Habits and Stuff You Shouldn't Do in Public

There are some things people do consciously and unconsciously that are viewed as distracting and possibly inappropriate. As a salesperson, if you are doing these things, you may be viewed as uncultured, impolite, and generally a person others would prefer not to be around. Bad habits are very distracting and can derail your intentions. Some people will view bad habits as a symptom that the salesperson is lying or trying to hide something. Whatever the reason, people will perceive a bad habit poorly.

The best thing is don't these things around customers or in public—or don't do them anywhere at all. Some of these habits are symptoms of nervous displacement and may be very difficult to break. You may need to get some help to break them. There are several ways to do this. Self-help therapies can be audiotapes, videotapes, chemical treatments—the list goes on and on. Therapy can be helpful to eliminate habits that are harmful. Hypnotism and acupuncture are other possibilities, but I have no idea how effective they are. I have heard from people I know that hypnotism and acupuncture do work with some people and can be effective.

Some habits are unconscious methods of getting attention. These are habits of behavior that you may not realize you are doing. I have seen salespeople display all of these habits directly in front of customers.

Chewing and Biting

Some people chew on their lip over and over while they are talking or listening. If you do a lot of chewing, there'll be open sores on the lip. Both the chewing and the sores are distracting and uncomfortable to look at.

Nail-biting is a common habit. Sometimes people do it when they drive or are at rest. They may not do this in front of customers or other people, but the results—open wounds on the ends of the fingers—are obvious to the detail-oriented. With the fears over exposed blood and AIDS, customers may have a problem shaking a chewed-up hand.

Smoking

These days, smoking is looked on as a dirty, smelly habit that will eventually kill you. I don't smoke, and I don't know many salespeople who do. If you don't smoke and someone comes up to you who just had a butt, you can smell it easily.

Many customer buildings or grounds do not allow smoking. I see some salespeople hanging outside the lobby to get a smoke in even when the weather is really bad out. They look so miserable. Smoking is an addiction, and it takes a big effort to quit. Try to get help if you can't quit.

Drinking

If you like alcohol and control your drinking, that's fine. But make sure when you go out with a customer that you imbibe at a conservative pace. If the customer has a drinking problem, you need to be careful not to insult him or her, but try to keep yourself from getting stewed in front of that person.

Do you think you may be drinking too much? Try to stop. If you can't, you should look into therapy or some kind of treatment. Many people drink responsibly. There is plenty of information in the public domain about how to control it. For some people this is very tough to manage.

Chewing Gum

Chewing gum in front of people is rude and distracting. Only do it if your customer offers you some. If you are going to be in mixed company, do not chew gum even if it is offered. Make sure your car isn't littered with gum wrappers and other indications of your habit.

Attention-Seeking Behaviors

This is a class of behaviors where the salesperson has a tilt to the head when talking or some other "acceptable" behavior that borders on normal but is different enough to attract attention. For example, I know of a person who always begins a sentence with a muted chuckle when answering a tough question. She doesn't even know it's happening. The chuckle makes it seem as if she finds the question amusing even when it is very serious. If you are doing this kind of thing, you are probably not aware of it. People who do this often overlook it consciously, but unconsciously it is viewed as different and not normal.

Another example is affective speech. This is when you put too much emphasis on words in a sentence. Sometimes it can sound like slurring your words or ending a sentence by saying the words too quickly. Some typical ones to control could be

- clearing your throat excessively while you talk;
- prefacing sentences with "With that said," "To be frank," or "To tell the truth";
- stuttering before beginning a sentence;
- repeating introductory lines over and over;
- saying "ah, ah" to fill in between sentences;
- talking too loud or with too much enthusiasm; and
- talking too much or too long or taking too long to make a point.

Clothing

Wearing clothing that is too new or controversial is another attention-seeking behavior. Make sure what you wear is appropriate for the workplace. Not dressing completely—leaving button-down shirts unbuttoned, for example, or your shirt untucked—is just sloppy and very distracting. If you do these things, I would guess you don't own a mirror. Go buy one right away.

Not cleaning your shirts frequently is another potential problem. Though this may not be viewed as a bad habit, it can be an obsession. I know of salespeople who are so cheap they refuse to clean their shirts frequently. The shirts end up stained around the collar and armpit. They smell. Detail-oriented people notice these things. Dress shirts should be worn once and then cleaned.

Not Paying Attention

This is more subtle than attention seeking, but it's very distracting and disrespectful. There are salespeople I know who can't maintain eye contact because they are always looking away. Not maintaining eye contact is rude and telegraphs a lack of interest in the conversation. Always make sure you look people in the eye when they are talking.

Other signs of not paying attention that may cause customers to think less of you include doodling during a meeting and checking e-mails or texting in a meeting or even a face-to-face conversation.

Electronics

Speaking of e-mail and texting, your electronic devices can get you in all sorts of trouble if you don't use good sense. Set the ringer on your cell phone to mute before meetings. When people don't do this, it's very annoying. This is a good way to get demoted in the mind of a senior manager.

Smartphones can be set to vibrate when you receive an e-mail. I have seen salespeople who are in conversation with customers stop in midsentence, reach down and grab their BlackBerries, and look to see who sent the e-mail. This is downright rude.

I have been in meetings where people have digital watches that beep on the hour. This is nothing but sophomoric behavior. Don't allow alarms or ringtones to distract from the message you're trying to deliver.

Body Language

The nonverbal messages you send with your body language are very, very important. Holding your hands in a tight-fisted way or showing you aren't relaxed will unconsciously transmit you don't like meeting with whoever you are talking to. How you sit in your chair can telegraph you want to leave now. Typing on a computer in a meeting is rude because nobody knows what you are really typing about. This is an unconscious negative signal. Sitting too relaxed can be a turnoff. Taking a seat in the back away from others can signal you aren't important to the meeting. Look out for these other body-language no-no's:

- cracking knuckles, which is loud and obnoxious to some people
- scratching the top of your head too much or itching yourself
- picking your nose or some other self-grooming habit
- inspecting your nails—a clear signal you're bored

Conversational Habits

There are salespeople who never let someone finish a sentence. This is very irritating. Stop interrupting if you want people to listen to you.

Overuse of clichés is another bad habit. I know of a salesperson who ends every encounter with, "You got it!" with too much emphasis. Another says, "Keep the faith." It gets really boring. It can even be the source of joking behind your back.

Improper use of words is another concern. I had a boss once who used big words to impress me and others. Trouble was, he used the words improperly in a sentence. In fact, he didn't even know what many of the bigger words he used meant. It was amusing when he did this in front of me, but when he did it in front of customers, it was embarrassing. It made him look unintelligent. Though I tried to talk to him about it, he continued to do it.

Some salespeople have very nervous laughs. They sound sort of crazy. You know what that's like—too loud or too fast. Sometimes the salesperson laughs at almost everything the customer says. It could be too forced. This is unconscious cheap pandering and insults the other person if he or she is perceptive enough to see it.

Gross Behavior

Always cover your mouth with your sleeve when you cough or sneeze, not your hand. Think about it. I sneeze into my hand and then shake your hand. Gross! Not covering your mouth when you cough or sneeze is repulsive.

Also repulsive? Burping and farting. If you do this in front of customers, I can advise you to get a job in another profession.

And think about this: You go to the bathroom and return with wet hands on your way out of a meeting. Everyone is shaking hands good-bye. You shake their hands while your hands are wet. To the other person, it feels as if you peed on your hands.

Wolfing your food, talking with your mouth full, and wiping your mouth with your hands are also unsightly habits. If you did this at home, your mother would be all over you. Make sure you know how to present yourself as a cultured human being and not like an escaped animal from a circus.

The best advice here is to try to break the habit and present the most normal face you can to your customer. Using a behavioral gimmick to try to stand out is a mistake. Be considerate of others and try to have your manners in check. If you are really good at what you do, you will stand out naturally. Clean it up and behave like a balanced professional. The web and your friends are good sources of feedback.

So you've done a check on your bad habits. Maybe you figured out you were doing something you shouldn't and made a mental note to try to be aware of stopping it. While you're at it, do you regularly monitor your health and try to improve it? This is an edge that will make you a better salesperson.

Your Health

It's just common sense that if you are healthy, you can be on top of your game. You should be constantly aware of what is going on in your body and brain and make sure you take care of them. This way, you will have an edge over your competitors. There are some simple things you can do to keep in tip-top shape.

Take care of the physical you. Make sure you have good hygiene habits. Exercise regularly as recommended by a doctor, no matter what your age. Get yearly physicals, and make sure you manage any cholesterol, blood pressure, or other potentially bad health issues. Follow the advice of your doctor. If you don't like his advice, seek another doctor. Why go to a doctor if you won't take his advice?

I have visited doctors who are rude idiots. One time, I was looking for a new doctor. I needed a physical, so I asked a friend of mine. My friend highly recommended his doctor, and I made an appointment. The day came for my physical, so I went to the doctor's office. As I sat there talking with the guy, he began to fall asleep on me. I couldn't believe it. After he was done with the physical, he gave me what I thought was canned advice and left the room without saying good-bye. I could understand him being busy; I was fine with that. But I really don't think he was listening to me. I couldn't trust him to give me good advice. As a salesperson, you can tell a good guy right away.

The message is, no two doctors are the same. Make sure you get one you can trust. I wouldn't recommend seeing different doctors whenever you get sick. Try to consistently see the same doctor and/or nurse practitioner for all your issues so that they can keep your complete history. This could avoid complications arising from incomplete information because you went elsewhere for treatment.

Another good reason to visit the same medical office is if you are on more than one drug prescription, it will help you avoid a potential drug interaction mix-up. Also, use the same pharmacy for all your drug needs. The bigger chains watch out for drug-interaction issues with your prescription. If you go to more than one source, a potential problem may be missed.

See the dentist at least twice yearly, or as frequently as he or she suggests. Even though you might feel great now, there are issues that can affect you as you get older. Better to find out about them now rather than when it's too expensive or too late to do anything about it. If you don't know a good dentist, ask someone who will give you good advice. Ask your doctor who he goes to. A lot of medical studies point to a strong correlation between good dental health and overall health.

Your mental health needs care too. Don't believe the people (even the ones in your own company) who think it's great to be a workaholic. If that's what you think, well, good luck. I'm not saying to take it easy either—I expect you will bust your ass every week. But as you work hard, make sure you play hard. Balance of work and play are key to keeping a strong mind cruising. You should have outside activities that excite you. Whether it's family togetherness or riding the trails on a mountain bike, do something you can get passionate about.

When you get home from work, immediately change your clothes. Put on something comfortable. The switch in clothing sets clear boundaries between what is work and what is play. As soon as you change your clothes, do something for yourself. Spend some time with your family or, if you are single, do an activity that mentally recharges you. If you have a hobby or activity like going to the gym, go do it. Make sure you can relax after work is over. As a salesperson, you probably need to keep your cell phone and e-mail handy while you are relaxing. That's okay as long as you can mentally separate yourself while still being on call. You should have time to yourself every day.

Some people choose to work from morning until late at night. They do this every day. They work on the weekends. They've made a choice to not be with family or friends and spend all their time on work instead. These people can have very successful careers. They are driven. They can make a lot of money.

If you decide to work at a start-up, you will have a very busy schedule. It can be very demanding. Before you choose to work around the clock, make sure you are aware of the contingencies of your behavior. Make sure your spouse and children agree with what you are doing. Many times people who are driven to work all the time and have families rationalize that their families understand when in fact they don't. It is really an addiction. You can't expect that if you spend all your time at work you can have a strong relationship with your family. What you put into something is what you get out

The rule on spending your time is true for work as well as family. If you spend a lot of time at work, you can be very successful. If you spend a lot of time with your family, your relationships will be stronger and more fulfilling for all. If you are single, you have more of an opportunity work longer hours, but your private time will be affected. This can take a toll on you mentally. Even if you don't have a family, you still need to recharge your batteries.

As you get older, you might have a family and children. Be aware that having a family seriously impacts your entire belief structure on what is important to you. If you are single and working very hard and then get married and have kids, the world is going to change, and you are going to have to adapt to it. Otherwise, you'll be headed for a disaster. No matter if you are single or married with children, it's all about balance. Make sure you know what that is and how to do it. That is what life is about.

Good salespeople naturally keep their health strong. This is done by carefully balancing work and play, making smart lifestyle choices, and taking care of body and mind. Most everyone knows how to do this; it's just common sense. With all the information available, it's easy to know what you should do. It's up to you to make the choice to maintain your health. You know better than anyone what to do to stay strong and healthy.

So you work out, eat healthy, and are in good shape. Nice. Your head should be clear and you're feeling good and pumped. Your appearance to others is very important. It's a sign of whether you are to be trusted or not. You're clean, healthy, and in good shape. You're almost ready to interact with people. How are your manners? Can you sit down at a table and behave like a cultured person?

Dining Out

Most salespeople will have to entertain. You may have to go out to dinner or attend a formal gathering. We were all taught by our parents how to behave at the table. Not all of us listened or were instructed on higher, refined dining etiquette. You need to know how to use all the hardware you may find at fine restaurant to keep from looking like an uncouth slob. Some of your dinners may be with very polished and cultured senior managers. Not knowing how to conduct yourself at a formal dinner can block you from access to senior people.

Formal dinner settings can be intimidating, but in reality the rules are simple. Sit only after your host sits. If it is a dinner where your factory people are present, your host may be your senior manager. Depending on how controlling your senior manager is, he or she may expect you to do the honors. Usually, whoever is the highest in the pecking order is the host. Despite this, you may be expected to assume some of the hosting duties, such as selecting the wine, ordering appetizers for everyone, and of course, picking up the tab.

If you find yourself elected as host but are afraid to expose your lack of knowledge of fine wines or any complex dishes the restaurant may have, go ask a waiter to help you. As your waiter retreats, follow him or her out of sight. Don't worry about your guests; if they see you approach the waiter, they will think you are making some kind of special arrangement. Take your waiter aside and ask for help in deciding what wine to order and anything else you have questions about. Your waiter will figure out real quickly that the tip will directly correlate to the quality of help. If the waiter is good, he or she will make it look like you are an expert at the culinary arts, impressing your guests.

Preparation is a good thing also. For very important dinners, go in the day before and meet the waiters and maître d' (which means *headwaiter*). If you are making the arrangements for a customer dinner at a nice restaurant, check to see whether it has valet parking. If it does, make arrangements with the valet to park your customers' cars. If there is no valet, tell your customer exactly where to park. Supply maps or diagrams.

Make sure everyone knows how to get to the restaurant. If you think some people may not have a good idea, send out an e-mail to everyone with the information.

Utensils

The general rule is to use the utensils from the outside in. You can't go wrong if you do it that way. Dessert utensils are always above the plate, oriented horizontally. If there is a tiny fork on the right, it's for the appetizer. Your server may bring additional utensils after you finish a course. These utensils are to be used with whatever the server puts in front of you next. Sometimes there may be a very small spoon in the group of utensils. This is for the sorbet, which is served between courses to cleanse the palate.

Your bread plate is on your left. Your water glass is on your right. The red-wine glass will be wider than the white-wine glass. The wide mouth on the red-wine glass is so there is more exposure to air to let the wine breathe.

When you are finished, rest your fork on your plate. This indicates to the waiter that you are done with your course. He or she will take the fork and replace it with a clean one or place your used fork back on the table in front of you. If you drop a utensil on the ground, wait for the waiter and ask for another one.

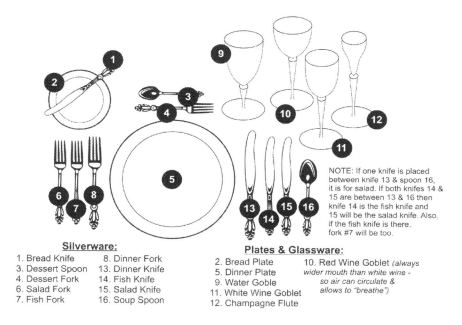

NOTE: If one knife is placed between knife 13 & spoon 16, it is for salad. If both knifes 14 & 15 are between 13 & 16 then knife 14 is the fish knife and 15 will be the salad knife. Also, if the fish knife is there, fork #7 will be too.

Silverware:

1. Bread Knife	8. Dinner Fork
3. Dessert Spoon	13. Dinner Knife
4. Dessert Fork	14. Fish Knife
6. Salad Fork	15. Salad Knife
7. Fish Fork	16. Soup Spoon

Plates & Glassware:

2. Bread Plate
5. Dinner Plate
9. Water Goble
11. White Wine Goblet
12. Champagne Flute

10. Red Wine Goblet *(always wider mouth than white wine - so air can circulate & allows to "breathe")*

Drinking

There are many options for drinking. Obviously, alcohol will be served as wine, beer, drinks, and after-dinner cordials. Keep in mind that one of your guests may be a recovering alcoholic and won't be drinking. Look for this information so that you can ensure he or she won't be forced into an embarrassing situation. Also, there are some religions that prohibit drinking alcoholic beverages. Carefully watch your guests for a sign they are abstaining from alcohol. Don't push drinking on anybody. If one of your guests decides to push someone to drink, try to mediate the situation before it becomes embarrassing for everybody.

At most dinners, mixed drinks and beer will be served first, and then wine with the meal. But that isn't always how it works. Sometimes your group may want to stay with mixed drinks and beer for the whole dinner, while others may want wine only. Make sure you ask your customers and factory people what they want. If wine is served at dinner, some will like white and others red. Rarely will all guests want only one or the other. You should pick a white and a red and have the waiter bring both for people to pick.

Selecting wines can be daunting, especially for a group of important, cultured clients. Know this: most of them have no idea how to pick wines, even though some may boast about certain wines on the menu. They will be watching you because they assume you are a wine connoisseur. Don't worry; all you need to do is act confident. If you are a newbie on wines, as mentioned before, privately ask for the staff to help you pick the wines and make you look good at it. If one of your guests seems to want to pick the wine—giving you nonverbal and verbal cues—let that individual do the honors if you want to. If you go to dinners a lot, invest in a quick course on choosing wines.

Don't drink too much. Nothing can hurt you more than imbibing excessively in front of customers and looking like an idiot. It will hurt your credibility and possibly your business. Drinking too much in front of your senior management can be career limiting. Should you be expected to drink with the boys but don't want to drink too much, you can arrange with the waiter to bring you a nonalcoholic drink every time you order an alcoholic one.

If one of your customers drinks too much, handle it carefully. You don't want to embarrass him or her. Arrange for alternate transportation if the customer is too drunk to drive. Do this very discreetly with the waitstaff. Most restaurants these days are accustomed to assisting customers who drink too much.

Some higher-end restaurants have a wine steward called a *sommelier*. This is your wine waiter. He or she will talk with you about the wines and make suggestions based on what you will eat. If you are uncertain about picking wines, approach the sommelier out of eyesight of your guests and ask him or her to help you with the wines without exposing your ignorance. Sommeliers do this all the time. Of course, after the dinner is over, you will be expected to give a generous tip for making you look so cultured.

Etiquette

There are some other basic dining etiquette dos and don'ts:

- Keep your elbows off the table at all times. At the end of the dinner, when the table is cleared, you can put your elbows on it. But that's it.
- Don't talk with food in your mouth. If somebody asks you a question while you are munching on something, hold up your hand to indicate you will done shortly.
- Take small bites and don't wolf your food down. Some people do this without even knowing how crude it looks.
- Your napkin should be placed in your lap after the first piece of food is placed on the table. It doesn't matter what it is or how small; as soon as the first piece arrives, the napkin goes in the lap. Usually this is the bread and butter, but it doesn't matter what it is. Some people will put their napkin in their lap when they sit. This is acceptable, but it is not correct protocol. If you are the host, you will be expected to set an example.
- Always hold your fork in your right hand if you are a righty or left if you are a lefty. When you cut with a knife, put the fork in your nondominant hand and cut with your dominant hand. Use the fork to stick and hold your food while you cut it. After you finish cutting, put the knife down and transfer your fork to your dominant hand. Always transfer the fork to the other hand after you cut. Never hold the food with the fork then swipe it into your mouth without changing hands.

If you have a large party, you may want to get up during the main course and briefly chat with everyone. Move around the table and have a brief conversation with each person. Don't skip anybody unless he or she is embroiled in a deep conversation with another guest.

Use your menu to communicate to your waiter. When your menu is open, an attentive waiter will interpret this as a signal you are not ready to order your food. Closing your menu indicates to the waiter you are ready to order. In most restaurants, when you close your menu or put it facedown, the waiter will appear to ask for your order, especially if you are the perceived host of a business dinner.

Toasting

You may want to make a toast. Study up on toasting. Most people are scared to death of toasting. Should you make a brief toast, some of your customers will admire you for doing it. A toast can be a simple line thanking everyone for being there, or be more centered on what business you are celebrating. You can even make a funny one as long as you are sure everyone will enjoy it.

If you attend dinners put on by other, more experienced salespeople, you will see how it's done. A toast can be on almost any subject. If there is a key person in your party, you may want to ask him or her to make the toast before the dinner.

Paying the Bill

When you are the one hosting (and paying for) a very expensive dinner, make sure you have the money to pay for it *before* you sit down. Nothing is more embarrassing than having the waiter return to inform you that your credit card won't accept the charges. Always a have a card with a lot of headroom for big charges. If you have credit problems, you can always bring cash. Always bring far more than you plan to spend.

Most high-end restaurants are very good at alerting the host his credit card has bounced without embarrassing him. Usually the waiter will whisper in your ear that he wants to talk to you and leads you to a private area where he can work it out with you. Sometimes credit cards are rejected for silly reasons, so it's always good to have a backup.

If you are a guest at a lunch or dinner and someone else is paying the bill, strongly resist the urge to gawk at the bill. Looking at the bill, especially while it is being paid, is rude.

Tipping

In most countries, you will be expected to tip. In higher-end restaurants, tipping happens often, and more people get tips. In the USA, a good tip for outstanding service is 20 percent of the total price of dinner. "As expected" service is 15 percent, and less if the service is substandard. The maître d' can get a good-sized tip if he or she gets you a special table, or nothing if all he or she does is hand your party off to a waiter. If you have a sommelier, that individual should be tipped. For larger parties, the restaurant will include the tip in the final bill. If you think the service was better than expected, add more to the tip. If it was below average, you might want to bring it up with the restaurant manager. Valets will need to be tipped too.

As you can imagine, the money will be flying out of your wallet at a good clip. Hopefully, your expense account will allow reimbursement for all these tips and the dinner. It isn't appropriate to ask for receipt for a tip, but your company should allow you to submit small cash amounts for reimbursement without a receipt. Tipping is one area this type of policy covers.

If you are new to entertaining, make sure you go to lunches and dinners where more experienced salespeople are the hosts. This is the best way to learn. The company culture will dictate certain acceptable ways of entertaining. It is at these company dinners that you learn the proper protocol for your culture, not in an etiquette classroom. If your business has you doing a lot of entertaining, you might consider taking courses in selecting wines and other liquors like the scotches.

Every country has its particular way of conducting dinners. Should you be traveling to another country and having lunch or dinner with an important customer, do your research up front. Not only use the web, but if you have access to friendly peers or others in the country, ask them for help understanding local customs. Know your etiquette and be cultured. It's one of the fun parts of being a salesperson.

Since you are entertaining, you will have to make conversation. Being a deeper, cultured person is a big part of making a strong statement to your prospects and customers that will make them want to associate with you. Being well rounded can give you a big edge against your competitors. Doing things outside of work is one way to make yourself a better person.

Outside Interests and Why They Are Important

Those who are dedicated to work and don't have time for outside activities are making excuses for a failed private life. If your job is the only thing in your life that has meaning, then you have no clue what life is about. It is vital to your spirit and self to meet your needs with activities outside of work.

A person who has outside interests is more interesting to talk to and more cultured. Customers will want to spend time with someone who can not only talk about work but is also passionate about outside activities. Salespeople who talk only about work are boring, and a customer will wonder why they have failed to have a private life. If you don't have an outside interest, get one. There has to be something you're interested in.

To figure out what would work for you, write down on a piece of paper some things you find interesting. Look at the list and try to imagine which of the things you could do outside of work. Do you like sports? Perhaps you like to skate and played hockey in school. There are leagues that businesspeople put together. Try one of those. You might also think about volunteering in your community. Many volunteer organizations would kill for a professional businessperson like yourself to add your two cents to their operation. If you like to teach, try volunteering at a local school. If you are the fatherly type, maybe being a Big Brother is for you. Museums are always looking for professional people to help with fundraising. Nonprofit theater is also an interesting place to volunteer, and it won't hurt your network, either.

All of these activities are rewarding and make you a more complete, cultured person. They also help you socially. If you are interested in a particular thing, it's likely other people similar to you are too. Be thankful that you are talented and have resources. Give back to the community. This will make you a far better person—and also a better salesperson with a bigger network.

I have personally volunteered all my life. I enjoy it, and I have made many friends over the years who I still keep in touch with. Customers are fascinated to hear some of the more unusual stories of my experiences.

You should read constantly. Heck, even reading romance novels or techno-thrillers can help you. Motivational books and sales-training books like this one can help you be far more effective. It doesn't matter what you read; just do it. There are huge amounts of reading material on the web. Sign up for online magazines, blogs, and other "push" and "pull" media. As a businessperson, you might want to sign up for a brokerage account and do a little trading. The information provided by your account can be invaluable to your job.

Overall, outside interests bolster your overall foundation as a human being and enhance your character. This makes you appear to be more experienced as a person. Being more experienced with life makes you a better person in private life and in sales. People enjoy associating with a more cultured, deeper person. They learn from you.

Your clothes also make a big statement about who you are, both consciously and unconsciously. Dressing improperly may keep you from ever reaching a goal. It's that important. Take heed. Your clothes telegraph who you are. Make sure you send the right signal and not an SOS. Time to don the uniform of the salesperson.

Dressing for Business

Ever since IBM's new manager, Louis Gerstner, changed the company from dark blue suits to casual attire, standards of how to dress for business have turned into a free-for-all. Friday casual has contributed to the confusion. It was so easy when it was just suits, suits, and suits. The only thing to worry about was which tie you were wearing. Clothing for women was more complex with colors, but it was still only business suits. These days, if you are a salesperson, you have to be careful about how you dress in this new environment. New York business attire is different from San Francisco. Tokyo is different from Paris.

My point here is not to give you a list of what to wear, but to make sure you don't take things too far. I have noticed salespeople who dress too casually for a job. To me, this could mean they have become mediocre, or they are clueless as to the message they are sending. I like it when I show up in a customer's lobby and see my competitor dressed too casually. Though this may seem like subjective judgment, it isn't. Being able to pick the right clothing for a customer visit is like knowing the right foods to eat.

When buying clothes, you should always select natural-fiber fabrics. No polyester or synthetics. Cotton for shirts; wool for jackets, slacks and suits; silk for ties. All-leather shoes from top brands. Don't be cheap with your clothes. Your outfit makes a statement that you feel good about yourself and you're successful. If you're cheap, it will show.

The question is, do you really know who you are dressing for? Some salespeople who dress down will say their customer is casual, so they should be too. On the surface, this makes sense. But they are missing something. Did you know your clothes are all about nonverbal communication? The unconscious person is more strongly influenced by clothing than the conscious one. What you wear talks to the unconscious person. If you dress down, you may be telling your customer's unconscious side that you don't care enough about him or her, or you aren't as professional as you should be.

It goes even further. Your clothes dictate where you stand in a pecking order. If you underdress for a meeting with someone who is dressed "above" you, you are in a weaker position psychologically. This is especially true in jobs of social interaction, such as sales and politics, where conscious and unconscious power plays are in constant dynamic interaction.

This is controversial, but even if you think there is only a slight chance I could be right, why risk it? I can read the body language of people pretty well, and I have seen the defenses go up when someone dresses too casually. You have to be aware of this when you consider what to wear. I am not saying you have to wear a suit all the time, but as a general rule, you should dress at least one notch up from what your customer is wearing. Knowing how to dress appropriately for customers is a fundamental skill.

Now you look the part. Nice. Time to go to work. But besides clothes, there is a bigger picture that broadcasts who you are and what you represent. Not only is how you dress important, but also the whole *you* that goes beyond the clothes. Part of the whole you is your car. Consider it an extension of your clothing. Your car, like your clothes, tells the unconscious person who you really are.

Your Car

Your car is a way station for business, and it is the chariot of a road warrior. It also makes a statement of who you are, both unconsciously and consciously. If you take customers out in your car, what you drive is important. How you dress should match the style of your car. There should be a balance between the two. Otherwise, a customer who sees you in a nice suit and then gets to your car and sees a piece of crap—or worse, a very dirty car—will note there is an issue. This is distracting, and it is something to avoid.

If you take customers out in your car, it should be a late-model four-door that is large enough to seat four people comfortably. The nicer the car you drive, the more successful you will look. Just as you keep yourself clean, you should keep your car clean too. Never transport customers in a dirty car. Never force them to push aside clutter to find a seat. It says you don't care about them.

Your car should be kept in good repair. Nothing is more of an epic fail than your car breaking down with a customer in it or, worse, running out of gas. Can you imagine the stories this customer will tell others about you afterward? Keeping your car in good repair and the gas tank full are very basic requirements. I hope you can see that.

You should make sure you have everything you need for yourself and any passengers who are with you. If you entertain customers, there are a few extra items you will need to carry with you. Below is a list of suggested items:

- first-aid kit—a good one—with vinyl or latex gloves
- small bottle of Purell in each door pocket
- tools necessary to fix a tire (your cell phone could be out of range)
- flashlight
- emergency reflector
- cold-weather package (if you are in a northern climate)
  - two or more space blankets
  - matches in two separate waterproof cases
  - string (colored)
  - blanket

- o   boots
- o   gloves
- compass
- Handi Wipes for all four seats
- Kleenex for all four seats
- change for tolls, or automatic toll-paying device (if your state has one)
- flares or road flasher
- breath freshener
- business cards (thirty to fifty) in glove compartment
- extra pens or pencils
- two pads of paper (small are preferred)
- GPS
- maps
- charger cable for cell phone (have two, one for briefcase, one for car)
- membership card for a car service like AAA
- hands-free earphone or headset for cell phone that secures firmly to your ear—one that you can leave in your car. Keep a separate one in your briefcase or pack.

Looks like you're set to go to work and start your first day on the job. You're almost ready to embark on your adventure as a winning salesperson. Let's just check to make sure you have it all down.

Looking Successful Is a Self-Fulfilling Prophecy

I drive a nice four-door late-model car that's big enough to seat four people and looks good. I wear nice clothes and make sure that all my sales tools—like my business pack, pens, and other things that customers see—are top quality. You can never go wrong with top quality. I like to look neat and professional.

Is this important? Well, obv ously, performance is most important in sales, but style counts. If you look at unconscious-person versus conscious-person perceptions, I truly believe that the "whole" customer wants to be associated with a successful salesperson, and his or her perception about what that is combines both performance and style.

Many people believe performance is all there is and everything else is fluff. But you can't ignore the power of style. Style appeals to the more primal and unconscious desires, and we all have these buried in our unconscious. Consciously, people will feel good about someone who looks successful. The root of some of these feelings is dictated by their unconscious motivations and desires. These aren't readily articulated by most people, and that is why style is controversial. Many people look at a polished person and admire his or her ability to color-coordinate and choose clothing, cars, and jewelry.

On an unconscious level, the primal instincts govern what is perceived as successful. This has nothing to do with the business objective and couldn't be further from it. These are powerful forces that are hidden deep within a person, and yet they push the person like a ghostly force to do what they want. They come to the surface of the conscious as masked feelings and desires.

A more polished person will look like a leader. That means that things like nice clothes and cars have an impact on a customer's unconscious desire to be associated with you. They will trigger associations of success, leadership, and power. This is very important and can be an asset to you. Performance and style go hand in hand.

Many salespeople can perform, but they don't understand style. Some salespeople rebel and purchase cheap cars and wear mediocre clothing. They will talk about how a cheap car doesn't intimidate customers and an expensive one does. Customers will meet and work with them. But when all else is equal, if one salesperson is polished and one is not, the customer will go for the more successful-looking competitor. This is an edge. You don't need the most expensive stuff or to go around flashing expensive jewelry. But you should look successful, and part of that is high-quality clothing, tools, and vehicles.

Looking successful will have an interesting effect on you. You will increase your cultural expertise and knowledge base. You will become worldly and cultured. Your ability to move in more diverse groups of people will increase. All this will expand you as a person and expose you to more things that contribute to your growth. Remember, style and looking successful are very important. They are a tool you should master to arm yourself against competitors and to build on your cultural strengths.

There are other things besides material objects that are even more powerful for you to master. Those things are inside you, and you have to figure out how to unlock them. Unlocking them is part of your path to self-actualization and character. These characteristics help unleash the abundant power you should be naturally radiating.

Now that you radiate success and have all the pieces together, it's time to buckle down and review some fundamentals.

CHAPTER TWO

GETTING STARTED IN SALES

Your First Day as a Salesperson

Your first day on the job is very exciting. Before you get started, there are a few things you should make a priority before you hit the road.

Benefits

Make sure you understand all the benefits the company offers. This includes employee stock purchase plans (ESPPs), "evergreen" plans, and other equity reward plans. I know one guy, we'll call him Peter, who worked for a high-tech company for many years. He was unaware—because he never asked and HR blew it by not telling him—that there was an employee stock purchase plan. The company's stock price was usually very low; it was in the single digits for many years, including when he joined. Years later, the market exploded and his company became a darling of the industry. The stock shot up from $6 a share into the $30-plus range. Many people who had been at the company about the same amount of time as Peter had enlisted in the ESPP and had been accruing stock for years at the single-digit price. When the stock exploded, they sold out, and some were able to retire early. Peter found out about the ESPP when he was talking to one of these people. They were saying good-bye to him as they gleefully discussed their good fortune. Peter wasn't very happy to find out he could have done the same thing.

If you're in a remote office, find out who the human-resource contact is and talk to him or her about it. Study these plans carefully and make sure they match your investment strategy. If you have questions about what to do, ask. I am stressing this because I have personally experienced companies forgetting to inform me of creative monetary plans that aren't usually offered in other companies. Missing out on one of these could leave you out of a potentially lucrative opportunity.

Technology

Check to make sure you get an e-mail account with an alias that isn't stupid or very difficult to type. Ask when your e-mail account will be activated. Test it. Get to know your IT (information technology) department, if your company has one. Treat these workers like family, as one day they will save your life.

Your company may buy you a smartphone and/or a notebook—find out if you have a choice. Get to know the e-mail client on the computer and your phone, if it supports e-mail. Get a contact database system and calendar planner. Maybe your company uses Outlook or some other software like it.

Find out who pays the bills for your phone and Internet access. Some companies take care of that, but others have you expense these charges. If you are going to use your personal cell phone for business calls, get a copy of an expense report with cellular calls on it. Some companies allow you to claim personal calls as a perk. From the beginning, you'll be making long-term relationships that will span multiple jobs. You want your contacts to be able to reach you anytime, even if you have a new job. If your manager is open and communicative, he or she will tell you about that.

There is a radio in smartphones that is used to establish your calls with the cell towers. The radios are based on certain strict standards imposed by the government of your country. Many countries have different standards for these radios. A smartphone that works in one country may not work in another. Sometimes these are referred to as two-band or three-band phones. If you travel to another country, you should check with your carrier or IT person to make sure your phone will work there. Also investigate whether there are excessive surcharges in the country you are going to. I have seen charges of thousands of dollars billed to unsuspecting salespeople.

Travel

If there is the slightest chance you may leave the country, go get a passport as soon as possible. In fact, you should just go get one anyway. Don't wait until you really need one. The lead time on passports can be up to several weeks. In some cases, you can get one in a couple of days, but you can't count on that. Why chance it? Passports work very well as identification for domestic air travel as well as international.

Find out what your company's travel policy is. If the company uses a particular travel agent, find out if there is a travel profile the agent keeps on the employees. Fill out the form and submit it right away. It may take the travel agency awhile to get your information in its computers.

If you have never flown, ask your manager to help you out. Sign up for the frequent-flier clubs for the airlines, rental-car agencies, and hotels. You never know when you might be flying somewhere.

Your company may have strict policies about which airline and rental car company you can use. Make sure you ask. You might hear they use American or Hertz or something like that. There may not be a strict policy but rather an unwritten one. If the company uses one type of airline all the time, you might as well try it. If you have an administrator who handles these details, it will make that individual's job easier.

Some companies will allow you to book business class for overseas flights. Others make you travel in the worst seats because those are the cheapest. I don't agree with insisting on the cheap seats. It demoralizes the employee. At least let employees fly coach in the aisle or window seat, not the center one.

Expenses

If you don't have a credit card already, you absolutely need to get at least two. I recommend a credit card like Visa or MasterCard and a charge card like American Express. If there is a problem with one card, you'll have a backup. Make sure the limit on the credit card is at least $10,000. Always keep good headroom on the card. If you don't want to use a credit card, use a cash card. Still, have a spare card even if you don't use it.

Perhaps your company will issue you a charge card for entertainment expenses. Make sure you understand how it works. Some company credit cards are actually issued under your social security number. Many companies won't even tell you they are doing this. You have the right to tell them not to give out your social security number. But these days, using the number is common practice. Just make sure they pay the bill every month.

There is a side benefit to having a company-issued credit card on your social security number. Many credit-card companies offer mileage points for every dollar spent. Because you'll be using this card to charge entertainment and possibly air travel, you'll reap a huge amount of points that will be owned by you. If you get a company card this way, make sure you enable the points system in your name.

If the company doesn't issue you a card, you will be expected to use your personal credit card for entertainment expenses. To be reimbursed, you will need to make out expense reports. Get a copy (probably electronic) and make sure you understand how to fill one out. Try to get a sample from someone that is already filled out. Have your manager give you one of his or hers as an example.

Your company may have rules about how much you can spend or some protocol about how you can entertain. Many times, there is an unwritten and unspoken protocol that allows a certain leeway in what you can add as an expense. This is called a *perk* or *perquisite*. If you find that your peers are doing this, you should look into doing it yourself. Just be cautioned that while many companies allow this unspoken flexibility, there are people who will abuse it. Using these people as an example may get you in serious trouble. You should make sure the person you are relying on for information about this is credible.

Some companies concentrate too much on regulating how much salespeople are allowed to spend and what they're allowed to spend it on. There should be rules about how a salesperson spends company money, but most of the decisions should be left to the salesperson. If a company is tight with expenses and tightly regulates how you can entertain, it doesn't trust its salespeople to make good decisions about what is right for the customer. Your manager should be able to explain the boundaries of how you can spend money for entertaining.

When you are interviewing for a job, try to find out about the company's expense policies. If one employer plans to tie your hands behind your back, consider another company. Entertainment is a strategic tool in your sales bag. Limits placed on how you can spend money also limit how successful you can be.

Getting Started

Your company may have an orientation session for you. Sign up for this right away. These are very informative, and you get a chance to network with people you may be working with.

Try to get as much data as possible about your accounts from everybody in the office and your company. Your manager will meet with you to discuss your account responsibilities; take careful notes. Ask your manager to prioritize what he or she thinks is important. Get lists of contacts with phone and e-mail addresses. There should be notes from the previous salesperson. If the company uses a customer relationship manager tool (CRM) like Salesforce.com, find out who the guru is on it and get to know him or her. Take the guru to lunch and build a good relationship. This person will save you on a regular basis.

Have your manager bring you in to the account and introduce you as the new salesperson. If the previous salesperson transferred to a different account, you might want that individual to introduce you to the customer instead. The hand-off of the salesperson is very important to get right. Your customers will appreciate the move, and it will help you get off to a running start.

Make sure you find out who the decision makers are in each account. Don't take anyone's word as law, even the past salesperson. That person may or may not have assessed the situation correctly. For the moment, though, this is the only data you have to go on, so work with it.

After you find out about your accounts, have your manager explain how your factory works and who the key contacts are. These workers are going to help you get things done for the customer, so the better you know them, the higher your value to the customer.

If your customers are local, you should ask your manager about good restaurants where you can entertain your customers. Talk with the other salespeople in the office about your accounts. You will probably get some good dirt about them. See if they have notes and organizational charts. Find out who the competitors are in your account. Get their names and look for them on the sign-in sheet in the lobby of your customer. Introduce yourself to your competitors—you never know what you can find out. Just remember to get more data than you give. (Some companies advise against speaking with competitors, as that can be construed as price-fixing. Follow your legal people's advice on this.)

During your first week or month, you'll be picking up where others left off. Your experience will be much like a detective getting all the clues to find out what is really going on. As I said before, don't think the data you get is law. Everything should be considered questionable until you verify it with the account yourself.

If your accounts are new and there is no history with your company, you will need to plan a way to get into them. Your marketing people could be helpful in getting you started. You should put together a sales plan outlining your sales objectives, which are usually based on your quota and how that is structured. Your plan should outline how you intend to find and qualify your accounts, move them through the funnel, and bring them to closure. (A sales funnel is a visual tool that captures a snapshot of the state of your business—see chapter 7). Closing an order may not necessarily mean a purchase order. It could be signing a contract. It should be related to how you get paid.

Always focus on how you get paid and the fastest way you can exceed your quota. If you get paid some salary and commission, the company will expect you to spend time doing sales activities not directly related to building your commission. Overall, your plan should be a direct map of how you get paid for your activities. Don't ever think that you are limited to the plan the company gives you. You should always be figuring a way to blow your commission away and make gobs of money.

Don't ever be satisfied with mediocre performance. Being a salesperson means you can be a mercenary if you have to. You should be a very clever expert at how to get around systems to make them work to your advantage. Be creative. Think of new ways to get more revenue.

Fill up your weekly appointments and get on the road as fast as possible. You can't close orders as well from a desk as you can in person. When you're in front of the customer, you get the real skinny about what is going on. You'll have conversations that a phone or e-mail can't possibly make happen, and you can carefully note the body language. Spend only off-business hours in the office unless there is something unique about your job. Just remember that if you are in the office, you're not in front of a customer.

There always is something to do. You could work twenty-four hours a day if you didn't need to sleep. This is how you should think. All of this is productive work. Never work on things that are not going to help you blow your quota away. Be focused on making money. Drive yourself. But always leave time for play. Make sure your play is as productive and intensive as your work. It should give you satisfaction and tremendous fulfillment. This will recharge your batteries so you can get back to work pumped up and ready to reach more goals the next day.

Find out what the company's vacation policy is. Plan vacations well ahead of time. Make sure it's really something you like to do. Be creative. If you work in a company office, they may have skeleton crews working the phones on the off-hours and holidays. If you can, pitch in and help. Be part of the team, but remember to focus on blowing your quota away. If you take some time off, make sure you are still available to get important messages. I don't even tell customers I go on vacations or take days off. I just limit myself to only receiving the important calls. Use caller ID, and if it isn't important, let the caller leave a voicemail.

For those times when you have to be somewhere you can't get e-mails, you can set up an automatic "I am out of the office until ..." announcement. But I think these messages are like having a sign that says you don't want to do business. You'd be surprised how few phone calls you get that need immediate attention. I'm not saying to ignore the phone. But if you're on vacation, you don't have to respond to every phone call. The message is to always be available for your customer and make sure you play during your playtime. It's okay to take a vacation in Neverland, but I always tell my manager where I can be reached if something important comes up. Most managers are good about this and don't abuse it.

Your first day will be full of many things you have to learn. Make a list of what you want to accomplish before you go in to work. Be upbeat and talk to as many people as you can. Tomorrow may be your first day dealing with a customer. If you know what to expect, you'll be better prepared. Understanding the sales cycle will adjust your expectations and allow you to take the next step with confidence.

The Sales Cycle

Selling is a basic step-by-step process.

Presales

1. Establish a relationship.
2. Determine need, unarticulated or articulated.
3. Explain how you can meet needs; establish value.
4. Ask and answer questions—this is how the customer understands you are meeting a need.
   - How much are they willing to pay?
   - When would they want it?
   - How many would they need?
   - Are there special conditions or legal requirements for delivery?
   - Do they need preestablished credit terms before you can take the order?
5. Ask for the order, get it, and leave.

Postsales

1. Make sure the order is delivered.
2. Study how the customer shops for, buys, uses, and disposes of the product or service.
3. Improve your service to the customer.
4. Build more relationships and start more presales cycles.

5. If there is a backlog of product, make sure it is continually filled by orders.
6. Discover more opportunities in the organization.
7. Go back to presales and start again.

If you follow this cycle, you will have a continuously full sales funnel. The above cycle is obviously simplified, but you are smart and can figure out how it might apply to your sales environment. Every salesperson has to do at least part of this list and cycle through it. Sometimes people call presales "hunting" and postsales "farming." Some companies hire salespeople looking for these clear distinctions in the people they hire. Usually they have large sales organizations and multiple people covering the same account, so they split the responsibility among the team.

Salespeople who classify themselves as hunters or farmers pigeonhole themselves. No matter how many salespeople you have on an account, if someone is a true farmer, you stand the chance of missing an opportunity if you turn that person loose in a big organization. He or she could completely overlook some new thing that presented itself because of a disruptive event. You want all salespeople looking for new opportunities. I don't understand how someone could really say he or she is a salesperson and not want to take purchase orders, close business, or discover a new opportunity with a customer.

I have called on customers with salespeople doing "buddy calls." Some of these guys were remarkable in how distorted their view of their job was. On one occasion, I was visiting a large network firm with a guy from a partner company. He claimed he was a superhunter. We went into the account and met several people. One of them was a high-level director of procurement. In conversation, the director asked the sales guy to help one of his buyers book an order—the buyer needed help with part numbers. The sales guy actually blew the director off, saying he didn't have time (to take an order!) and we had to go. When we got to the parking lot, I asked why we didn't go into purchasing and get the order. He claimed it wasn't his job; other people did that job, not him. As we got into his car, he told me his time was too valuable to take orders. I made a mental note never ever to visit a customer with this guy again. A few months later, he was canned.

Selling is a full-time position. It's about generating revenue for your company and making money. You are your company's face to your customer. It's your job to extract as much revenue as you possibly can for your company while making the most money your quota will allow. This means you have to be opportunistic in all situations and not personally bound by silly rules about what you can and can't do. Opportunities may present themselves at the most unusual times, and your job is to recognize what is going on and seize it. *Carpe diem*, baby. Book it.

As a salesperson, you are a conduit for getting the product or service out of the factory and to the customer for consumption. This is commonly referred as the *channel*. There are several types of channels.

What Is a Channel?

You've seen the commercials on TV. The pitchman is telling you how great a chemical cleaner is. All you need to do is call the phone number and give them your credit card and *bang*, the product is shipped to you. They make it so easy for you, the customer, to buy their product. But the people who do the TV ad don't make the cleaner. Those people were hired by the manufacturer to figure out the best way to make it easy for customers to buy the product. Those are channel people. That's the point of a channel: to make it easy for customers to buy your product so you sell a lot of it.

While this may sound simple, it isn't. Many companies build fantastic products and then never figure out how to make it easy for customers to buy them. Have you ever been frustrated because you wanted to purchase a product that's supposed to be on sale everywhere but when you look for it, you can't find it? That's an example of poor channel execution. People actually want to buy something and they can't. It sounds stupid, but it happens all the time. Some do it very well and others stink at it. Amazon, for example, is an incredible channel. It doesn't manufacture anything. It is only a channel, and a big one at that.

The simplest type of channel is a direct channel. This is where your customer buys directly from the manufacturer. Direct sales make the process of getting and tracking orders from your customer easy. Your customers like it because they have one call to make to get product directly from the manufacturer. So why doesn't everyone do this? It all depends on your product and the type of market you're in. It gets complicated to do it well. You will need salespeople to sell it. The salespeople will be responsible for creating and fulfilling demand. As long as this works, a direct channel may be the way to go.

There are problems with "going direct." Your customers may need product with "just in time" delivery, but your manufacturing lead time is over eight weeks. Your customers expect the delivery immediately, but manufacturing may take up to eight weeks to deliver it. Don't get on their case; they are doing the best they can. You need to have a buffer inventory. If demand is high, this means carrying a huge inventory. Your CIO won't want to hold inventory. If a bug is found in the product, the product has to go through a revision that makes all previous products obsolete. If there is inventory of older product, it may need to be purged. This costs a lot of money.

Your customers will make even more demands of supply. They may want the right to return unused product. If your competitor is doing that, you will have to do it to. Logistics systems in companies can be unpredictable. A salesperson wants to call in an order, but the customer wants the lead time before he orders. The salesperson calls and is quoted six weeks, and then tells that to the customer. The customer takes a day or two to get the purchase order to the salesperson. So two days later, the salesperson enters the order. But in those two days, a huge order came in from a high-profile customer that consumed production for ten weeks. When the delivery date comes back to the original customer, it is now out four or more weeks from when the salesperson quoted it. The customer is upset.

If your company ships large amounts of product to a few customers, a direct sales system will work well. But most manufacturers have both large and small customers. Your customer may be delinquent on a payment for understandable reasons. But your accounts-receivable people are detail consumed and seem determined to reject and piss off all customers as much as possible. Your customer goes on credit hold. Nothing will ship to them, and you find out the credit hold freezes all shipments to your customer, which will stop their production and ability to make revenue. Right after you find out about this, you get a call on your office line. Looking at the caller ID, you realize it's the VP of production for your customer. Your day is just beginning.

As my daughter likes to say, "Oh, joy!" Depending on how badly your factory treats your customers, an indirect channel may work more effectively.

On paper, an indirect channel seems the perfect solution to sell to your customer. The channel will hold inventory, provide order logistics, have a large a sales force, and manage terms of credit. They are the interface your customer sees for your company—other than you, that is.

The indirect channel can be a distributor, retailer, VAR (value added reseller), or any in-between resource that helps your customer shop, buy, use, and dispose of your product or service. A very important thing to know is that the channel creates "pull" pressure on your customer. If the channel wants something changed or a new product or feature, they will tell your customer to build it into the product or create a new product.

If you have a customers who are driven by their channel (most are), then you have the means to create a "push" campaign for your product. You go to your customer's channel, after signing them up with agreements including terms and conditions (Ts and Cs) for how you'll do business. Get some time with them and convince them that your product's features would make their lives better—but more importantly, everybody will be awash in huge amounts of cash. If you do a good job, word gets back to your customer to put your product in from the channel salespeople. You go to your customer and continue selling to them.

This is "pull" or demand creation. You persuade your customer your product or service is better than cold fusion. They get rabid and call the reseller and tell them they have to have your product. So you have harnessed the forces of "pull" and "push" to create an unstoppable force that converges to a purchase order for your product or service. This is a very powerful method of selling, and under the right conditions, you can take a marginal sales opportunity and turn it into a big success.

Indirect channels have their downside. Some salespeople think they can set and forget the indirect channel. They go in, present and train for a few hours, and then leave for more "important" tasks. The reality is that it takes just as much effort to manage an indirect channel as a direct channel. You have to closely manage the indirect channel. Sit on it. If you really understand how it works, it can be a powerful tool that multiplies your efforts.

I know many salespeople who think they are channel masters. The reality of indirect sales is that many people talk about how well they do it, but few really leverage it to its full potential. Even a moderate amount of effort will yield some decent results. You have to do training, buddy calls, training, more buddy calls, and favors, and you have to be very, very patient and spend a lot of time sitting on them. Develop a strategy together and set goals and objectives. Visit them on a regular basis.

Every indirect sales organization has distractions. This is a big problem. It's about you getting attention for your company's staff. Most indirect-channel companies like distributors and resellers have many lines of products. All these lines will be striving for attention. The bigger lines that drive large revenue will receive the most attention. If your product line is smaller, you will have to devise a cunning plan to differentiate it from the bigger guys. Many of these organizations are relationship based. Put on your entertainment hat. Use your expense account and convince these guys you should be favored. It's what you do, right?

While you're booking all this business, you may notice your to-do list is growing faster than you can manage it and demanding more and more of your time. Immediately you realize you just can't do everything on the list. Some things will have to be overlooked. But which ones? Time is your most precious resource. How you manage it is one of the most basic fundamentals of a successful salesperson. To manage your time, you have to learn how to prioritize. Do what's important first and leave the rest for later. Well, it's not that simple, but you know what I mean.

Prioritize

Nothing could be more important than reviewing your to-do list and prioritizing it. You will quickly drown and perish if you can't set priorities in an order that makes sense for you. Sales is all about setting priorities. It's a large part of what makes a successful salesperson. If you can't distinguish between the importance of two or more things to do, you might want to look at other careers.

First, you need to admit there is always too much to do. You could work twenty-four hours a day and still not have enough time. So the real art of being in sales is getting your priorities in the right order. The more meetings you have, the more data and action items you'll have.

Shortly after you start a sales job, your list of to-dos will quickly become overwhelming. This is where a good salesperson will shine, by knowing what is important and what can be put off.

I have heard many salespeople complain they work too long and don't have time for fun. If this is you, it could be you're not doing a good job prioritizing your work. There are a lot of books written on this. Sit back and reevaluate what you're working on. Consult a mentor or peer as to how they prioritize. Read up on it. The web has lots of information on the subject. Get advice if you still have trouble. Fail to solve this problem and you'll be overwhelmed, bitter about your job, and eventually out of a job altogether.

You can pretty much divide your work into two distinct priorities. Start by making a list of everything you have to do. Some salespeople use software to capture action items; others use pad and paper. It doesn't matter how you do it as long as it works for you. Once you make a list, the challenge is to decide what is important and what can wait.

The first and highest priority is the one that if it isn't done, your job could be in trouble. Maybe it's going to the customer to get a purchase order or getting back to your manager with the answer to a question. Life is about choice, and you need to make a clear distinction between important and less important. Once you tag the items that are of highest importance, arrange to get them done, making sure you're realistic about the time needed to complete them. You'll have to do some prioritizing among your top priorities.

Lower-level priorities may become high-level over time. This could happen if you've delayed a low priority too long, and now it must be completed. In reviewing your list, if you discover a low-level priority that's become urgent, make it a high priority.

You are going to have to make tough, complicated choices. You will probably have a quota, and that is what you live for. To make your quota, you have to close business. But not all deals you are working on will help you make your quota. Some will be large, but they may be too far out to matter. Some you may be able to close within your quota measurement period. These are the most important ones. There may be lots and lots of small deals begging for your time. Add them up and you have a good amount of revenue, but they all need time to close. Maybe too much time.

Then there's your boss. He may be asking you to call on accounts that won't pay much but have a high priority for him or your company. One favorite of mine is when the CEO cuts and pastes an announcement from the paper about a deal you didn't know about and copies the company demanding you close it. Some customers know they are small revenue and will not get much attention, but they excel at being the "squeaky wheel," burning up your precious time. Successful salespeople have these and many more variables to deal with. A good salesperson is an expert at bringing order to chaos.

Some priorities may never get done. This is normal. If you find very low-level priorities lingering for a long time at the bottom of your list, make a decision to either forget about them or bump them up. Usually these get taken off. If you remove them, make sure there won't be any issues if you don't do them.

There will be occasions when your list is impossible to manage. It becomes so long and arduous you can't even finish all the highest-priority action items. You're spread too thin. Reasons for this vary. Your business could be growing too fast. You could be in a start-up company that doesn't have the resources to fund an expensive sales group. No matter how the situation has evolved, you need to have a discussion with your boss to make sure he or she is aware of the situation and knows you are doing the best you can. The implication is that some customers may not be serviced in time and could complain. Your boss may have to let the customer know you are doing your best.

Review your list daily or even more frequently, depending on how your action items change around. There are many tools on the web that assist in managing action items. Check out videos on how people manage their priorities, and you will probably get some good ideas. Good luck with your list. Excuse me while I go check mine …

Speaking of priorities, a formula that clearly shows what is more and less important is helpful in determining what really should be done now versus later. One very useful formula is your quota. Every salesperson is measured in some way by a quota. Since your success is clearly linked to it, using your quota to set priorities is not a bad idea.

The Sales Quota

This is where the rubber meets the road. This is the single most important thing that drives your decisions on where you spend time. Of all the things you do, your quota is what you live for.

Many people don't understand working with a quota and fear it. They prefer jobs where they have 100 percent salary. This is why it takes a certain kind of person to be a salesperson. You have to understand there is risk but also reward—and the reward can be very large. More risk. More reward. Bring it on.

Since so much of a salesperson's time is devoted to quota, how it is structured facilitates sales behavior that closely follows how the commission is paid out. There are many types of quota systems. All are derived to motivate and shape the behavior of the salespeople. Some companies are very aware of what kind of behavior is created with a certain payout structure and others are clueless. Most are very aware of the contingencies of their payout formulas. For example, if salespeople get paid only on large orders and there is no incentive to reward servicing small orders, those smaller orders will be ignored. When this happens, the smaller customers get frustrated at the lack of support and take their business elsewhere. This may or may not be a good way to run your business, but it's management's decision. Your job is not to question it, but to use the formula to drive the way you order your priorities.

As a salesperson, your pay will have two components: salary and commission. Usually, commissions are paid at the end of a quarter, but that isn't always the case. Some bonus plans are paid on execution of a close. It depends who you work for and what market you're in. Generally, most salaries are around 50 to 80 percent of total. Some companies have plans that are 100 percent quota. They do this because their products are in demand.

A quota of 100 percent costs the company nothing in overhead but has other issues associated with it. Salespeople in these plans have no real allegiance to the company and will quit if the market turns down or the company can't meet demand (if there are barriers beyond the salesperson's control). When a market turns down, a company really needs salespeople. These companies suffer when a market or economy collapses and they lose salespeople just when they need them most.

Salespeople on the 100 percent plan can make huge amounts of money as long as the market is up, their company has a large enough manufacturing capacity to meet demand, and they have no limit or "cap" on how much they can earn. These plans attract a very specific type of salesperson who thrives on high risk. If you want a little less risk and a more predictable payout structure (no sales plan with commission is totally without risk or predictable), you should not take a full-commission sales job.

When you are hired as a salesperson in a non-full-commission position, one of the first things you will do is negotiate your pay. Your prospective employer will offer you a base plus commission. The final offer will be the base plus the calculated commission based on achieving 100 percent of quota. The plan should include how the commission works. Since a good salesperson is never satisfied with achieving just 100 percent of quota, you should know what happens if you go beyond it. This is very important, because some companies will actually limit what you can make and others won't. In one company I worked for, you maxed out in commission if you achieved greater than 125 percent of quota. Any more revenue you generated in the quarter beyond 125 percent you would lose commission on.

In negotiating your pay, ask about the calculation the company uses for your payout. You may find you need a PhD to understand it. Some have a ceiling and others don't. The ceiling or cap will be calculated using some kind of math. One company I worked for had a cap at 125 percent (very common), and the calculation on how you were paid was a sine-cosine curve. Others offer a list of individual components that add up to a number. These components can be based on a particular product they want to motivate you to sell. Other components can be the company achieving certain revenue or profit numbers.

Some of these components may be out of your control. They may or may not be fair. If you have less control, you may reach your personal quota, but end up not getting paid because of other people or the economy. This is why it's important for you to discover exactly how you will get paid. Have your manager explain it to you. If your manager has problems explaining it, you can assume you will not understand it either.

Salespeople can be very creative in finding loopholes to exploit, especially when it comes to maximizing the quota payout. Years ago, in a company I was at, we had a cap of 150 percent on our quota. At the end of the quarter, if we were reaching past 150 percent, we would try to find a way to move those billings to the next quarter. The trick was to get to know the accounts-receivable people really well. A few salespeople and I would wine and dine them profusely and just have a great time with them. We got to be great friends.

As we neared the end of a quarter and I saw that I would max out a few weeks before it finished, I would call in and ask the accounts-receivable person to put my largest customer on credit hold. Credit hold is a scorched-earth policy that companies use to withhold all shipments because a customer has run into credit problems. Credit hold cannot be overridden unless a senior manager releases the shipments. My largest customer was driving over 90 percent of my backlog, so by putting that company on credit hold, I stopped shipments for the rest of the quarter.

This works only when you're close to the end of the quarter, but that's when almost all shipments for the quarter went out anyway. I couldn't do this earlier, as it would eventually be discovered, and I would probably be fired along with the accounts-receivable person. I only did this a couple of times, but it allowed me to push revenue into the next quarter. While I don't recommend that you do anything like this, it's a good example of how salespeople can exploit weaknesses in any factory or customer system.

I should mention the "draw." This is when your company pays you in advance for sales you will "probably" attain. They give you a lump sum of money up front, based on the expectation that you will reach your sales goals. Companies do this because many salespeople make a lot of money and spend it. They don't want their salespeople to have money problems, which will distract them from their jobs. The draw is like getting a loan with no interest. I don't recommend it, but in a dire situation, you may be forced to go to your manager and ask for it. If you don't make your quota, your company will probably ask you to pay the difference, which could be a lot of money. Don't get yourself into this situation unless you feel the reward is worth the risk. Sales is all about measured risk, and if you think the risk can help you, then do it. But be aware it could end catastrophically.

Some plans will have three components: an easy, medium, and stretch goal. Others can be very straightforward. Just remember, your quota will always go up after every pay period. So manage your superiors' expectations appropriately. If you have wild stories of huge orders coming in the near future, you can bet your manager will incorporate that into your next quota. But leaving him or her guessing can backfire on you also. There is a careful balance you have to maintain between making sure your boss knows you are successful and tempering the perception of how successful you will be in the next quarter or quarters. You obviously have to report in on big orders or successes, but make sure your superiors clearly understand how big or small it is, and the risk associated with landing the deal.

Quota is a huge topic. The best thing you can do as a salesperson is clearly understand how you get paid commission and what you need to do and not do (distractions) to reach your goals. Selling is fun, and making quota is like scoring a huge goal in an important competition. But what it really does is prioritize what you do. When you get your quota and understand how you get paid on it, you can quickly figure out what you should be spending your time on. Everything else is a waste. If you have a sales funnel, (see page 151), look at it. It should tell you (on the right side) what prospects will be very likely to book business. These are the ones to spend your time on.

In working toward a quota, you may find your sales process is broken into two areas. One area is where you have a prospect, which is a potential customer (no current business). The other is a customer who is booking business on a regular basis. To get business from the prospect, you have to generate business from scratch. To get business from the customer, you have to take orders on existing business and see areas where you can grow. Working a prospect is called *demand creation*. Working an existing customer is called *demand fulfillment*, but in reality, you'll do both functions with an existing customer.

Demand Creation and Demand Fulfillment

These two buzzwords have been popular for a long time. The processes are also called presales and postsales, or hunting and farming. Though these terms get overused in sales jargon, they point out two very important and distinctly different processes that together provide a stream of ever-growing revenue.

Demand creation is the process of identifying a market for your product, discovering new customers with a need, and convincing them to place orders. Creating demand is necessary for any business to get revenue. Demand creation fills the left side of your sales funnel. Revenue can't be sustained without it. The role of the salesperson in this process is to work with marketing to identify a market for your product, identify likely prospects, and tell the salespeople to go get them.

The salespeople will use various methods to reach out to prospects to get a first meeting. They will cold-call, use cold-calling services, use various kinds of online/contract databases, or if they have a large list of contacts, use that to obtain information to reach prospects. Once the list is generated, they will begin to call or contact people to get meetings. Making first contact with a potential prospect can be difficult, and many people don't like doing it. But cold-calling and setting up first meetings is a skill every salesperson should have experience with.

There is no best way to contact prospects for the first time. Some salespeople use e-mails and others use the phone. My opinion is that there is little if any chance an e-mail will get your prospect's attention. These days, everyone gets so many junk e-mails, it's easy for yours to end up in a junk folder or simply ignored. On the other hand, the number of e-mails you can send in a day is much greater than the number of phone calls you make.

Once you convince a prospect to meet, a normal sales cycle of discovery of need, pitching the value of your product to the need, and closing begins. Hopefully, the salesperson will succeed in convincing the prospect to place an order.

After the demand is created, you need to fulfill it or keep a steady stream of orders coming into your factory from all the customers who placed their first orders. You need to make sure the customer remains happy with your company and wants to continue doing business. Demand fulfillment (sometimes referred to as order fulfillment) is the process of managing existing business. In this phase of selling, the salesperson is taking new orders, managing backlog (making sure orders are shipped on time to meet the customer's expectation), keeping the backlog filled, negotiating price changes, notifying of product changes, and even making a product obsolescence transition smoothly. There can be many more processes going on, like entertaining customers, public announcements, and other peripherally related activities

Some companies like to separate demand creation from fulfillment. This is more of an idealistic approach, as most salespeople who are talented do both. Salespeople come with all sorts of expertise and abilities. Some are good at getting customers and signing them up, some are good closers, and some are very good at keeping the postsales customer happy. No matter which category you fit into, be careful to not get pigeonholed by taking a position that restricts you to one side or the other.

If you take a job as a demand-fulfillment salesperson, your resume will show that. If you take a demand-creation job, your resume will show your experience as good for finding and closing deals, but weak at maintaining them. Most good salespeople have a balance of the two. I find some salespeople like to think of themselves as good at demand creation and others are good at fulfillment. In many cases, it's just a preference and what they feel comfortable doing.

Don't be fooled by people who think a salesperson should be a "hunter" or a "farmer." These metaphors are widely used to describe a salesperson or a need by management to pigeonhole. I am speculating, but I think these terms came about because many salespeople are uncomfortable with creating demand or doing demand fulfillment. To rationalize their weakness in one area, they claim they are a fantastic hunter and farming is for the mundane. Or they will claim they manage galactic-sized backlogs and drive huge growth in revenue by keeping their Fortune 50 company in love with them. They always get invited to the president's club. Hunting is for scrappers, they'll say.

Many salespeople prefer to do one or the other type of selling. Any good, solid salesperson can do both. Anybody who tells me they do well with only one or the other is idealistic and probably doesn't have good experience as a salesperson.

As an example, take a salesperson whose job is to manage a moderately sized customer who has a healthy backlog. The salesperson is responsible for the account, and he alone calls on it. He goes into purchasing one day to give it to the manager on the delivery status of a key product. While in conversation with the manager, he discovers the company is starting a new line of products. The salesperson gets the contact information of the key decision maker and sets up a meeting. The salesperson has transitioned to demand-creation mode. The point is salespeople have to wear both hats.

On larger accounts, the responsibilities get split up sometimes into purchasing (where demand fulfillment is) and engineering (possibly where demand creation rests). Somehow, people think these two can be separated in sales. I strongly disagree with that. Salespeople should be able to create demand and manage a regular stream of orders. I mean, you can do all the demand creation you like, but if you get someone to place a purchase order, who is going to take it and manage the process?

In large corporations, the sales organization may be segmented into very specific functions. One salesperson may be responsible for purchasing while others may call on departments that generate new business. It's been my experience that, even in these segmented roles, a salesperson who has experience in demand creation is more valuable covering purchasing than a person who doesn't.

I strongly recommend that if you are starting out in your career, you begin with a job that requires both creating demand and fulfilling it. When a company segments the two activities, they may call them by different names. *Presales*, *business development*, *evangelist*, or just plain *salesman* can be one of the demand-creation titles. If you are very aware of your strengths and weaknesses and clearly understand your talents, go ahead and do it. Otherwise, my advice is to make sure you have a job that gives you experience with both pre- and postsales. It all depends on you.

Demand creation is pretty straightforward, but it is very hard work. First, you have to clearly understand your product and what markets it serves. Then you need to discover the customers and penetrate the market. Getting into accounts can be a frustrating task. If you don't know anybody, you need to be creative about getting names and reaching out to give your pitch. After you give the pitch, you have to find out if the people you're pitching to are decision makers, influencers, or a waste of time. This can take awhile, especially if the company is big. Organizational charts (see Organizational charts p. 160), come in handy here. After you work hard on finding and winning over the decision makers, you need to close. If you close, then you get the order or contract and move into demand fulfillment.

Demand fulfillment is more hard work, but different. You've established an account that is now doing business with your company. But that business can go away one way or another. It's your job to not only keep the customer happy with the current deal, but to keep exploring this customer for new deals (more demand creation). This is where mediocre salespeople fall down.

There is an easy way and a hard way to do demand creation and fulfillment. If your company offers many types of products or services, some will be good and others probably won't be. Selling is getting an order using the easiest way possible. Who wants to work harder than they have to? Or, who wants to use more of their precious time than they have to? You may find some of your company's products sell better than others. There is a reason for this. Your management may want you to sell everything, but you shouldn't care. You should sell what your customers want. Knowing the good products from the dogs will make your job easier and keep you from wasting your time or your customer's.

Know What Your Company Is Good At

Every company has a set of products or services it wants people to buy. Also, the company will try to be and do many things for its customers. All companies have to expand to grow. When expanding, one way is to offer even more goods and services. There comes a point when the company becomes less efficient in producing products and services that are in demand. The more products and services a company offers, the better the chance that some of these products will fall short of meeting customers' needs.

With all these things, the reality is the company will be good at only a subset of what it sells and what it can do. Most senior managers in a company are acutely aware of this. As a salesperson, you will be told to sell everything, and the factory will deliver on everything as promised. As you get more experienced, you will find out there is a limited number of things your company will do very well. The rest will be crap. How will you find out about these things? You will promise something to the customer and your factory will fail to deliver it, the product won't meet the expectations you were told to set with your customer, or the product or service won't meet the needs of the customer.

For whatever reason, you will discover that some subset of products or services your company produces are in demand and others are a waste of your time. Knowing this, you will only sell what you can quickly move and stop selling what nobody wants. You have to do this because your quota dictates your priority, which is to make money. You won't make money trying to sell stuff nobody wants.

This also applies to supporting your customer. Your company will be very good at supporting certain things and not others. Getting to know this as soon as possible will allow you to set the correct expectations with your customer so nobody is disappcinted, in case you know your factory will fail to deliver on something.

You have to be careful, as your manager or factory will want you to sell everything. You need to be passive-aggressive (saying you will but not really doing it) and politically correct with your factory people, who want you to sell something that won't sell. If your factory realizes how important feedback from the field is, there will be a mechanism for it. It can be just e-mails, sales conferences, or some other method, depending on the culture and how receptive your company is to this valuable information. Hopefully they listen carefully and use the information to make changes and improvements.

When you expose your company's products to a customer or prospect for the first time, you must be careful how you begin your sales process. Even when you know the customer will want it, you have to always make sure the customer perceives value in what you are selling first. Some customers may demand the price up front without even knowing how good a product is. This is a mistake many salespeople make. You have to establish value before price.

Price and Value

Why would anyone give out a price to a customer before the customer can appreciate the value of your product? It makes no sense, but many salespeople lead with pricing before the customer has an opportunity to learn what about the product or service is compelling. This happens because customers almost always ask for price first.

This is especially true in high-tech, where the products tend to be complicated and the customers will think your product is just like everyone else's. Always avoid discussions about price if you suspect the customer doesn't understand the value. After you have determined the customer clearly understands the value, and he or she is showing buying signals, you can discuss pricing. Value before price is all part of the sales cycle.

Understanding the needs of the customer is vitally important before you can paint a picture of how you meet those needs. If your product does a fantastic job of meeting the customer's needs, that could be very compelling. If it's compelling, your customer should perceive your product or service is just what he or she needs. It can get more complicated than that, but that's basically it. Getting your customer to understand value makes it easier to ask for money for it. The more the customer perceives value and the more strongly your product appears to meet a need, the more the customer will want it and the more he or she will pay for it. Coupling need to value is part of what you get paid for. Selling the value is how you make your money.

What You Sell and the Value Proposition

Before you talk to a prospect, you'd better understand your company's products or services. Going in to a prospect without understanding what you sell or how to articulate the value of your product is shooting blind and can make you look like an idiot. Carve out some time to get educated on your company's products or services and why customers buy them. This is called the *value proposition*. You have to be able to do this or you won't close a single deal.

If your company's products are highly technical, you may be paired with an engineer who has people skills to help you explain in depth the technical aspects of the value or your product. Some companies have training programs for their salespeople. These can be good or bad. It all depends who teaches. Product knowledge is absolutely essential to a salesperson's competence. The better you are at it, the more deals you can close.

It just makes sense to have a deep understanding of your company's products. Not every company requires salespeople to know products with any depth. If your competitor is more articulate in stating value proposition than you are, though, you'll look incompetent to the customer. So get some education on your company's products and become an expert. You'll be well on your way to closing those big deals.

If you're technical and selling a technical product or service, you'll be ahead of the game. Not all sales organizations hire technical people to sell technical products. If the product is a commodity or the customer clearly understands the value proposition before you walk in the door, then this strategy can work. But if it isn't entirely clear to the prospect what the benefit of your product or service is, having a deeper understanding will help you be more influential in selling. If it's a technical sell and you are technical, your chances of closing are much higher than for a salesperson who isn't technical.

The message should be clear: the better you understand your products and services, the faster and more likely you will be to close deals. It's really that simple. Once you master the art of establishing need and selling on value, customers should be interested in talking price and acting like they want to buy.

Buying Signals

There will be times when you're in a customer meeting and people are positive about what you are selling and even helping you win others over. The body language is all positive, and everyone is enthusiastic about what you are selling. Your antenna is telling you they will probably buy your product. You get excited because the customer is excited. Buying signals are both verbal and nonverbal. Everything is positive when you interact with the prospect, and your feeling is that you can close soon.

Not everyone shows buying signals, but when you see them, you know exactly what they are. Some of them could be: the prospect brainstorms about how they will use your product, or they say they must get the decision maker involved right away. There are many ways people show they are in favor of buying your product.

Buying signals don't mean you can close a deal. It means whoever you are selling to has mentally accepted your value proposition. There may be many more steps to actually closing, but you know you are making good progress. If the decision maker is showing buying signals, you may test to see if he or she can be closed. Or, you can try to close if there are no barriers left to overcome. This is how you can tell a good salesperson from a bad one. It's all in taking the customer from talking about buying to actually buying.

Buying signals are very subjective. As you get more experienced meeting with customers, you will begin to appreciate this phenomenon. If you are passionate about selling, buying signals are a key indication you are making progress on successfully pitching your product. Buying signals are a huge psychological lift for a salesperson. They're validation that you are doing the right thing.

Many times salespeople will discuss buying-signal stories because they are fun to hear. I have had people call me when they are talking to my customer to tell me, "I must be doing my job because they are showing buying signals." When it happens to you, it's a great feeling. I hope you can experience a lot of buying signals.

So there you are with your customers. Your senses are telling you they want to give you an order. So ask for the order. Sounds simple, doesn't it? It's not always as easy as it looks, though. Once you have buying signals, you have to shape the environment correctly or the situation can be very awkward. It takes a lot of careful judgment to figure out when it's the right time to close.

Another challenging activity for salespeople is lead generation. Some companies may hand you a list of prospects to call on. Other companies expect you to do it. Once you get your lead or contact, you either have to call on that individual or try to catch him or her in person. When the contact is someone you have never met, you have to introduce yourself and begin to pitch. For many salespeople, this is a daunting task. It's called cold-calling.

Cold-Calling

Cold-calling is an essential part of sales, and one of several activities that can fill the front of your sales funnel. It's when you call people you've never spoke to before. The process of cold-calling follows these steps:

1. Identify a market where your product or service could be sold.
2. List the top companies in that market that might buy the largest amount of your goods or services. Prioritize the list.
3. Get a list of contacts at those companies and sort them by their titles as to who might be a decision maker or influencer in purchasing your product or service.
4. Compose a short, concise "elevator pitch" to quickly convey the value of what you're selling to the person you're calling. Try to imagine the objections people may bring up. Anticipating them will help speed calls to a close.
5. Practice your pitch by yourself and then ask people to listen to it for feedback. Make revisions and when you're satisfied, go to the next step.
6. Develop a spreadsheet or other method to track your progress as you make calls.
7. Start calling your list of prospects to set up meetings or move to the next step in the sales cycle. Or, if you have to visit people, walk in and begin talking.
8. Note your progress and stop frequently to evaluate how your pitch is doing. The more times you speak your elevator pitch, the better you will be at it. After a few times speaking it, you may want to refine it.

The purpose of cold-calling is to generate leads with new prospects who might want to buy your product. These new prospects may or may not have heard from you before. It requires unending patience, coping with rejection, and tolerating the frustration of scores of calls where nobody picks up the phone when you call. It is like picking up the phone and calling random people.

Most salespeople hate cold-calling. It is a tedious and frustrating activity. A few love doing it. Those salespeople look at it as a challenge much like a game of sports, where you score a goal when the prospect agrees to a meeting or follow-up action item.

Cold-calling doesn't have to be done by phone. You can send e-mails and even visit the prospect and try to engage people where he or she works. Social networks are another place to develop leads with people you've never met before. But most cold-calling is still done by phone, as that is the most effective way to engage a person in real time. Using the phone and having a conversation allows you to counter any objections the prospect might have.

E-mails can be easily ignored by the prospect and don't give you the opportunity to counter objections. E-mail is a very poor vehicle for attempting to persuade someone. On the other hand, you can send thousands of e-mails to huge lists of prospects to try to generate leads for you to call. Usually bulk e-mails have a very low return rate, but a reply to an e-mail is an opportunity that can't be ignored. If you send out enough e-mails, you will get replies. A cold-calling strategy should encompass all different ways of reaching out to prospects.

If you are calling people, you'll find that some are approachable and others are not. Those who are will pick up the phone and give you a minute to make your pitch. In most cases, you will make many, many calls before someone picks up the phone. Of the people who pick up the phone, only a few will be interested in talking with you. People stress how important the pitch is. I really think it is less the content of the pitch and more how receptive the person you reach is. It's binary—people will either talk with you or they won't. People who will talk are already receptive. So don't sweat the pitch too much.

Of the people who talk with you, only a few of them will be valid prospects who are a decision influencers or decision makers. I can almost guarantee if you make enough calls, someone within your target company will talk to you on the phone. Some of these people will actually help you out. I have cold-called people within target companies who received my unsolicited phone call and spent a significant amount of time chatting. I have called senior vice presidents I had no previous relationship with and found some of these guys to be very friendly and willing to help me out. The people I am talking about were not low-level individuals. The whole point is that you need to be patient and persistent. The more people you call, the better the chance you will get someone who will talk with you. Many businesses are based on cold-calling because it works.

You can increase the likelihood of reaching a valid prospect by having a high-quality data set of contacts. You get what you pay for. There are many free databases available that provide contact information for thousands of companies. The data on these lists is questionable, but I have had success using them. If you have a budget for cold-calling, you can pay for higher-quality lists that are vetted so that the contacts are accurate. There are organizations that will cold-call for you, if you are willing to pay a lot of money. It all comes down to how much it's worth to you and how you want to spend your time.

If you have no idea where to start getting phone numbers for a prospect, try the web. Searching will usually yield some names at a company, even if they are private. Public companies are easier, as they usually list names of managers on their websites. Check the financial reports. The directors and vice presidents will be listed somewhere in the text.

Sometimes a public company's number isn't listed. These types of companies usually have something to do with consumers, and they don't want to be inundated with customer-service calls to their corporate headquarters. They want customers to use their 800 number instead. Examples of this are cable TV operators and health-care providers. Still, if you look hard enough and are creative enough, you can find the number.

Once you get the number, you need a name. If you don't have a name, you can ask for the vice president or director of whatever department would be the one you want to sell your product to. Another great way to find information on companies is to use an online stock account. E-Trade, TD Bank, or Scottrade are a few of the many online brokerage firms who have huge amounts of information on public companies.

The point is that you have to do some hard, creative work to penetrate an organization. The web is a fantastic tool for salespeople. I find it amazing that so many senior executives (who don't want to be bothered by pesky salespeople) put so much information about themselves on social-networking sites. These days, getting a list of contacts to call is very easy to do.

Cold-calling is a necessary activity for any sales organization. How an organization goes about it can be efficient or not. Some companies have very highly paid salespeople do their own cold-calling. If these salespeople do demand creation or demand fulfillment, their time is better spent in front of prospects/customers rather than sitting behind a desk, cold-calling. Cold-calling can be done by inside people as long as they can be trained and scripted in how to present the elevator pitch, qualify a lead, and close by setting up a meeting with a salesperson. This is a much better way to utilize sales resources than having your highest paid people spend hours and hours cold-calling.

Some companies don't do this very well and don't have a good cold-calling strategy. Politics, egos, and tight budgets among other things can impede such a strategy. What ends up happening is the most expensive salespeople waste their time cold-calling because they need their sales funnels filled up. If they can't get a resource to do it or do it effectively, they end up doing it themselves. In the end, it has to do with meeting quota, and the buck stops with the salesperson.

Cold-calling is one way to generate leads. Every salesperson should know how to do it. Practice makes perfect, and the more you do it, the better you will be at it. Small companies may not have the resources to cold-call people. Their salespeople will have to do it. But if you want to accelerate lead generation, putting in a cold-calling resource can help with that. It all depends on the need. There is a lot of information on the web about it, so get out there and start cold-calling.

Once you get your foot in the door, you need to worm your way around the prospect to find the right people to pitch to. The more decision influencers and decision makers you know, the better penetration of the account you will have. The better your penetration, the faster and more efficient you will be at qualifying business opportunities.

Account Penetration

If you have one or more customers, you will be expected to be the expert about them. Penetrating an account means first getting to know everyone in a decision-making role and second, everyone else. The more you know, the better penetration you have, the more information you have, the more effective your account strategy will be.

Organizational charts will be very helpful to you and your management; they're a good gauge as to how many people you really know or could know. Another aspect of penetration is clearly understanding what is going on there and where to spend your time. I am sure you don't have unlimited time, so you have to prioritize. What can help is making up a presentation or spreadsheet set for each of your customers that outlines what projects are in process, which ones are likely to succeed or fail, funding data, who is working on what, and what is their marketing plan, channel plan, forecasted revenue, projections, barriers, etc. If your company has a CRM (customer relationship manager tool), you can use that. The point is to develop a detailed system that you can use to keep track of how much you really know about your customer(s).

The process of putting this together will help you organize your thoughts on how much you really understand about the account and what you could do. You can outline it or even make a business plan. Just write something down to force yourself to think about the best way to spend your time. If you trust your peers, ask them about it. Or even bounce your thoughts off a mentor. The whole point is that organization of your activities will help you be better at penetration. It will give you an edge against your competitors.

Even when salespeople have good penetration, it doesn't mean they have control of it. Just because you know a lot of people doesn't mean you have influence or can execute a plan. There is another step in the sales process in which you "own" the account, a step beyond penetration called *account control*. This is when the salesperson not only has many contacts at a company, but is considered by the factory and the customer as a respected consultant for that account and is trusted to direct all activities. The salesperson dictates what happens and it does. The customer listens and the factory takes direction. A salesperson who is in control will make things happen.

Account Control

If you can't control your account, don't expect your strategies or goals to ever materialize. Any success won't be because of what you did. A good company will realize its salespeople are on the front lines and need to be the ones calling the shots. Never work as a salesperson for a company that insists on managing what you do and what happens with the account. Never.

Account control is when you (as the salesperson responsible for an account) know everything that happens. You control all the conversations, make sure all the action items are completed on time, orchestrate meetings, maintain the relationships, and drive the strategy and goals. And win. If you can't account for 100 percent of the previous items, you are not in control. Loss of control keeps a salesperson from being effective. It is a vulnerability your competitors will exploit. Too many cooks will spoil the broth. You will not be able to confidently forecast winning business simply because you don't control all the variables.

Loss of control happens for various reasons. Senior management can be too controlling of their salespeople. This happens with high-profile accounts where everyone is overly concerned about success. A controlling VP or CEO feels the need to "go around" the salesperson directly to the customer. If it happens a lot in your job, try to get inserted into the discussions. Offer to set them up, and of course, listen in. What is bad about this if it happens a lot is that promises may be made during a discussion without you knowing it. If the customer has access to a senior manager who has better information, why would he or she need you? Situations like this can make a salesperson ineffectual at an account. Good salespeople never let this happen, and if it happens a lot, they quit their job and go to place where the salesperson is responsible for control.

The depth of your relationships and how well you support your customer is the fundamental basis of account control. Having strong relationships with influential people will naturally keep anybody from being overly intrusive or someone from taking control. More than likely, you will get a call from one of your customers if someone from your company tries to go around you. Also, a strong account presence will keep your competitors at bay. In fact, your customer may prefer to buy a less competitive product from a strong salesperson than a highly competitive product from a weak salesperson.

On the other hand, if you are a weak, mediocre salesperson, you aren't concerned about account control or have fooled yourself into thinking you have it. You let other people access the account without any status as to what they are doing. They will develop their own strategy and exclude you. Having access to the customer makes someone important internally to the company. It's about the information. In meetings, insecure people will make themselves look important because they know something about a major customer nobody else does. They talk confidently as if they are in control. Managers don't care where the information comes from as long as it's important.

As a salesperson controlling an account, you will be faced with strong personalities vying for access to your customer, whether or not it's pertinent to the overall strategy to win. This is normal, and a strong salesperson will control it. Weak salespeople will rationalize why it's important for them not to know everything that is happening at their account while someone is stepping all over them.

You may have an internal support team helping with important customers. Your team will have access to customers without you being directly involved. You still need to know what is going on with your customers and mutually agree on what they should do, though. You drive the strategy and tactics, not the team. Mediocre salespeople let things run without getting involved. This is a mistake. Management may allow this if they have a culture of mediocrity.

Obviously, if you have a large account where a team of people are responsible, all the team members must share the work and do their part on their own. However, a good team meets regularly to review what they are doing and all agree on an overall goal. Frequent communication among team members is vitally important to keep everyone up to speed. This is how account control is maintained with a group. Rogue players shouldn't be tolerated and should be called out or at least managed. Otherwise, they will hurt the effectiveness of the team.

A good salesperson should have a flair for detail and control. These two traits will make controlling the account natural.

CHAPTER THREE

MEETINGS

Arranging Customer/Factory Meetings

If you have account control, the outcome of any meeting is determined before the meeting happens. The meeting is only a formality. You set the agenda and the expectations and manage the meeting in such a way that it closes as everybody thinks it will. It is only a vehicle to take you one step closer to closing business. With good preparation and careful thought, most of your meetings can be productive and predictable. There are some simple rules for arranging a meeting.

Before the Meeting

- Clearly define what you want to achieve in the meeting.
- You are the salesperson, so you rule how this meeting is planned and run, and you decide what the action items will be. If you have senior managers with big egos going to the meeting, don't be surprised if they try to wrest control from you. Your best tactic is to control the meeting as best you can without getting them mad at you. Always remember, the salesperson on the account should call all the shots. Your senior management can override you, sometimes for good reason. But if they control the customer too much, you won't be effective as a salesperson.
- Make sure it is clear that customers are getting something they want from the meeting, something of value. It should be clear up front that the meeting is addressing either an articulated or an unarticulated need.
- Develop an agenda with the customer and make sure he or she approves it. Circulate it to everyone early enough that you can make changes and still have time to get it to everyone before the

meeting. Note anyone who might object. This could be a problem if it isn't addressed.

- If you and a customer are planning the meeting together, go meet with that individual and discuss who talks where in the agenda. The more professionally the meeting is run, the better your chances of getting the senior managers to talk and not be distracted by screwups. If the customer is an ally, then you are in good shape. Any way you look at it, if this person is in part responsible for setting up the meeting, in most cases you can be sure he or she will want and need to look good. So you don't have to worry too much about that person purposely causing failure. On the other hand, if the individual is incompetent, you need to take over control of the planning and "help" him or her be successful.
- You should do introductions and state the purpose for the meeting right at the beginning. Put this in the agenda.
- If you have multiple people from your side going to the meeting, have a premeeting strategy session. Anybody who does not attend shouldn't be allowed to go to the customer. Someone who avoids this type of meeting could have an unconscious agenda for the customer, which could be destructive. Of course, some people have legitimate excuses for missing meetings. If certain people can't make it, talk to them individually about the strategy. Listen very carefully to how they talk about it. If they have an unconscious or conscious agenda, your sales antenna will tell you something is wrong. If you do sense something is wrong, you might want to consider leaving them out of the meeting or trying to get them to agree to your strategy or discuss why they don't like it. You have to make sure the meeting goes smoothly, and if some people don't understand that, you should pull the plug on them. If you are in a bind, discuss it with your manager.
- Consider what might go wrong and how you will overcome it. Discuss it during your planning session so your team members are aware of it too.
- There could be people on the customer's side going to the meeting who want you to lose and will try to make you or your people look stupid. Make sure you are prepared to counter that behavior. I really enjoy it when a hotheaded customer starts to shoot off his mouth in a meeting in front of one of his high-level managers. If you can keep your people from engaging in his ranting, you will gain credibility points with the senior manager.

Make sure your people are prepared beforehand about any hotheads or bad agendas. Discuss how to neutralize them.

- Any materials you need to bring with you should be ready at least a day before the meeting. If you are publishing an agenda for the meeting, make sure it goes out two or three days before.
- Send reminders a week ahead of time to both your customers and your factory people. Then send them out again the day before. If there are senior managers going, call their administration person to confirm their attendance.
- If people from your company are coming in from different destinations to the meeting, give them directions, both printed and electronic. The best way is for you to drive everyone to the meeting. This is important so you can go over last-minute strategies on the way in and do a debrief in the car afterward.
- For early-morning meetings, plan to bring some food or whatever is traditional for morning snacks. If it will be a long meeting, make sure there is food and refreshments—either you bring them or the customer can provide them. If you do it, you know it will be done right.
- Confirm the meeting with the person or people you are visiting. If the meeting was scheduled more than a few days before, call or e-mail the person a day or two ahead of the scheduled meeting to make sure it's not forgotten.
  - o If you don't get a return confirm from the person, leave additional voicemails and e-mails. You never know if the person is out sick or was called out of town unexpectedly.
  - o If you still don't get a return confirm from the person setting up the meeting or a colleague, be concerned that the ball's been dropped or someone is avoiding you. If the individual doesn't contact you, he or she could be preparing a plausible denial, such as "I forgot about the meeting." If you can't reach that person, the chances of the meeting happening are very slim. There will be a point at which you have to pull the plug so that anyone traveling in for the meeting can cancel and not waste their time.
  - o If you still can't reach the person and this is a really important meeting for you, be a pest and e-mail and call repeated times. Leave multiple voicemails on the person's office and cell phones. If you know other people

who work for the customer, ask them to find this person. Face it, if your contact is avoiding you, the meeting isn't important to that individual, is it? If this was a surprise, you are missing out on something and really don't know what's going on in the account. I would say you have a big hole in how you understand what is going on with this customer. You should have known about this possibility. Fix it.

- If something happens where you need to cancel the meeting, do it immediately. If it turns out that the reason is because of new data that indicated you were walking into a trap or something popped up that your contact wasn't who you should be talking to, make up an excuse that doesn't make the person think he or she is unimportant. You don't have to be direct. Also, you are never obligated to provide details on why the meeting was cancelled. Sometimes the reason is simple. If you were bringing a senior manager from your company to the meeting and his schedule changed, there's not much you can do about that. But make sure you frame the reason so that the customer doesn't feel unimportant. Just saying he had to go to another meeting is weak. The customer may be fine with it but unconsciously will resent it. You can say there are travel problems with flights or other innocuous reasons. No matter what, the meeting isn't going to happen. So don't spend a lot of time with elaborate excuses. Keep it simple.

- Make sure you bring whatever is needed for presentation materials or visual aids. Unless you know this customer like the back of your hand, don't count on him or her to provide everything promised. Especially if the meeting is very important and there are plenty of senior managers attending, always bring extra, as more people may show up than you were expecting.

- If your company is presenting, make sure you have a backup copy of the slide set on your computer. Have it on a flash drive, or back it up on Dropbox or similar online cloud storage. Also, print out a hard-copy version and keep it with you. Even if the customer is providing a projector or other multimedia device, consider bringing one as a backup. Be paranoid about this, and you'll be well prepared.

During the Meeting

- Before the start of the meeting, get all the customers to give you their contact information. Get their business cards. If they don't have cards, give them one of yours and tell them to write their phone and e-mail on the back of it. Make sure they spell out their name and give you their phone and e-mail address at minimum. If the group is large, circulate a piece of paper. Make columns at the top that have name, phone, e-mail, and any other data you want. Don't make too many columns. You should pass the paper to the customer and supply the pen. Watch it go around the room. It may stall, or someone may be missed. It's okay to get up during the meeting and keep it going. Make sure it gets back to you.
- Make sure everyone gets your business card.
- Take notes during the meeting. People will be watching you. At minimum, you need to take out a pen and a pad of paper. If you don't, your unconscious message to the customer will be that the meeting isn't important to you. Let me tell you, they will notice, because you are controlling the meeting. Make sure to write down important details:
  - o date
  - o who from your side attended
  - o all customer names and titles
  - o what the purpose of the meeting was
  - o all the action items, marked with some delimiter that allows you to quickly scan the page and pick them out, when they're due, and who owns them
  - o all the issues brought up
  - o key points, including any potential roadblocks
  - o any product details
  - o ideas you have during the meeting (whether or not they are germane to the meeting)
- Watch the time carefully. Check with your customer before the meeting as to how much time you have. Try not to run over. If you are running behind, find a way to speed it up. Give a ten minute warning before the end. Leave time near the end to conclude and review action items.
- Don't doodle. People sitting next to you will notice and take it as another sign you are bored and they are unimportant. Even if you think you can get away with it, someone will notice the

doodles when you pick up your pad. Assume someone is always watching you. You may even drop your doodle page and the customer may pick it up for you, which is worse. Everyone will want to know if you take better notes than them. Of course you do, right?

- Don't type on a laptop or tablet. If you do, nobody will know if you are typing notes or doing e-mails. They will assume you are doing e-mails. Looking at a screen means you aren't paying attention to body language and nonverbal communication. Remember, 67 percent of the communication at your meeting will be nonverbal. Take notes the old-fashioned way. Then you stay engaged.
- At the end of the meeting, everybody will want to leave. Don't let them go until you review all the action items verbally with the group, when each is due, and who owns them.

One-on-One Meeting with a Customer

- After your customer agrees to the meeting, send an e-mail to confirm it. In the e-mail, be very specific about which day of the week it is, the date, and the time.
- If the meeting was scheduled more than a few days away, either call or e-mail the customer with a reminder of the meeting.
- If you don't get a return confirm from the customer, leave a voicemail and send another e-mail. The customer may be trying to avoid you to have the excuse that he or she "forgot" the meeting.
- If this is a meeting you really need to have and there's a chance the customer may cancel it, become "unavailable" until the meeting happens. (The reverse of the strategy above that the customer might pull on you.)
- Be very clear with yourself what you want to accomplish in the meeting. That is, know the goal of the meeting and the expected outcome.
- You have to bring value to the meeting. Customers are always looking for information about the company or other tidbits that will make them more interested in meeting with you.
- Make sure you take notes during the meeting. At least take a pencil out and a pad of paper. Otherwise, the unconscious and

sometimes conscious cue to your customer is the meeting is unimportant to you.

- At the end of the meeting, review the action items with your customer. Make sure everyone is clear about which ones are yours and which ones are the customer's.
- Communicate regularly with the customer afterward on your progress completing the action items.
- Keep reviewing the action items and keeping them on track until they're done.

The Conference/Web Call

- Make sure you know what you want to accomplish with the call.
- Use a service that gets you good connection. Cheap services usually have poor quality. Nothing is more frustrating than loud echoing or noise on a call, especially if you have to redial. Anytime you need to redial, you may lose people. This is very important, yet many salespeople overlook this.
- Try to avoid making the customer pay for the conference call, although sometimes you can't avoid this.
- Before the call, make sure you confirm with everyone via e-mail, calendar invites, and voice (or voicemail). If someone doesn't get back to you, you should assume that person won't be on the call. If the call is over a week away, reconfirm with everyone the day before. When you send out confirmations by e-mail, include
  o date of the month;
  o day of the week; and
  o the time for all time zones people are calling from (12:30 p.m. EST—9:30 a.m. PST—9:30 p.m. TWN). Some calendar clients like Outlook can be very confusing on the times set in the calendar. If the person you are inviting is in another time zone, the actual time in Outlook may be very different from what you want it to be. I always state the time of the meeting in the subject header just to be safe. If one of the times is another day because of dateline crossing, put in that day along with the time. If you are unsure of time zones, go to worldtimeserver.com.
- Those receiving your e-mail confirmations will notice the CC: of all the people involved. If people from your company are going

to be on the call, you should think about whether you want to expose their e-mail addresses to the customer when you send the e-mail confirmation. The point of your job is to be the main point of contact. Exposing e-mail addresses could open up a back door of communication that may get out of control. My recommendation is to avoid exposure unless you want it to happen. While we're talking about copying, you should be careful about blind copying. I don't recommend ever using it. E-mails aren't private. Just watch the news on TV for evidence of that. If you feel strongly about sending a blind copy, consider the consequences if it's exposed to the wrong people. Is it worth it?

- Make sure any of your internal people who will be on the conference call are clear on what the outcome of the meeting is. You may want to have a separate internal-only call to discuss the strategy and who is going to say what. Make sure you rehearse what the customer is likely to say. Your people are depending on you to instruct them on how to behave. As in any meeting, there may be people who want you to lose. Make sure your people know who they are and what they are likely to do to sabotage the conference call. Rehearse how you will respond.

- If you will use visual aids like a presentation on the call, make sure you can use all the controls for the presenting software before the call happens. Nothing is more frustrating than having several people on a call and you look like a dummy because you don't know how to use the presentation software. Practice using it before your call.

- Your company may be cheap and not provide services like WebEx for their salespeople. This is shortsighted and reflects lack of support for the salespeople. If you do a lot of calls using visual aids and your company is too cheap to provide the service, you might think of getting your own personal one.

- It never fails that someone is in the car or a coffee shop with a lot of background noise. He or she may not realize it and keep the phone unmuted. Additionally, this individual may not even be listening, so when you ask everyone to mute, nothing happens. Most conference-call services allow the person running the call to mute one caller or everyone. Get familiar with the control options.

- Some services are difficult to use. They have menus that are very long, and it's sometimes difficult to see what number to call in to and the password. If this is the case, make it easier on your attendees and put a note in your calendar reminder with the number and password.

Now that you know how to run a good meeting—whether in person or on the phone—you will want pay close attention to who controls it. Controlling a meeting is like account control. If a group of people are driving it, chaos will rule, and you won't get close to completing any strategy. You should be *el capitan* of the meeting, the head honcho. Everyone, customer and factory person alike, should be looking to you as the supreme overlord for guiding the group through it.

The Salesperson Controls the Meeting

At one point during my career, I had worldwide account responsibility for a Fortune 100 company that was also one of the top five revenue-producing customers for my company. Needless to say, what sales did with the account was very visible and always had the eye of senior management. In addition, many of the senior executives of my company desired to visit this big customer and speak with management there for various reasons. On one occasion, I had the president of our company with me.

I had set up several meetings for him, and the schedule was very tight. This was my first time in his company. Our first meeting was with the vice president of manufacturing. This meeting was particularly important for several reasons. This VP happened to be a close friend of our CEO and the president. Plus, there was political turmoil within the company, and there was a chance this VP could be promoted to president in a shuffle. Our company would have the high-level access we lacked with the current president.

This was our first formal meeting with the VP. The second meeting was with an influential manager who could help us win an important design that represented a substantial amount of revenue. We had never met this manager before, and he was anxious to be introduced to our president.

The first meeting went better than I expected. Though they knew each other well, the VP kept bringing up ways for us to work together more closely. I could see that our president was enjoying the meeting. This was going really, really well. Of course, this made me feel really good, because I had the idea for this meeting; it was going well, so I looked good to my president. Everybody was happy.

After a while, I noticed that we were beginning to run late. But this meeting was going so well, I felt I couldn't interrupt them. Their conversation became personal and deeper, so I felt it would be very insensitive to interrupt them. The time went by, and we became seriously late for the next meeting. Finally, the meeting ran down and we all said our good-byes. When I was alone with our president, he asked me what was next. I told him that we were very late for the next meeting. He turned to me obviously agitated and asked me why I didn't interrupt the meeting.

In a second, I realized that is exactly what I should have done. My president expected me to have account control, which meant I should have interrupted the first meeting and moved to the second. I had no good answer and told him I made a mistake. I drove him over to where we were supposed to meet the manager, but he had gone. It took me three or four months to repair the relationship with that customer. Fortunately, everything worked out for our company and for me. And I had learned an important lesson.

Your senior managers should let the salesperson call the shots on the account. You have the privilege of interrupting them in meetings to keep them on track, to tell them they have fifteen minutes left before they have to go, or even to point out that a customer has been waiting to get a question answered (while they went on and on without answering it). Your job is to exert dictatorial control over meetings and what goes on with your customer. Period. If you can't control the account, how can you ever succeed at implementing a strategy there?

Companies vary in how much account control they allow the salesperson. As you may notice, companies that limit what the salesperson can control end up with mediocre salespeople. Companies that allow their salespeople complete control end up with powerful, professional salespeople who frequently win. If you are a great salesperson, you won't want to work for a company that doesn't let you do much. Working at one of these companies is a horrible experience.

Controlling a meeting is a vitally important skill. Controlling a large, important meeting requires a whole new level of attention and strategy.

These types of meetings easily cascade out of control, sometimes very badly. A salesperson who screws up on one of these puppies may be looking for a job. If you stick to the details, plan carefully, set expectations, and stick to your plan, you can cruise through and make things happen.

People have different styles of conveying their message to the customer. Some are articulate and others aren't. Some can deliver a crisp, concise message and others present a confusing mishmash and never get to the point. You should understand the strengths and weaknesses of the people who will accompany you to customer meetings. I have found that even the smartest CEOs can have trouble making a point or understanding what the customer needs to hear.

One time I was with my CEO visiting the CEO of a prospective customer for the first time. My CEO was very technical, so his comfort area when he communicated was to be technical. The prospect CEO was not technical but a very effective manager. As we began our dialogue, my CEO reverted to his comfort zone and began to describe our product in very detailed technical terms the prospect CEO did not understand. I could tell, because I saw the prospect CEOs eyes glaze over (nonverbal communication). While my CEO was very perceptive, I believe he unconsciously ignored the visual cues of boredom the prospect CEO was giving. Finally, I interrupted my CEO, turned to the prospect CEO, and asked her if she knew what our product's value to her company would be. She looked at me and replied that she had no idea. I responded to her with a very concise description of why her company would benefit by doing business with us. She immediately got it, and I could tell she appreciated my interruption. Thankfully, my CEO got the cue and skillfully transitioned to a more meaningful conversation. The meeting ended successfully.

Interrupting your companion at a meeting may or may not work out. Some people get infuriated over their own people interrupting them. The role of the salesperson should be to guide the meeting in the right direction. Many times, people like to hear themselves talk, and in so doing deviate from the topic because they are so into themselves. Usually, their egos are very large, and they can't imagine themselves screwing up. Interrupting is a judgment call you have to make. You may have to interrupt because the subject got off track and has to be brought back to the reason why you are there.

I like to have a discussion beforehand with the people I bring into the meeting about the fact that I may interrupt them to keep the meeting on track. I am the salesperson, I control the account, and that means I control meetings and can act as a referee. If someone is deviating from the subject, I steer the conversation back on track. It helps to discuss the way you will run the meeting before you go in and come to an agreement on your tactics. It would be great to have only people who are well behaved in a meeting, but that won't happen. Besides, this is part of why you get paid so much. When you visit a prospect with one or more people, you essentially have an orchestra for which the salesperson should be recognized as the conductor.

Never correct people (your people or the customer) in a meeting. It publicly humiliates them and diminishes their credibility. If one of your people tries to correct someone, interrupt in a tactful way and say you will take it offline. If one of your people said the wrong thing in the meeting, confront him or her afterward about it, one on one. If it was bad, you'll have to figure out a way to fix it with the customer. If your customer said something bad in the meeting, you may or may not want to confront him or her about it. That all depends on your relationship. Hopefully, you will have an ally in the meeting you can go to and ask why the customer spoke in that way.

A good meeting is one where the salesperson has set it up so the result is predetermined. This level of control is necessary if you want to execute a strategy to obtain an expected result. One of the tactics for doing this is to rehearse with all the members of your team as to exactly what they will say in the meeting. You may even rehearse their lines, something like a stage manager will do with actors during rehearsal. The meeting can be your factory people visiting a customer site or your customer visiting your factory. It doesn't matter. You have to exert control to achieve the goal of the meeting. Scripting ensures that what is said in the meeting moves you closer to that goal line.

Scripting

Scripting is a fundamental skill for any salesperson. When you conduct meetings, you may have factory people supporting you, and they'll need to know what to say to contribute to the goal of the meeting. Get everybody together beforehand, either in person or by other means, such as a conference call. Review your strategy for closing the meeting. During the premeeting prep, you should clearly state to each person what you need him or her to say. Everyone must agree with your strategy.

Some people will say they agree, but inside they have another agenda or just don't care. Either way, this attitude could disrupt the customer meeting. You need to solve the problem before you get in front of the customer. A benefit of scripting is that the process can expose to you if someone isn't mentally cooperating. After you script a person of what to say, have them repeat it back to you. Listen to each person carefully. Watch for body language. This is important, because if people aren't buying into your agenda for the meeting, you will discover it here. Your sensitive salesperson antennae will detect a problem. You'll know something isn't exactly right with the way they say it.

This is the time to get it out on the table and confront the individual. Tell him or her you think he or she isn't buying into your idea. You can say something like, "You know, Peter, I have a feeling you don't agree with this. Is that right?" This allows malcontents to get their issues out on the table. Be objective as you listen to their counterargument. Consider what those who disagree have to say and try to see if they are right. Don't be upset if someone has a better idea about a strategy. You are interested in results, not in being the smartest person. If this person's idea is better, use it. Rescript everyone again and have each person repeat what he or she is supposed to say. Now everyone will be prepared, and you have controlled the entire meeting so the outcome will be as you want.

When you script people, you may do it directly or indirectly. If you are direct, you tell them what you want them to say and why. It's important to tell them why so they don't feel they're being treated like an idiot. Indirect scripting is when you are more subtle with people you want to script and work together on how the meeting is supposed to end, and then rehearse what they will say. You don't tell them you're scripting them, you're just making sure they agree to say things that you mutually agree on, which will bring the meeting around to what you both agreed on. This way, everyone will say what is needed.

Scripting is useful in many sales situations. Some salespeople don't do it at all or don't do it enough. Knowing when to script is important. Every encounter in which one of your factory people will communicate to your customer should be scripted. You should always be thinking about the final result of the conversation or meeting and how people should be scripted to have a successful outcome. It can be as simple as asking someone what he or she will say to the customer. The more you script, the better you will be at it, and the better you will know when to use it. Scripting is easy to learn to do If you are new at it, watch your peers do it in meetings.

After you get the hang of scripting, not only will you be able to script, but you will know when someone has been scripted by other people. The easier it is to catch someone who is scripted, the less sophisticated the scripter is. Hearing a script will clearly divulge what the strategy was behind the scripting. This gives you important information on what the scripter's strategy is. It's very revealing.

People who are willing to be scripted are allies of the person who scripted them. You may discover in a meeting that someone was scripted by a competitor to sabotage your meeting. This will reveal that the scripter is not your ally and is willing to work against you. Also, the script will reveal important information about what the scripter knows about your weaknesses. This whole scripting thing is rather powerful and sophisticated.

While you are busy crafting scripts for a meeting, you might take a break and make sure you have more of the basic meeting skills down. One of those is presenting. Every salesperson should be able to create and deliver a rousing presentation. Presenting to an audience is a skill that is necessary for making good money in almost any profession.

Presenting

Being able to present to customers in front of an audience is a skill that will ensure you can break into a six-figure income. Not many people have the talent to

- speak in front of people,
- smoothly articulate using visual aids, and
- deliver a value proposition that is clear and concise.

This is an absolute requirement for a successful salesperson.

Presenting takes lots of practice and watching others do it. Not only do you have to speak publicly, but you need to make your point using visual aids like Microsoft PowerPoint. Additionally, you need to be familiar with what you are talking about, which takes a lot of studying and watching others present.

Presenting requires you to have a deep understanding about your product's features so you can clearly convey them to the customer. If you can't teach it, you don't know it. If you don't know it, you will look like a fool if you try to present it.

You will need presentation material. Unfortunately, not all companies generate presentation material that is of good quality. In many cases, marketing people will generate a slide set and gives one to sales for presenting. Sometimes you aren't that lucky and have to put one together yourself. Having a good command of presentation software and how to use it is very important.

When you first begin to present, you will only be able to give a very basic presentation and probably not answer many questions. This is because your understanding of the product will be shallow. The more you present, the more you will understand about the product, the better you will present. The more you watch others present in your company, the better you will understand the product and how to present it yourself.

Don't get too fancy with your presentation. Keep it simple. Avoid using a lot of complex features unless you are a guru at it. Presentations that are complicated find a way to fail when you are showing them to customers. Remember, the point is that this is your platform, not the presentation's platform. If your visual aid is too rich, it will distract from your message.

Practice by yourself or with peers. Even use a video camera on yourself. If you have to present to large audiences and do it often, you might want to sign up for a course on it. Sometimes your company may sponsor an internal course on presenting. Take it. Get a book on it. Train yourself to be the best.

Save your old presentations. It never fails that I want to make a point and remember a great slide on some old presentation somewhere. Now where was that? I hope I didn't delete it!

As you present, you will notice more subtle points to talk about with the customer. The customers will ask questions. The more experienced you become at presenting, the more detailed and complex questions you will be able to answer. Sometimes you will have revelations while you are presenting. This happens to me all the time. You have a stroke of brilliant insight that allows you to see a big-picture aspect of the product that no one in your company told you about. Write your insight down.

No matter how technical your product or service is, if you can't articulate its benefits in a simple-to-understand way, you can bet customers won't understand it either. Don't get mired down in detail when you present. Don't read the slides. If you do, everyone will think you are wasting their time. Remember, the presentation is about you and what you have to say, not the presentation itself. You are the focus, not the slides.

Another interesting phenomenon I notice is there are two different feature sets for the same product. One set is when your factory people explain the product to you directly without customers present. The other set is the one they describe to customers when they are presenting. This isn't a deception or a way to keep you from getting information. When people are relaxed, they behave one way; when they are in front of a customer, they are under pressure, and they behave another way. This is true even if they seem outwardly confident and relaxed with the customer. The core of the story stays the same, but be prepared to hear a slightly different version when you sit in front of the customer.

Make sure you take notes when others are presenting. You will hear them talk about features you didn't know about. Write these down and check with them later to make sure you heard correctly. This way you develop a thorough list of all the features of your product that you can incorporate into the presentation when you give it.

When you first go on the road and start presenting, keep a notepad close by while you are in front of your customer. As you present, three things will happen. First, you will think of new questions to ask about your product that didn't occur to you before. Second, you will think of ways to improve the presentation. Third, you will have small revelations about your product that you didn't realize previously, as I stated above. Your understanding of the product will deepen.

On your notepad, jot down quick notes to yourself about these thoughts. If you do it quickly, it shouldn't bother your audience. Later, bring what you took down on your notepad to someone in your company who can answer your questions or hear your ideas. Usually, this is the person who made the presentation or some other marketing person. Also, don't be afraid to ask your peers. Observe as much as you can and practice, practice, practice. If you do, in no time you will become a master at presenting.

While you're up in front of all those people presenting, you have a great opportunity to look around the room and see who is really listening and if your audience is engaged. The way people sit, their posture, where they put their arms, and even eye contact are all providing nonverbal communication as to how you are doing. Body language is a huge component of nonverbal communication. Mastery of this subtle but powerful communication is another important skill for a salesperson to have.

Body Language and Nonverbal Communication

As a salesperson, you are undoubtedly perceptive and already have a talent for reading nonverbal communication, including body language. You should have a sense for it, since it represents 67 percent of all communication. People's unconscious selves are always looking for a potential clue that what you say is not what you say out loud. The more you interact with people, the deeper their assessment of you accumulates. During this process, they build an opinion of whether or not to trust you. The more time you spend, the deeper the trust, and the more opportunities you have to blow it.

Nonverbal communication really tells the truth. Verbal is all talk. If nonverbal communication is consistent with what is being said verbally, it's confirmed as true. Now, we all sometimes trust what is being said. But that is after a deeper assessment has been confirmed. This is why when you meet someone for the first time, you take what he or she says with a grain of salt. Not understanding this process will have you effective at only 33 percent of your game.

Most nonverbal communication is done with facial expressions, but not all. Probably at minimum, you should feel confident that you can go into a meeting, look around, and get a sense of who is relaxed and who isn't. If you're better at it, you can tell who is going to listen and who isn't. There will be plenty of visual cues available when you sit down. Can you pick them up? Are you sensing the overall feelings and noting who needs convincing and who doesn't? When you interact with someone or a group in a meeting, as soon as you walk in, quickly assess what people are doing.

- Watch gestures, body geometry, and facial expressions.
- How do people sit? Arms crossed, tensed up?
- Do they look relaxed or like they're at a starting block for a sprint?
- Do they look you in the eye?
- Are they fidgeting?
- When they speak, where do they look?
- Do they sit facing you, close, or far away?
- Are they positioned to dominate (like behind a desk) or close to you?
- What is the tone or inflection of their speech? (The words may be completely different from how they say them.)
- Do they sit or stand facing you or turned?
- What are they doing with their hands while you speak?
- Are their hands on top of the table or below, doing something you don't quite know?

If you are speaking to one or more people, make note of how they are paying attention. Some people can be very rude in meetings and check their e-mail on a laptop while you are talking. This is a good nonverbal cue they aren't interested but are using the meeting to burn time. Do you have their attention? Look around to see who is and isn't paying attention. I can tell in less than fifteen seconds who is interested and who isn't.

I teach a communications merit badge for Boy Scouts who are aspiring to their Eagle rank. When I start the first class, I tell them I already know who will pass and who will get partial credit (and have to take more time to pass because they won't complete all the requirements). Body language is an important tool that shows whether or not you are making progress or being persuasive with a prospect.

Some people are very unaware of their body language, while others use it as a subtle tool to communicate with you. To be successful in sales, you have to be able to read body language and interpret nonverbal communication. The unconscious person communicates nonverbally. Pay close attention. If you can do it well, you can distinguish between what someone says and what he or she really means.

Once you are more aware of the importance of nonverbal communication, you can appreciate how really influential it is. Meetings are rich in nonverbal communication. Not only are others sending you messages in a meeting, but you are also sending messages to them. You are being carefully watched, though it may not be apparent. Taking notes or at least appearing to take notes communicates your level of interest. Note-taking will reinforce your memory of the event and provide a log to refer back to later when you've completely forgotten what happened.

Taking Notes

People have all sorts of ways of noting what was said in a meeting. Some people take copious notes and others take none. What is right? There are people I know who don't need to take notes. Their memories are so good that much of what is said—most importantly, the key points—they will easily remember. This type of person is the exception. Most people will forget or take away only a percentage of what was said.

Regardless of your memory, though, taking notes has more to do with showing interest and attention than with actually noting the salient points of a meeting. By taking out pen and paper, you show your interest in what will happen. This action is far more important than actually writing down the important points of the meeting. If you don't put paper in front of you for notes, you will probably announce to every unconscious and conscious side of your customer that you aren't interested in the meeting.

Notice that I specify pen and paper for notes, not a laptop computer. If you take out your computer, open it up, and start typing on it, there will be some concern, however small, that you are uninterested in the meeting and choosing to surf the web instead. Nobody can see what you are typing or looking at, and they will assume the worst.

If your customer chooses to bring out a laptop, there's nothing you can do about it, but don't you do it. I have been in group meetings where over half the customers are working on their laptops while I presented. How do you think I felt about that? I really doubt they knew what was going on in the meeting or what I was saying. I think I could have put up pictures of dogs and cats on the screen and they wouldn't have noticed. I can assure you that if the roles were reversed, they would feel the same way. So resist hauling out your laptop. Tablet computers are okay, as long as you can write on them in longhand. Typing is not good etiquette.

As the salesperson at the meeting, you are responsible for all notes unless you are presenting. If someone from your company is with you, have him or her take notes. If you are alone, you will have to both present and take notes. Your customer won't mind you stopping the presentation to take notes every now and then; it shows you are interested and want to support him or her.

Notes are very important. If you forget your notebook, ask the customer for a piece of paper. Always take notes, no matter what. This is a fundamental.

While you are scribbling away during the meeting, an action item may come up. It is vitally important to get the complete details. Meetings that get things done usually have action items. If those items aren't completed, the purpose of the meeting is negated. The salesperson is the keeper of the action item even when someone else owns it.

The Action Item

An action item (AI) is a building block that helps move a sales cycle to the next step. Salespeople live for action items, which are dynamic, perishable, and numerous. If you have an active set of accounts, you will have a myriad of action items to follow up on each day. Even when customers aren't giving you action items, your factory people will. When they stop giving you action items, there will be action items that are endogenous—not triggered by an outside event. These are things you need to do for yourself, professionally or personally. Action items are a to-do list.

Once an AI is completed as follow-up to a meeting, you are poised to go the next step. Usually with customers or prospects, you can't reengage without finishing the AI. Think about this: if you owe a customer some data and you want to move to the next step with that customer in a sales cycle, he or she has the obvious expectation that you owe something. You can't reengage because you will be asked where the action item is, and if it isn't done, your interaction will be distracted by discussing the incomplete AI.

Even if you think you can still see the customer without finishing the AI, there will be an unconscious expectation that you need to do it. This can complicate your relationship and cause unpredictable and possibly undesirable behavior. It's better to clean up the AI than make things more complicated for yourself. Aren't things complicated enough already?

If you are very active in sales, you will always need to keep track of all your action items. Large numbers of unassociated action items can get very unwieldy. Keeping track of what to do for whom and when it's due can be very difficult. To manage AIs effectively, you need some kind of system that works for you. There are literally hundreds of systems to keep track of things. Some people think their system is perfect and may even try to convince you there really isn't any other way to track AIs. Don't get sucked into that thinking. How you manage action items is very personal. Something that works well for one person could be totally impractical for another. You need to find one that works for you. Remember, all you want is good results.

Some people like to incorporate technology into managing action items. Smartphones, tablets, and notebook computers can be powerful options. But I know very effective salespeople who use a simple small notebook to track action items. So whether you like to do it manually or digitally, it doesn't matter. Find something you like and use it. As time goes by, you may see something that catches your eye. Go ahead and experiment. As you get older, your needs and preferences will change. It's expected that what you are doing now may be very different from what you will use in a few years.

Most systems offer a way to prioritize and categorize. AIs are very dynamic. A simple system has three levels of priority, the highest being the one where you will lose your job if you don't do it—something like your CEO telling you he needs the data on his desk by the next morning over a critical issue. The next level is something like an important customer needing a report from you by the next business day so he can look good in a meeting. A low priority might be a rock fetch given to you by a customer who is a pest and doesn't buy anything.

AIs must be juggled by priority because they are perishable. They are basically a to-do list, and as we all know, managing a to-do list successfully can be daunting. Old, low-priority action items that you put off have to be escalated if you run out of time to do them. You have to regularly review your entire list to avoid forgetting an old low-priority item that suddenly becomes very important. Some AIs will never get done. You just won't have the time to do them. Every salesperson wrestles with this problem.

Use all the resources at your disposal to complete AIs. If you're lucky, you may have inside people who can assist you in completing AIs. Use them in the most efficient way you can. If you really depend on these people, treat them like family. Don't be cheap, as they are helping make you successful. Maybe at certain holidays, you give a gift as a way of saying thank you? Communicate with them regularly and don't keep them in the dark as to why they are doing these AIs. They will appreciate you telling them why this AI is so important to complete. Make them feel as if they have privileged information.

If your inside helpers are a shared resource, you will have competition for their time. Being appreciative and collaborative will ensure you get a disproportionate amount of it. It's remarkable to me that many salespeople have abusive relationships with their inside people. It's so easy to displace such salespeople by treating those same workers with respect. Usually the salespeople will not even know why their AIs were so late.

There is a lot of information on the web about AIs and various techniques. Peruse the information and try several methods. Some cost money, but completing AIs efficiently is critical to your success. If you think a system will definitely help you, don't be afraid of putting out some cash for it. It's all a very personal decision, so go with what seems like a good solution for you. Don't let someone tell you your system is foolish or old. It doesn't matter as long as it works for you.

CHAPTER FOUR

BASIC SALES SKILLS

Preparation

As a salesperson, you must be a master at preparation. Whatever you are planning to do, you have to anticipate every move like a chess game. Look at all the moves and evaluate what will happen at each step. Being prepared is about anticipating what comes next and getting ready for it. If there is a barrier to the next step or some action that needs to happen, it's you who has to make sure it does. It can mean sending a brief to your manager for an upcoming customer visit, sending reminders to attendees of a meeting, or anticipating what customers need to make it easier for them to order from you. Every day, you will spend time making preparations for all the things you have to do. Each item you prepare for makes your job easier later and paves a path to success.

The first thing you learn after you become expert at preparing is that sometimes you don't have time to prepare. Even though you may be very thorough and a good planner, you'll become frustrated because there is not enough time in the day. Well, there never will be. This makes many salespeople frustrated, because they can't complete all their plans on time. Just be good at prioritizing.

Not everyone you depend on will be as good as you are at preparing. So you may need to prepare for them too. Your management may stink at it. Don't blame them. I know salespeople who roll their eyes skyward when their management changes the schedule for the fourth time or decides to make arrangements for travel at the last minute, when the airline fees will be exorbitant, and decides to cancel because of it. Why can't these people plan better? Instead of stewing about how inept your management is at planning, you might look at yourself to see why you get so pissed off about this whenever it happens.

Your job is to fix problems. Your factory people, including your management, will create problems all the time for you—and so will your customers. Fixing problems is one of the things they pay you to do. If the job was easy, they wouldn't need you, would they? So if you find yourself getting pissed off about your manager's lack of preparation, ask yourself if you're really just unhappy with your job. When you focus on criticism instead of being constructive, it's a good indication you're ready to go or just burned out.

Preparation is, in part, a learned skill. If you are new to sales, look to your peers, managers, and mentors to see how they prepare for stuff. As with anything in life, it's a balance. Strive to be good, but also understand you can't control the world. Strive for lofty goals, but also know you can only do what you can do and nothing more. Don't sweat it if you prepare like a master but still fall short. It's only normal.

Now that you are prepared, nothing will get in your way. You have anticipated all the moves ahead and are ready to act. Acting on a plan won't help you, though, if your timing stinks. Being punctual to appointments is one fundamental most, but not all, salespeople understand. Being late to a meeting is sometimes unavoidable, but it should be a rare occurrence. How important is it to be on time?

Being on Time

It's so important to be on time that I'm writing a section on it in this chapter, even though you would think it was just what every salesperson did automatically, without prompting. Unfortunately, I have noticed that many salespeople—even capable and brilliant ones—lose touch with their basic fundamentals, including punctuality. I have seen highly professional salespeople be habitually late. Their execution in all other areas is flawless but is tarnished by tardiness. Over and over again, I see how being late hurts them with customers. I hear customers talking behind their backs. If only they could just be on time, their business would grow. What is even sadder about this is that the salesperson is unaware how bad his or her reputation is. Someone else is getting the larger share of business, and these individuals don't even know why.

It is incredible that so simple a task should be so hard to do. No matter what you rationalize for the reason, being late is a problem, and it pisses your customer off. The customer may not say anything; he or she may even be very cordial and show no trace of resentment. But let me tell you, being late can put you seriously afoul of your customer's unconscious being, and you don't want that to happen. If you are late habitually to this customer, you run the risk of developing a reputation that will diminish your credibility and, in the end, your ability to influence. You might as well pack it up.

In your career, you will have many very, very important meetings to go to. They could be with your CEO or senior management. A poor performance could be job-limiting, and arriving late will contribute to that. If you are flying to another city for the meeting, consider the possibility of a flight cancellation. You may want to fly in the day before rather than the same morning as the meeting, just in case. Be paranoid about being on time to high-level meetings.

Even when your travel is well planned, there are instances when you'll be delayed. If this happens, always call the person you are meeting with to explain that you will be late. Ask if this is okay, and offer to reschedule if necessary. Be apologetic. In most situations, the person will appreciate the alert and be willing to wait for you.

Being on time is a ridiculously simple principle. Yet many salespeople can't seem to understand the message that tardiness telegraphs. How does something like this start? I would say it's probably an unconscious problem. You leave at the last minute. You stop looking at the time. Instead of planning to arrive at least fifteen minutes before the meeting, you plan to arrive exactly at the agreed time. This is something a mediocre performer does, just a lazy thing.

Punctuality shows respect to the people you are meeting with, is professional behavior, and will differentiate you from mediocre performers. Always be on time. If you do that, know there is a percentage of your competition that isn't. Some salespeople can't fix a tardiness habit. They usually end up being let go. Don't end up in that category.

Be on time, and the world will be at your disposal. Well, at least most of the time. In some cases, the world will tell you to bug off. Being rejected and turning it around is one of those annoying things a salesperson is paid to handle. Getting people to be reasonable and consider they made the wrong decision is what it's all about.

Handling Rejection, Failure, and Barriers

History has demonstrated that the most notable winners usually encountered heartbreaking obstacles before they triumphed. They won because they refused to become discouraged by their defeats.—B. C. Forbes, financial journalist who founded Forbes Magazine

Obstacles are necessary for success because in selling, as in all careers of importance, victory comes only after many struggles and countless defeats. Yet each struggle, each defeat, sharpens your skills and strengths, your courage and your endurance, your ability and your confidence, and thus each obstacle is a comrade-in-arms forcing you to become better or quit. Each rebuff is an opportunity to move forward; turn away from them, avoid them, and you throw away your future.—Og Mandino, motivational speaker, writer, and World War II pilot

That which does not kill us makes us stronger.—Friedrich Nietzsche, philologist and existentialist philosopher

Sales starts when the customer says NO.—Old sales saying

Rejection is one of the most basic issues a salesperson has to deal with. It comes when the customer says no—to something as big as an order or as simple as an invitation to lunch. In your personal life, the situation is the same. Many people in everyday life loathe rejection. They avoid it as much as possible. I think it's obvious that rejection is a painful experience, and it makes sense to avoid painful things. But if you constantly avoid rejection, your chance of moving forward is zero.

A salesperson has to embrace, manage, and overcome rejection. This is one of the reasons salespeople make the big money. Not everybody wants to do this. The most fundamental reason salespeople are needed to sell a product is that they know how to overcome objection. They are absolute top guns at doing this. Period.

Sales isn't about taking orders, it's about overcoming objection and rejection. When a customer says no, that's when good salespeople begin to earn their money. Many people don't understand that rejection in sales isn't personal. The rejection is not about the individual but the product or service the salesperson is trying to sell. Still, many people don't understand the difference between the two. If you are a salesperson or just thinking about becoming one, you already have a gut feel for this distinction. It's not personal—though I will say that the rules in this section apply to personal rejection also.

If you are rejected—that is, the customer says no—the first thing you should think of is how to reverse that decision. To reverse a rejection, you need to understand the real reason you were rejected. This can be very complicated. Many times the customer won't reveal the real reason for your rejection because he or she wants to get it over with. You will find that many customers hate telling someone no. They want to avoid a long drawn-out confrontation, so they make up something simple and clear-cut that you can't respond to. This way, they get it over with quickly and don't have to spend a lot of energy with you. People want closure. It allows them to leave a painful situation and move on.

The moment after someone tells you no is your best chance to find out why. Make sure you ask what you did wrong or why the decision against you was made. Try to say something to get the customer to talk about it. If you can get a discussion going, there is a good chance he or she will tell you why the decision was made. If you get the real reason, you may be able to offer a counterproposal. If you get new information about why you were denied, you have a chance to reverse it. This process is called *loss recovery*.

You have to be careful about choosing the right time to counter the decision. If you bring it up right away, the customer may get pissed off at you for trying again. You are making that individual go back to the pain of telling you no. Timing is everything. If you won't see the customer again for a while, then you have to bring it up at the moment. If you visit frequently, you might consider waiting until you've thought out your strategy completely. Either way, once you receive the "real" information, you can try to turn the decision around. You need to keep trying until it looks completely hopeless. Customers will inwardly appreciate your persistence in trying to win.

I have personally experienced how being persistent can reverse a decision. Key factors to winning against rejection are

- making sure you understand the real reason for their decision,
- formulating a new strategy if you discover new information,
- choosing the right time to turn the tables on the decision,
- persistence, and
- knowing when to keep pushing and when to quit.

When the customer says no and you have no idea why, that may be a sign you're lacking seriously important data about the opportunity. Another red flag that important data is missing is when you are implementing a strategy and nothing is happening. You can't get any traction, and you don't know why. This should warn you that something is happening behind the scenes that you aren't aware of. This is where your crystal ball should help you. Trust your feelings. If it feels bad, try to get creative and develop some hunches as to what is missing and the reason things aren't working the way they should be. Sometimes the most obvious thing you are missing is the one you're in denial about.

One last point on rejection: you can't take it personally. The customers aren't saying you suck. They are only saying they don't want your product or service. If you find yourself agonizing over being told no, it will cloud your ability to solve the problem. If you can't see clearly, you are hosed. You've got to detach yourself from making it personal and focus on finding and removing the barriers.

Sales is a vast ocean of rejection. Take it personally, and you'll be one unhappy guppy. Not letting rejection get to you is fundamental in sales. Get over it! I have seen potentially great salespeople burn out early because they couldn't get over being rejected. If you have trouble with this, it could be a good time to have a chat with a mentor.

How bad can rejection be? I was thrown out of a company one time—literally told to get out. I was with some factory people making a pitch to a group of high-tech prospects. My factory guy was doing great until he unknowingly described how we had copied a circuit that the prospect had invented. I could see something was wrong when the prospect began to turn red. I tried giving my factory guy some body language signals to change the topic. He was so enamored with how we cleverly copied the circuit to avoid lawsuits, I think the building could have burned down and he wouldn't have noticed. He continued until the prospect jumped up and told us to get out. My factory guy was dumbfounded. He even tried to finish his story as we were walking out, which infuriated the prospect even more. I think he came close to getting punched in the face. The prospect described, in a very agitated manner, how he had already sued one company over the copying of his invention and might consider suing us. His parting statement was to never come back.

The problem was that I had a lot of potential business riding on this individual. My quota was getting larger, and I really needed this guy to book business with us. My first mental note was to never bring this factory guy anywhere again, unless to a shooting range where he could hold the targets.

I knew the customer didn't want me around. I could have left and felt sorry for myself, wondering how much damage was done and how many people he would tell that my company sucked. Since I had learned to detach myself from taking these things personally, I immediately set about finding a way to turn this into an opportunity. I immediately began to strategize how to use this to get more business.

Because I assumed the prospect wasn't mad at *me* but at my company, I could reach out to him personally. Of course, I let a few days go by to let him cool down, and then I called him. He was still perturbed, and he vented about my factory guy. In talking with him, I discovered he was under a lot of pressure and was upset about everyone copying his invention. I did a lot of active listening. Fortunately, over a short time I was able to resume meetings with him and even got some more business.

Sometimes it does get personal. There will be times you may be trying to rationally discuss an issue with someone who has no interest in listening to you and thinks it's a good idea to bring back the head of the vendor because it will impress management. Ideally, someone else from your company brings bad news to the customer, not you, and it's his or her head the customer takes. But it doesn't always work that way. In this situation, be level-headed and utterly rational no matter how bad the situation is. Hopefully you can do damage control later.

There will be times the factory makes a promise that you relate to the customer, and then the factory breaks it and causes the customer to lose credibility within his company. Even though you had nothing to do with the decision to break the promise, you may end up getting blamed by association. This can seriously harm a relationship. Customers may be very hurt, and in some ways you can't blame them. They may not have the skills to understand you are only the messenger. Not everyone can see clearly all the time. To recover from this may take some time, or you may get a lucky break. All you can do is look for opportunities to recover the lost credibility. This takes a long time.

To beat the constant stream of rejection in a sales job, you have to tap into your reservoir of optimism. Getting to know yourself and feeling that you can do anything will help you scale the mountain. To do that, you need a huge amount of positive energy, which comes from within you. Believe in yourself and that you are very good at what you do. If you can do that, there isn't anything you can't do.

When customers get to a point of making a decision on buying your product or service, they may or may not indicate their intentions very clearly. A good salesperson can sense when a customer gets into this state of consciousness and knows it's time to ask for the order or close.

Closing

Closing is a true art form that is mostly appreciated by salespeople and some of the customers they call on. Everyone closes every day. When you ask for something, you are closing. In sales, closing is the point in the sales cycle when the salesperson has demonstrated he or she can fulfill the prospect's need and determines that it's time to ask the prospect to buy the product or service. This is a very subtle and important step.

There are literally dozens of ways to converge to a point of closing. There are hundreds of ways to get the prospect to commit to buy. All of these depend on very subtle complex nuances that fit the best and offer the highest likelihood the prospect is at the exact point of being ready to be asked for the order.

If you look on the web, there are many sites that list closing techniques. How do you know which technique to use? That is one of the things that make salespeople such valuable assets to your organization. Most salespeople have an ability to just "know" the right way to set up a close. Like any profession, if salespeople are good, they have a talent for it. Also, like any professional, they train for it and get even better with practice.

Closing is a fundamental skill for a salesperson. Once you know most all the ways to close, you hope that you've chosen the right one. These methods go by many names, including test close, empathy close, doubt close, exclusive close, opportunity cost close, have-to-do-it-now-or-lose-it close. Get the picture? The salesperson has demonstrated the product can meet the need of the prospect, but it is at this point he or she has to use one of the many types of close methods to get the customer to commit to buying.

Experience and training are the only ways to get to be a great closer. Most salespeople can get to a close. Some don't use the best method. Some get the order anyway, and some fail because they didn't approach it correctly. Then, believe it or not, there are salespeople who are afraid of closing and never ask for the order.

My grandfather was a successful salesperson. Before he did that, he sat on the other side as a high-level purchasing director for Alcoa Aluminum. He would tell me stories of his days as a buyer and the salespeople who called on him. Some he had tremendous respect for. He was an ally for some. Then there was this one poor soul of a salesperson. My grandfather said this guy would visit him every two weeks. He would come in and talk about golf, which my grandfather was passionate about. Then he would leave. Remarkably, my grandfather never knew what this guy sold! All the guy did was come in and talk about golf. Eventually, my grandfather was too busy and stopped seeing him.

Can you imagine a salesperson who never even began a sales cycle or closed for an order? I have known some salespeople who just can't close. How do they get in this position? Lack of oversight. Some companies have customers who book regularly and fill backlog with orders. Some salespeople who service these types of customers can get mediocre and are overlooked. I can't imagine not asking for an order. Just remember one of the basic rules of sales, the ABC rule: Always Be Closing!

Even when the prospect commits to buy, a salesperson can lose the order. If the customer has accepted the terms and has indicated an intention to buy, there is no need to provide more information. Yet some salespeople continue to close even after they get the order. This is a big mistake. If the customer has decided to buy, why is there a need to keep closing? There is no upside to continuing to sell. There is only downside.

You need to shut up when you have a deal, even though you may be excited about winning. Talking excessively could be interpreted as a sign of nervousness, which may make the customer reconsider. Exposing information about what you are doing or chatting too much increases the risk of killing a deal. If you have the order, you are done. The best salespeople know when to shut up and get out. If you have a deal done, get away as soon as possible. Sit around after you have the order, and you make it easy for customers to tell you they changed their mind. If you leave, it's harder to reach you. Of course, they can call you, but still it requires more work to reach you than if you were in front of them. After you get the order, stop talking and politely leave.

Study up on closing. You may be surprised to find out how many ways there are to close a deal. Remember the ABC rule, and may you close many deals!

You know your quota and what you get paid for, you can articulate your value proposition, and you are well prepared to begin selling. You are a picture of a valiant knight of sales, crusading for your company's kingdom. But to make a sale, you have to go to your prospect's kingdom and encounter the subjects on their land. Who are these people and what of their ways? Perhaps, knight of sales, you can prepare for your encounter by doing some study on who these people really are and which ones will help you make a sale. Many will talk with you, but few will actually be empowered to make the decision. Knowing a little about the structure of how decisions are made will save you time and enhance your rate of success in landing business.

The DI and the DM

Obviously, not everyone on your organizational chart will buy your product or service. Also, more than one person may be involved in the process of making a decision to buy. It can get rather complicated and confusing. The organizational chart will show you where the group will be but won't identify who among the group will make the decision.

You already know some people on the organizational chart won't be of any help in closing a deal. The faster you can isolate people who are really important to making a decision, the faster you can make money. How can you get to the right people and identify their roles? You know you have to be efficient at this. You are thinking this is more like a job for Sherlock Holmes. Time to do some detective work and figure out who is making the decisions at the prospect.

When you call on a company, you need to influence the right person to make a decision to use your product. If you are calling on companies that have more than five to ten employees, it may not be obvious who is making the decision. The larger the company, the more difficult and time-consuming it is to find the right person. There are three classes of people you will meet at a customer: the decision maker (DM), the decision influencer (DI), and the person who has nothing to do with the decision (the NP or nonplayer). It should be obvious that you want to spend your time with the DM and the DI. Ideally, these are the only people you need to talk to, but in reality you will need to talk to everyone. You have to do that in order to not miss a DI or DM.

Any company may have more than one DM and DI. It's your job as the salesperson to determine which people you need to get to. If the company is large, the first thing you need to do is make an organizational chart and use it to identify who you should be talking to. These people are the ones you should spend your time with to close the deal.

Determining the DMs and DIs is made more complicated by the fact that not all people are approachable. On the other hand, some people are very approachable and engaging. In fact, they may want a lot of your time. Many times, the people who are the most approachable are the ones who are the least important to you—the NPs. To further confuse you, the DM may be a very approachable person. Identifying a DM or a DI is one of the key talents of a professional salesperson.

Sometimes DMs have people as barriers. DMs may be pestered by many salespeople. After a while, they get sick of it and naturally put in place people and administrators to help filter out the noise. Find someone who has a lot of barriers, and that's a good indication you've identified a DM.

Whether or not this person is key to your business is something you have to decide. It takes a lot of work to reach these people, and you don't want to waste your time reaching a DM who won't have anything to do with your business. Get as much data from the people around the DM as possible. This will help determine if you should go for it.

You may be stunned to have someone tell you directly he or she is the decision maker and you only need to deal with him or her. This is a clear signal that this individual is not a DM. Besides having insecurity problems, people like this are an issue for a salesperson. They insert themselves into your path to the real DM and create barriers. Handling them is tricky. You don't want to piss them off. You need to make them think they are important, give them attention, but in parallel plan a path the real DM. Many times, people within the organization know about this behavior but tolerate it because these delusional folks make excellent barriers to salespeople. Unluckily for you, they may be in a position to hurt you with the DM.

A high-level DM may be very difficult to reach. You may be told he or she doesn't want to deal with salespeople. This is either a solid wish on the DM's part or a test to see if a salesperson is good enough to get a meeting. Either way, if this is a DM who is key to making a deal, you have to find a way to get through. If you company has a relationship already established and is a strategic vendor, it will be easier to reach high-level execs. If not, you have to be creative. Sometimes it may take months and months to set up the right conditions for a meeting.

If you are new to this, the best way to find a DM is to call on as many people as you can. After a while, you will notice everything points to one person, probably a high-level manager. Some people you call on will be helpful; others won't be. Many times people who want to meet with you will bring some value to the meeting. Employees at a company will agree a good salesperson knows more about their company than they do. That's your value. If you can manage that, people will want to meet with you to find out what is going on. Having a piece of juicy information is a great way to get meetings. Watch out, though—NPs will be even more motivated to meet with you, as they are hungrier for information than DMs or DIs.

Don't be duped by titles. There are always two organizational charts—the formal one on paper and the one that shows who really makes the decisions. Always start by finding the topmost position on the formal organizational chart. As you get information from people around this person, you may discover it's not the right person for you to reach.

If you sell commodity products or services, the DM may be at a lower level in the company. I know very successful salespeople who only call on shipping-dock managers. They have no need to "call high." If you sell a very expensive/key product or take large-dollar orders, you will deal with DMs higher up in the organization. Your managers may want you to "call high," but you're the one who determines the right level, not them. Sometimes the advice is right on. Always check it out. Realize, though, that trying to reach everyone in a large company is a waste of time.

There may be only one DM and no DI. If you sell strategic products or services, you will need the attention of higher-level management to win the business. The influencers will be all around the DM. It is important to study how the DM makes a decision. The DM may talk to other people before making a decision. These are the DIs. Also, the DM may "hear" good things about your company. This is indirect influence that you can create. Indirect influence can be very powerful and may even cause the DM to discount a direct DI. If the business is very important to you, this is an absolute must-do.

Find the DMs and find out how they make decisions. Some do it alone; others may seek advice. Find out who they get their information from, the DIs. Do they do it informally (in hallways) or formally (at meetings)? This can give you insight on their trust level with the DI. If a DM is best friends with a potential DI, that tells you something. Do they play tennis together? Are they neighbors? Brothers? Sisters? Is the janitor the brother-in-law of the CEO? Is the administrative assistant to the VP his wife? Make sure you understand the relationships within your sphere of opportunity. Overlooking someone could kill a deal or hamper your ability to close it.

The DI is the person who will either recommend or reject your product to the DM. Hence, the DI needs to believe in your value proposition and think the DM should buy from your company. The DM will listen to the DI and take that individual's advice or throw it out. DIs are not DMs because of political and/or organizational reasons. They can't make the decision but are involved in the decision-making process in some way.

DIs can influence DMs either directly or indirectly. If it is direct influence, they are in the trust of the DM. The DM will ask them for their opinion. A DI who has direct influence cn a DM is in a powerful position. Indirect influence can be a person or team who are chartered with doing a formal evaluation of your product. Though these people may never talk directly to the DM or direct DI, their report may be very influential. Also, indirect influence may come from a groundswell of subordinates talking around the water cooler about how great your product is. If this talk gets to the DM or direct DI, it can help push a decision in your direction.

Remember that all this influence can also work against you. There is no guarantee that when a DI is meeting with you, he or she is gathering information to evaluate it objectively. The DI can work against you and try to make you fail. Why would DIs do this? There are several reasons. They may like your competitor's product better. Even if the competitor has an inferior product, the DI may like that company better than yours. What if the DI is an ally to your competitor? There are a lot of reasons why a DI would work against you. On the surface, the DI may be very friendly and even seem helpful. All the time, he or she is sucking information out of you to use against you.

This is why it's necessary to do a background check on DIs before you open up with your full pitch. Observe who they talk with. Talk to other people in the company about them. Do they meet with the competition a lot? Sometimes you can find that out by checking the sign-in register in the lobby. Sometimes you can tell by the type of questions the DI asks you. These questions may sound as if the competitor was asking them of you. What is even more deceitful is when you sense the DI is repeating questions that were scripted by your competitor. This is a clear sign of danger.

If you leave a meeting with a potential DI and feel something isn't right, it probably isn't. Your gut can help you see this. Review your meeting with your manager and replay what happened. It may come out in the replay that the DI was using you. If you are sure the DI is using you, you need to come up with a strategy that counteracts the DI. This is hard to do. You are in a difficult position, because you need to work with the DI. Just going away may make the DI mad at you, further emboldening him or her to work harder against you.

This situation is very difficult, but there are things you can do. Minimize the amount of information you provide the DI. If you can, work directly with the DM. If you do that, it will be the DI's word against yours. While this sounds like an unfair fight, some DIs may contaminate their "objective" opinion with the DM because they push the competition too hard. If the DM is perceptive, he or she will see what is going on and discount the opinion of the DI. This is an uphill battle, but it can be won. Don't be surprised if you are suddenly blindsided one day by a DI. It's very hard to detect a DI who is going to betray you. Some are obvious and others aren't. Depend on your gut to identify a friend or foe.

Large organizations can be very frustrating because many people can be involved in a decision. Identifying them correctly is very important. Also, you should watch out for people who are "invisible" within the organization. These are stealth people who are very influential and are adept at being transparent. These invisible people won't show up at your meetings, but you may hear about them. They are difficult to speak with and usually don't respond to e-mails. Getting them in a room with you will be a challenge. You have to flush them out by developing a strategy aimed specifically to trap them.

First you need to find out as much about them as possible—who they hang with, what they like or dislike, whether people quote what they say. Build a profile on them as deep as possible. Eventually, something will surface about them that catches your attention. An ally is an invaluable source of data on these invisible people. So are their administration people, if they will talk to you. Until you are able to see these stealth DMs, consider your prospect of closing insecure at best.

For some key giveaways as to whether someone is invisible, listen to what other people say about him or her. Things like, "Other people need to hear about this," or more obviously, "Jason has to hear this before we can go on." Don't be surprised to find out nobody wants to help you get this person in a meeting with you. Generally, these invisible people are intentionally unapproachable not only to outsiders but also to their own people. This is how they are able to disappear.

Some invisible people put up this persona as a barrier to help them find the most clever and resourceful salespeople. Since they're in a decision-making position, every salesperson wants to call on them. If they make themselves very difficult to reach, their life is more peaceful and only the most clever salespeople can get access to them. Some strategies are going to their boss, confronting them in the parking lot, bumping into them in the lobby or hallway, or just finding exactly what they like to talk about in meetings and structuring your pitch like that. Being creative is the way you will differentiate yourself from the rest of the salespeople trying to reach them.

Once you identify all the DMs and DIs, you are in a good position to close your deal. Always be paranoid that you are overlooking someone. If you are working on a large project review it with a respected peer or your manager. Listen to their questions and criticism. I, myself, have been victim to the blindness of being too close to the account to see everything that is going on. I got blindsided and blew deals because I neglected to call on one or two people I decided weren't influential enough to count. Other times I failed because I hadn't done enough legwork to find out about everyone involved in the decision. I got lazy. Be thorough and leave no stone unturned.

You need to talk to everyone at least once, if not on a regular basis. The decision making in companies is fluid and changes with reorganizations, new projects, new people, business upturns and downturns, and power struggles won and lost. The organizational information you acquire is perishable information. That is law. After a short period, what you know will become stale and obsolete. Count on it. You have to constantly be meeting with people and reclassifying the decision-making structure.

This is where mediocre salespeople fall down. They get comfy thinking they own the account and become lazy. Changes happen right under their noses, and after a while, they become a storehouse of out-of-date information. Eventually they begin to blow deals and possibly not even know the competition is taking their business. Don't let that happen to you. Update your organizational chart on a regular basis and constantly refresh your relationships. If you do that, you will stay on top of who is making the decisions, who is influencing them, and who is just waiting around until they show up on your radar.

People will give you advice on who they think the DMs and DIs are. This may be the salesperson who used to call on your account, your manager, or employees at your account. Take this advice with a grain of salt. Be wary of these opinions, as they could be wrong. I have known salespeople who call on a company for years and never truly understand who is making the decisions. It may sound pathetic, but mediocre salespeople do this all the time. Advice from these people is useless. So when someone tells you some guy is the "key guy," just note it and move on. Those giving you advice don't stand to lose anything by getting it wrong. It falls to you to be the detective and sort out the DM from the DI from the NP. You'll become a master at separating the chaff from the wheat.

In your interactions with DMs and DIs, you may be asked for some action item or favor. Or you may have promised delivery of a product to your customer only to later discover your factory has delayed it. There are many situations where something won't get done unless you get help. You will have to bring your problem to management's attention and convince them it's important enough for them to help you. Escalation is an art and requires salespeople to use their best skills at influence.

Escalating

Escalation is one of the tools a salesperson has for punching through barriers and making things happen. Many barriers to progress are best solved by directing management's attention to the issue. You'll need to learn when to escalate a problem, how to get management to engage, how to present important facts to persuade, and how to follow through. As a salesperson, if you can't escalate successfully, you won't make any money.

During a sales process, you may encounter a problem that blocks your ability to bring a customer to close an order. The problem can be a price that is too high, allocation relief, a rule that is overreaching, even an individual who is uncooperative or unresponsive. Whatever it is, if you can't solve the problem, you are stuck. Your only choice is to ask management to use their authority to override the system or person who is in your way.

Many salespeople have trouble escalating. It's really not hard, but some salespeople hesitate to go higher because they are worried they are unable to compose a compelling argument and/or they are uncomfortable confronting authority. This is normal with new salespeople who might think, "What do I say?"

When you think of it, we escalate every day. When we need something, we ask for it. The technique of escalation is straightforward, yet you'll need to use some common sense in deciding when and how to do it. Management is a tool to help you solve problems, and you should use it. Sometimes picking a manager to help is obvious and easy. Other times, you'll have to tread very carefully because some people may not like you bringing something up. You may have to go over someone's head, which he or she will not like.

There is a proper protocol for this. Work up the ladder one rung at a time until you get the answer you need. Skipping over people can make you some steadfast enemies, especially if they are insecure. Should you have to skip over someone, find a way to include the person you are going around so you minimize hurt feelings. But if you can't avoid it and have to skip over someone, make sure you've weighed the pros and cons carefully. You can always do damage control as a last resort.

Escalation requires preparation. First, understand exactly what you need and be able to articulate your argument clearly so it's persuasive. Once you know what to ask for, you should anticipate any questions the manager might ask you. Review in your mind what might come up. The better you anticipate your manager's thoughts or issues, the better prepared you will look.

In larger companies, senior managers are continually peppered by salespeople asking for resolution to their problems. This is very tiring and takes a lot of time. A good portion of the salespeople hitting on them will be poorly prepared, and their requests will be shot down. This will frustrate a good manager, who would rather have salespeople make compelling arguments than ill-prepared requests. So if you are well prepared and have a compelling argument, the manager will appreciate your request and might even give you a little more leeway. The better prepared you are, the greater the chance you'll convince the manager to help. Ask yourself the following questions:

- Do I really need to escalate this issue or is there a solution I haven't tried yet?
- Can I quickly and accurately articulate the problem?
- Do I have a convincing reason for escalating?
- Am I confident I know who the right person to escalate the issue to is?

- What might the manager ask me to clarify his or her thoughts?
- Is my argument persuasive enough?
- Will my action put the manager at risk in a way he or she may or may not be aware of?
- Are there any negative aspects to getting a manager to help me? Will other people resent my actions?

Your effectiveness at escalating is coupled with your understanding of the organization and your relationships. If you have previously formed relationships with managers, going to them about someone below them who is a barrier makes escalating a no-brainer. It's much harder if you are meeting for the first time to discuss a subordinate not giving you what you want. If you know the manager, the subordinate who is a barrier will expect you to report the problem. The issue of pissing that person off is moot. You have more power to do what you want when you want. The importance of building relationships high, wide, and deep within an organization can't be stressed enough here.

People who are generally insecure will resent you going over their head. There are other reasons they may resent it, but you need to make sure you know how they will react. If you believe they will try to block you, then they aren't going to be of much help to you anyway. But if you have to deal with them on a day-to-day basis, you will need to make the process of escalating as painless as possible but also control the situation. Escalating strategies are very situation-dependent, but focus all on reaching the higher-level decision maker to present your case.

If you need to retain your relationship with the person who is the barrier, then you must make it look like you tried to keep him or her in the loop without actually doing so. You can go to the boss and present your case, and then call the barrier right after and let him or her know you are doing this. (Better to ask forgiveness than permission, right?) This has to be done quickly, because the barrier and the boss may talk with each other. You don't want barrier people to find out first from their boss that you were going around them. You need to be the one giving them that information.

With luck, you will get their voicemail and leave a short message about what you are doing. If you get them on the line, the message doesn't change. You tell them you spoke with their boss. You should tell them everything that was said in the meeting. If they have any relationship at all with their boss, they will find out anyway. It's more important for them to get the information from you rather than hear it indirectly. If they do hear it from their boss first, they will be pissed at you and you'll need to do damage control.

Another way to get around a stubborn barrier is to have one of your associates or your boss go to that person's boss. This way, you can deny you had anything to do with it. You will retain your relationship with the person who is the barrier and still get your way. The downside to this method is that you lose the opportunity to connect with that person's boss and build a relationship with him or her. I'm not saying to restrict your boss's access to higher-level managers, it's just that you should be making relationships all the way up the chain, and if someone else is doing it in your place, you have lost an opportunity. Doing it yourself is better, but each situation is different.

You may find out you aren't the only one who needs to go around this barrier person, and the boss probably knows this. I have dealt with many people who were barriers for no other reason than to hold power over me. I used both methods mentioned above but preferred doing it myself. I've been pleasantly surprised to discover that the higher manager was receptive and helpful. My feeling was that the manager knew the subordinate was being too excessive as a barrier and didn't mind being escalated to.

Some people don't care if you go around them to get an answer. This is much easier. But you still need to keep them in the loop. Even though they might not seem to care, they do. Always make sure you are letting them know about your conversations with their boss. With some customers, you'll find there's an expectation that you will go around them if they can't help you. This is just the way their corporate culture works. Just flow with it. Still, the rule is, you need to keep them in the loop unless they really don't care.

If you work at a company that has a good sales team, part of your measurement will be how effective you are in escalating. This is one of the top skills good salespeople have to have in their bag. Developing this skill takes practice, a little keen perceptive ability, and aggressive behavior. If you can't effectively escalate, you might as well find another profession. Part of sales is knowing where to go in the organization to get things done.

Have questions on technique? Look at how your peers do it. Talk to your manager about it. Maybe he or she has some good stories to tell you. You will make mistakes and sometimes be embarrassed when a manager tells you that your argument is a waste of time. Learn from all this but keep escalating. A good salesperson is a pest. Part of being a good pest is having a talent for escalating.

Sometimes you don't have to plead for help. Escalating requires you to ask people to help you get to a goal you can't reach yourself. You can't ask for help all the time. It wears people down—and, like crying wolf, if you do it too much, your requests will fall on deaf ears. There is another option, and that's figuring out a clever way to get what you need without asking for it. Once you get to know your factory well, you may notice loopholes in the way they do business. Some of these can be subtly exploited to get what you need to make your number. The same goes for a customer's factory. You may be able to get access to people, even get information you couldn't by using normal channels. Successful salespeople have a knack for exploiting loopholes to get things done.

Going around Systems

Being a salesperson means figuring out ways to get orders and close. As you strive to reach your goal, you will be confronted with barriers to progress. Among the myriad of barriers you will deal with are those presented by highly structured systems. These systems can be phone, organizational, political, and bureaucratic, to name a few. Each one has a set of rules you are expected to follow on any number of subjects:

- how you place an order in the system
- what is allowed to be written off on an expense report
- how manufacturing determines which customer gets product that is on allocation
- the rules purchasing sets up for salespeople to follow if they want to interface with people within their company
- how pricing is determined for a particular sale
- what you are allowed to tell a prospect about new products
- how data is to be entered in a CRM

The number of rules salespeople deal with is daunting. It's amazing any business gets done. If you perceive a barrier to closing an order, one of the first things you can do is see if there is a better and faster way to close it. Always be opportunistic. A salesperson will gladly take a risk on a shortcut that can bypass a rule or system to land the order more quickly and easily. Most companies expect their salespeople to do this. This is one of the reasons salespeople get paid so much. In a way, companies are quietly admitting that without salespeople, the customer wouldn't be able to do business with them.

The more experience you get dealing with all the barriers these systems create, the more productive you'll be as a salesperson, and the better you will get at discovering shortcuts. Sometime you may get your wrists slapped for finding an exploit and leveraging it for your customer. If your management is good, they may outwardly punish you but inwardly respect the fact that you discovered something nobody else knew about. They know you are looking out for your customer's best interest.

This is normal for a healthy company. Salespeople are constantly testing weaknesses in the rules in an effort to make it easier for their customer to do business. While salespeople test for weaknesses, the company responds with more rules and barriers. Ever adapting to change, salespeople regroup and find other weaknesses to exploit. This cycle goes on and on. Some people think salespeople are bad and create chaos. These people are clueless and don't really understand how successful salespeople get things done.

If you are in sales, you already question authority. Just because the sign says you can't park there doesn't mean you can't park there, right? Knowing when and where to test authority and rules is what separates the men from the boys. The spoils go to the salesperson who frequently tests rules and breaks down barriers. This makes you more competitive against your peers, who compete for the same factory resources, and your competitors, who vie for time from your customer.

Customers just see that you get things done. Sophisticated customers will expect an accomplished salesperson to get them an unfair share of attention and support. Slicing through barriers is the hallmark of a top-notch salesperson. Always ask yourself if there is a better way to do something. Hone your perceptive skills to catch the little piece of detail that's a clue to getting around a barrier. Test systems by breaking rules here and there. If you don't experiment, you will never become more productive. Make mistakes and learn from them; before long, you'll be a master at cutting through the crap.

Going around systems and barriers carries some risk. The more daring your exploit, the more risk it will have. High risk has the downside of creating a potentially bad situation for you. You have to decide on the level of risk/reward you're comfortable with. Do it too frequently, and you will get caught. You may have to be ready to defend yourself.

We all do bad things at some point. Other people do them too. In a sales situation, you may be the perpetrator or it may be someone or something else. It could be something you did or forgot to do or something someone else did. It could be a total surprise or something you knew was eventually going to happen. No matter, you are suddenly presented with a serious problem, and it falls directly in your lap.

Failure and Damage Control

> *When you make a mistake, don't look back at it long. Take the reason of the thing into your mind, and then look forward. Mistakes are lessons of wisdom. The past cannot be changed. The future is yet in your power.—Hugh White, US politician; president pro tempore of Senate, 1832*

> *The winners in life think constantly in terms of I can, I will, and I am. Losers, on the other hand, concentrate their waking thoughts on what they should have or would have done, or what they can't do.—Dennis Waitley, psychologist, motivational speaker, and Korean War pilot*

> *Success is the ability to go from one failure to another with no loss of enthusiasm.—Winston Churchill, prime minister of England and a brilliant orator*

During your career, you will probably make a serious error. Maybe more than one. Someone else you are working with may make one. It can happen to a friend or family member. Whatever or whoever this thing happened to, there is no turning back. You need to sit back, take a breath, and clear your head. If you screw up, the first thing is to make sure you fix the problem quickly. If you get into trouble, don't try to deny it or see if it blows over. Make amends, take responsibility, and fix whatever you can.

If you get fired, then face it. You might be able to talk to your management about the problem and get another chance. If they want to roast you, they will anyway, and it may not matter what you say to them. In fact, you can get roasted at any time whenever they choose. Either way, it will work out in the end for you if you have a good character and know everyone makes mistakes.

I know people who were fired because they screwed up, but they probably would have been fired anyway. I know salespeople who were fired for screwing up, and it was the best thing for them. Now they are very happy with another job. If someone you know made a blunder, he or she probably could use some common-sense advice. Don't try to make the person feel good. It's better to give guidance as to how to manage the problem. That's what is really needed. If people don't see that, get them to, but also know when to back off. They may be feeling lousy, and when you can help them sort things out, it will be very helpful. Most people really appreciate that.

The whole thing about damage recovery is that it can get emotional. If that happens, people tend to make bad knee-jerk decisions and focus on blame rather than a solution. Usually, the decisions made are to focus blame or make someone feel good. The best thing to remember is that you cannot turn back time; what's done is done. Dwelling on what happened will only put off constructive progress. You need to begin where you are now and fix things, get over it, and move on with your life. Learn from what happened and make sure you try not to do that again. Look at it as an important life lesson and an opportunity to grow.

If someone else you're involved with made the big blunder or it's your factory, you have to be the instrument of repair and help everyone sort it out and move on. In some cases, the damage is widespread and will contaminate everything it touches. Be careful of situations where it's clear the individual or entity has to fix it on their own.

Sometimes people at your factory will really screw up with your customer—even getting a customer potentially fired from his or her job. Again, you have to be the mediator and use your leadership skills to keep everyone calm and sort it out rationally. Damage control requires a clear head, a good understanding of the situation, and the communication skills to speak in a way that will make everyone listen objectively. You may have to bring two warring parties together who despise each other. You are probably thinking this is beginning to sound more like working for the State Department than being in sales. If you are good at what you do, people will look to you to mediate the problem. This is one of the responsibilities of being a professional salesperson.

There isn't a lot to this. If you make a big mistake, you have to live with it. You can wallow in it and be miserable, or you can just move on. If you are good, your choice is to fix whatever damage you did, make amends, note that you did a stupid thing, and try not to do it again. Psychologists call something very negative that happens to animals *one-trial learning*. They call it that for a reason. Be smart. Make sure that is you. Go to your inner reserve of confidence about yourself that you are a good, strong person. Everyone screws up. Time will heal it. Just make good choices in the future.

Hopefully when you screw up—and you will—it won't be that bad and you can gracefully recover. Failure and damage control are transitions we all go through in life. In sales, as in life, you can't dwell on a failure or what you should have done. All it will do is hold you back, and if you tell people about it, you'll be viewed as a person who whines. In sales, this behavior will lead to failure. Time to move on, so get over it!

Get Over It!

> *Even though you may want to move forward in your life, you may have one foot on the brakes. In order to be free, we must learn how to let go. Release the hurt. Release the fear. Refuse to entertain your old pain. The energy it takes to hang onto the past is holding you back from a new life. What is it you would let go of today?*—Mary Manin Morrissey, minister, counselor, teacher, and founder of the Living Enrichment Center

As you go through life, you will get into situations where things don't go your way. It can be as simple as someone beating you to a parking space. You get upset because you had been driving around and around and finally when you saw one, you sped up to get to it, and just when you did, someone denied you your goal. Or you could be expecting a promotion and someone you really think is an idiot gets the job you wanted. You drive home wondering in disbelief what your management sees in this person. When we get into these situations, it is hard to really step back and look at them with naked objectivity.

These things happen to me too. I can't count how many times I've been faced with situations that astound me as to how unfair they are. What's important is to notice how you feel. Why are you so upset? Is it that you were denied something you thought was rightfully yours? In fact, you lost the parking space because your timing was too slow. Other people thought someone else was better for the job. This may sound rather oversimplified, but the plain truth is that life isn't fair. I don't mean it's *unfair*, just that it isn't bound by some set of rules that is supposed to mete out things evenly to everyone. Sometimes you're lucky, other times you're not. Sometimes someone else is luckier.

When you get into these situations, you may get upset. You have to ask yourself, *What am I going to do next?* You can consume yourself in fury, and for the moment that might make you feel good. You can hold on to these feelings of rage for as long as you want, even years. But if you do, you miss the whole point of life. The answer is to get over it and get on with your life. When I say *get over it*, I really mean that. Not only do I mean to give up on obsessing about it, but drop it and don't mention it again. Don't even think about it anymore.

It's okay to mention to someone how during the day today some aggressive jerk took a parking space that was meant for you. Or if you're speaking to a confidant, how you saw that Joe So-and-So got the manager's job and not you, and you were the one who really deserved it. If you hold on to this gummy negative residue, though, you will spend your precious time lamenting things you can't control or do anything about. What a waste of time. It's like listening to someone talk about the same thing over and over again.

If you have trouble with this type of thing, sales may not be for you. In sales, this type of thing happens all the time. It happens with your job, and it happens with your customers. Someone at your company can betray you. Your closest customer can suddenly decide to choose your competitor despite the long relationship and good business you both enjoyed. What do you do? Just move on and treat it rationally. Chalk it up as a valuable life lesson. Learn from it.

To cling to these feelings is destructive and will get you nowhere. If you have trouble letting go of things like this, you might try talking it over with friends, your spouse, or someone you can share your thoughts with. If that doesn't do it, I would recommend therapy. The reason is that if you can't go on with your life and stop obsessing about someone who betrayed you, there are other deep-seated reasons you are doing this. To continue in this state has to be frustrating, and you should do something about it.

The other thing is that you have to forgive people. I don't mean to treat them as friends after they just stabbed you in the back. You don't have to like anybody you forgive; just give up your pent-up focus of hate. It may be hard to swallow, but if you really want to have an enjoyable and full life, you need to forgive. Forgiveness is a very human thing to do and shows you have character.

One way to think of your life force is as a big tank of energy. This tank supplies the energy of your life. Lingering thoughts about how someone got luckier than you and didn't deserve it are negative energy. It sucks energy from your life tank, leaving less for you to use to enjoy life. You've got to look at why you're mad about a situation and *get over it and forgive*. You'll have a much better life and a successful career in sales.

CHAPTER FIVE

FACING THE CUSTOMER

Get the Names Right

Nothing is more of a turn-off than mispronouncing or misspelling someone's name. This will seriously distract the person you are dealing with—or worse, alert his or her unconscious mind that you are not to be trusted. I am sure someone has misspelled your name in the past. Do you remember how you felt? Always, always take the time to make sure the name is spelled correctly and that you pronounce it as the person wants to hear it.

Don't be afraid to ask how to spell or say an unusual name. You'll show that person's unconscious self that you care and are interested. It might even be a great conversation starter. Many people like to tell stories about their unusual name and how it came to be. Remember, people like to talk about two things: themselves and what they do.

E-mail is another potential epic fail when it comes to names. Make absolutely sure you type the name correctly. If you are unsure, take the extra time to check it. I can't stress how important this is. If you do make a mistake, correct it as soon as possible and apologize immediately. This will tell the other person that he or she is important to you. Watch out for spell-checkers. Sometimes they get aggressive at correcting and when you hit send, at the last second the name is changed.

You should always be very paranoid about making sure the name is spelled correctly. If you are unsure, stop and check it. I mention this here because even today, I see salespeople misspelling names. It's a sure sign of an unprofessional, lazy, mediocre salesperson. Don't let that be you.

While you're checking your contact list for misspelled names—I bet there are one or two in there—you might think about whether you make your customer do more work because you cut too many corners.

Make It Easy for Your Customer

This may sound obvious, but you wouldn't believe what some salespeople put their customers through because they cut corners. It can be big things or little things, or little things adding up to big things. This may sound trivial, but if your competitor is making it easier to do business than you are, the difference could add up over time.

- When sending information to a customer, do you make it easy for the customer to get it, or do you make him or her work for it? For example, in sending e-mails that refer to documents online, do you just send the link or do you send the actual document, knowing the person will have to download it anyway? If you do send a link, do you test it first? Or do you just assume it's okay?
- If you are sending something to your customer, say a visual aid like a presentation, is it in a format he or she can open? Do you bother to check?
- If you are meeting a prospect for lunch, do you confirm a day ahead of time and make sure the customer knows how to get there? If the answer is no, do you send directions or make the prospect look it up? Also, you know a great place to park—do you tell your customer about it?
- If a customer is having trouble understanding what your product does, do you just send a pointer to web page for the product, or do you get on the phone and walk the individual through, describing it to make sure everything is understood?
- Do your technical people insist on telling your "stupid" customer RTFM ("Read the f******g manual") or get on the phone to help him or her understand it?
- You ask your factory for a document that describes a principle on how your product works. They send you an e-mail telling you, "Here it is." Do you open it and read it to make sure it's what your customer needs? Or do you just forward it on? Also, let's say you open it and find it really doesn't explain things very well. I have seen documents sent by the factory with notation for a competitor on the pages. Knowing customers need to understand it first

before they will buy it, do you get your factory person on the phone with the customer to help explain it? If you can't do that, can you find someone to edit the document to make it clearer?

- If you are sending a presentation to a customer via e-mail, does it look professional or is it messy? If it's messy, do you clean it up first or send it as is?
- Your company is very cheap in providing a conference-call service. Everybody complains about the echoing, noise, and how some people get cut off or can't dial in. Do you find a better-quality alternative or do you continue with the frustrating service, apologizing to your customers about how bad it is, saying there is nothing you can do about it?
- You are going out to lunch with a new prospect. Do you offer a ride and get quality car time with the prospect, or do you just meet at the restaurant?
- When making arrangements for dinner, do you pick a spot close your house or to your customer's house? Does it make a difference if your customer lives a long away from your house?
- You are having an early-morning meeting with your customer. Do you just show up, or do you bring coffee, bagels, and donuts without asking?
- Your customer has been waiting a long time for a critical part your company makes. The customer has called you several times for help getting it. Finally, you find out the part is going to ship to your customer. You know your company will ship it via a slow method. Knowing how critical it is, do you convince your factory to ship it overnight or do you just let it go via slow boat?
- One of your factory people is visiting your region. This individual does work with your customer. Your factory person comments that he would like to see your customer, and he has a car and will drive there. Do you offer to pick him up at his hotel or just give him the address and hope he gets there on time?

I am sure you can think of many situations where you could make it easier for your customer or factory person. Do you do this? Or do you intentionally overlook situations to make things easier for you, despite mediocre sales? Make a difference with the little things. They always add up to big things.

A large part of your role is to guide a strategy to its goal. Part of that process is ensuring it doesn't get derailed in-process. One pitfall that can derail the best plan is to miscalculate the perceptions and expectations of your customer or factory people. It's all about minimizing surprise. Part of account control is carefully guiding everyone's expectation of what will happen next so that your strategy ends as everyone thought it would.

Managing Expectations

Expectations are one of the most important things a salesperson has to manage with customers and prospects. Setting the correct frame of mind for deliverables can mean the difference between success and failure. In fact, if expectations aren't managed correctly, even if you deliver to your customer on an important action item, you still may fail. Not only do you have to manage your customers but also your factory and your manager.

Many times, we're asked to deliver something and find out we can't do it, or it will be late or not exactly what the customer was expecting. If you don't set the expectation on the deliverable correctly, you can do some serious damage to your deal and worse, your personal credibility. What may seem like a small thing to you may be a huge thing to a customer or your manager. You've got to be good at putting yourself in their shoes to imagine how to set the expectation. Perception is reality. If the perception is different from what you set, you've got a problem.

Don't let people set expectations for you. In meetings, you may have factory people who are willing to commit to anything the customer asks for, whether or not you can deliver it. This is why before any meeting, you have to make sure everyone is scripted and agrees on the expected outcome. No matter how good you are at scripting, there are always people who never listen to your advice and think they know better. Sometimes they may even call your customer without you knowing and say things that set unreasonable expectations. Part of your job as a salesperson is to have a strong enough relationship with your customer, prospect, factory person, and manager that you can reset any damage that was done. This is called *damage control*.

It all comes down to knowing what you can deliver and shaping expectations so that you slightly overachieve your goal. Big surprises aren't good. Keep everything on an even keel. Don't overpromise, even with your manager. Don't overexpose your opportunity. Remember that despite all your hard work at controlling a very complex environment, you will occasionally fail. Usually this is due to factors beyond your control. You can recover; usually, it just takes time and a lot of work to earn back lost credibility.

Just as you manage expectations with customers, you have to do it with your factory and your management. Someday you will take your manager into an account you think will be good revenue for the company and expect him or her to be impressed. To your surprise, your manager leaves with a negative impression.

Recently, I visited a very large financial company where we made a small inroad into a group that liked our products. I brought my manager to lunch with some of their managers, and afterward we walked back to our car and chatted about what they said. He remarked how they enthusiastically told us they would be booking huge business with us—twelve months from now! My manager joked, sarcastically, that he couldn't wait for that order, which was telling me not to spend my time on them for now. What he didn't realize was that there were other programs that would go to revenue much sooner.

My mistake was not preparing him for the statements the other managers would make (as I knew they would). So now I had to do damage control with my manager to convince him there was a more near-term opportunity and to support me and them. Had I spent more time before the meeting telling him what they would say, I wouldn't have had to deal with his bad perception about the account.

If you are new to sales, it might be a good idea to do some visits with more experienced salespeople to see how they construct the correct expectation. Some salespeople are very, very good at it. It's a great skill to have and can be learned. After a while on the job, you'll begin to get the hang of it. Just make sure you look at where you want to end up and set everything in place to reach that end.

So now you are a master at setting expectations. If you get very good at it, the customer will take bad news in stride. More importantly, you will have given them bad news without getting shot. On a lighter side, if you've done a superb job relaying the bad news, don't be surprised if your customer starts hinting around at giving you some business. If you are good at managing expectations, you won't be associated with the event.

While it is rare, I've been given an order right after delivering bad news. When it happens, it will blow you away. You should pat yourself on the back. Sometimes customers want to order, but the context of the situation is awkward for them. You should understand these cues and help the customer through the process. Recognizing this very subtle behavior is very important to your success.

Setting expectations takes a lot of work. Work takes time. You don't have a lot of time. So you need to be careful that the time you spend on something is worth doing. This all gets back to setting priorities. You can't set priorities correctly without data. Not every account will yield business, no matter how hard you try. So you have to prioritize which accounts are more important than others—in other words, which accounts you will spend time on and which you won't. The process of understanding the potential business of an account is called *account qualification*. The more thoroughly you qualify an account, the better you will understand its potential.

Account Qualification

This is another of the fundamental skills of a salesperson. Qualification is the process of discovering whether or not you can sell to a particular prospect. It means gathering a large amount of general information about your customer's company, products, people, and needs to see if there is a fit. You have to understand how they are organized, draw up an organizational chart (if the company is large enough), and figure out who will make the decision about whether or not to use your product or service.

The phase of beginning to gather data about your customer is called *discovery*. The more data you get during discovery, the better your ability to put together a strategy that will assure the time you spent on qualifying the account was worth it. Cutting corners, or behaving like a mediocre salesperson, may leave you short on data and long on inaccurate assumptions. Without data, you can't have a worthwhile strategy. It's like shooting in the dark.

The more thorough you are in obtaining data, the better you will understand the landscape. The better you understand what is going on with your customers and how they make decisions, the better your chances to win business. Qualifying small accounts is much faster than larger ones, for obvious reasons. But sometimes you luck out, and in a large company, you reach a decision maker who already knows your product and thinks it fits into the company's needs.

Before I go on, one of the most important actions in qualification is estimating the true size of the opportunity. If you aren't aware of how big the opportunity is, it really doesn't make sense to put a lot of resources into it until you do. Part of your qualification will be to get multiple data points on the potential size of the business. This will affect how you apply resources. An opportunity that is small but easy to get may be worth grabbing.

A carefully executed qualification will gather enough data to determine if any opportunity is worth pursuing. During your qualification, you may realize you need factory resources to win an opportunity. Convincing your factory people to fly out and help you with a long shot may be difficult if you haven't done enough qualification and received convincing data. Your credibility could be in question if you call out all the troops to help you support what turns out to be a bad business opportunity.

You don't have to be a genius to know that the best way to get good data is from the customer's mouth. Using phone and e-mail is important, but deep, confidential information is only supplied verbally. The more time you spend in front of the right people, the better your chances of getting key information. If you are new to an account, you have to practically live with the customer. Whenever I get a new account, I first do research on the web for a day or so, make appointments for the next week, and then immerse myself in their facilities. Some customers have places for salespeople to conduct business. If your customer is smaller, you may need to find a place nearby to work, such as a Starbucks or some place with Wi-Fi access.

There isn't any information that is useless when gathering data. If you have to travel to the account, stay a day or two longer. Work from your hotel room or at the customer. Be as productive as possible. The point is to get in as deeply as possible to find the right people and information.

How much is the right amount of information? There is never enough information to be able to say your qualification is complete. You should always be qualifying your customer, even when you move from discovery to developing and executing a strategy. Information is perishable. Data on a customer that is over three months old should be used with caution. The more data you get, the better your qualification.

At some point, you will need to transition from gathering data to developing a strategy and moving on with your sales cycle. You will know when that happens. One day, you will realize that you need to get going and compose a strategy. Even though you are moving on with the sales cycle, though, you still are qualifying. You should always be looking for that piece of data that tells you your strategy is right on or off the mark.

Important data can come at any point in your sales cycle, so don't get cocky and think the order is in the bag before you close. I have seen many well-executed sales cycles blow up at the very end because a key piece of data wasn't revealed until the very last moment. Always be qualifying.

As you speak more and more with customers, you will continue to get new pieces of data that may influence your plan. Be flexible and adapt. I have experienced many curveballs when I thought I had the discovery all wrapped up. Secret projects, internally competing projects, there really wasn't any funding for the project, sudden interest from senior managers—these are just some of the scenarios that can suddenly show up just before you try to close. Always expect the unexpected. When it happens, figure out how to make it work in your favor. This is what makes sales so fun.

Be creative and use this new information to your advantage. Consider yourself lucky when exposed to new information. There will be times you will never know about important hidden details. You may be derailed without ever knowing what hit you. No matter, it's just another chapter in the life of salesperson. Get over it and move on.

Qualifying the account is something we all do in assessing the viability of an opportunity. As you get more experienced doing it, you get faster at picking winners and losers. The better you are at it, the more efficient you become at telling a good opportunity from a bad one. All it takes is experience. The more efficient you become at qualification, the less time you waste and the more money you'll make. Watch how others in your company do it. In no time, you'll become very efficient at qualifying an account and knowing the difference between a waste of time and a winner.

In order to really qualify an account, you have to visit it. There is no other way to assess potential business. You can't rely on the salesperson who used to call on the account. There could be residue from a bad experience, or the salesperson could be incompetent. Why risk overlooking a valuable find? The only way to determine potential is to qualify it yourself. To do that, you have to walk in and talk to people there. Phone, e-mail, or other indirect communications doesn't cut it. You have to do it face-to-face.

Face-to-Face Is King

If you are going to be a successful duck hunter, you must go where the ducks are.—Paul "Bear" Bryant, one of the most successful college football coaches of all time

You should always be in front of your customers. Don't hide behind e-mail, phone, or other indirect contact methods. When you are face-to-face with a customer (or factory person), you get information that is never provided in e-mails or phone calls. Many times this information is strategically more important than the main topic. Also, people are apt to offer more information in general when they are meeting with someone.

E-mail can get meetings. Phone calls can too. You can even close deals using these indirect means of communicating. All of these are important methods salespeople use to communicate. But if you want to get the whole story plus additional gravy, face-to-face is the only way to do it.

It amazes me how some salespeople spend more time e-mailing than face-to-face. I have even heard a sales guy say he "talked" to a person when he had only sent an e-mail. What is this guy thinking? Deals can be lost to the person who spends more time face-to-face.

There is a fine art to how to keep in front of a customer. As you get more experienced, you will develop methods that help you frequent customers without becoming tiring to them. Much of this has to do with how you distribute information. Another factor is whether they like you or not. I can guarantee that your customers have some real jerks calling on them. Some salespeople don't like their job, and people can sense this. If you come across as energetic, likeable, and trustworthy, customers will want to spend time with you, not that competitor. Hobbies and outside activities are very important too. They give you more to talk about.

Face-to-face gives you so much more data than phone, e-mail, or even texting. As I've mentioned before, over 67 percent of communication is nonverbal. This means when people communicate, they do it mostly with body language. So just by using indirect methods, you are missing two-thirds of what is being said. I mean, just by understanding the way nonverbal communication works, how could you ever depend on e-mail?

Some people will rationalize using indirect methods by saying, "Things are different these days. My customers prefer using e-mail, and that is the best way to contact them." I will agree that it's easier to e-mail someone than meet with him or her. But why do customers prefer e-mails? Well, they can hide behind them. It's far easier to avoid someone or tell people what they want to hear with e-mail. It's also easier to blow somebody off with e-mail. Salespeople view e-mail as a fantastic way of reaching people. Customers view it as a great way to filter who they see and to limit information. They can fib all they want in an e-mail and without nonverbal cues, salespeople will never know if they are being taken for a fool.

Face-to-face meetings are a must and a fundamental part of a salesperson's job. Rationalizing that your time is better spent using indirect communication with prospects and customers is the hallmark of a mediocre salesperson. Don't let anybody convince you otherwise. Face-to-face is king.

You will quickly find that many managers you need to meet with can't be accessed directly. To set up a meeting, you need to speak with an administrative assistant. This is an often overlooked individual who can be instrumental as an ally. Administrative assistants wield a subtle but extraordinary amount of power. Time to gain an appreciation for someone who can make or break your opportunity to reach DIs and DMs.

Administrative People Will Help You Succeed or Fail

Though they're easy to ignore, administrative people are the backbone of many organizations. Many times their jobs are thankless and sometimes stressful. You will deal with these people at your company and at your customer. You may even have one or more reporting to you, either directly or indirectly. For a salesperson, an administrative person can be the single most important factor to success … or failure.

If you need to access management as part of your business, you will have to work with administrators and assistants. Because of his or her relationship to the manager, the administrator will have direct access, will be entrusted with booking the schedule, and will determine who should meet with the manager and who shouldn't. Many senior-level admins act as confidants to the manager and are trusted to be filters. The manager will ask the admin's opinion of people and treat him or her as a friend, trusting that person's opinions. In some cases, this individual can get the manager to meet with a salesperson who normally wouldn't have a chance. Get the picture of how important the administrative people are?

If you are nice to these people, they can be powerful allies. They can provide information and can possibly influence a DM. On the other side, their influence can be used against you. Should you do something to irritate them or make them resent you, they can work behind your back to make your job very difficult, sometimes without you even knowing what is happening to you. Ignoring or disrespecting them will end in disappointment.

You should recognize that administrative people can be valuable allies and treat them as such. Always be respectful and treat them the same as you would the manager. This is true both for people in your company and your customer's. I mention this because I have seen many salespeople be disrespectful to administrative people. I am dumbfounded as to why a salesperson would do this.

When you approach administrative people at a customer to set up a meeting, give them the details of why you want the meeting. Keeping them in the dark will only make them suspicious of your intentions. Put yourself in their shoes. If their manager is influential, they will be constantly bombarded by people trying to gain access to their boss. Much like a cop who pulls people over for speeding, they have heard every excuse possible to gain access. You can assume many of the salespeople talking to them are wasting their time, and it's frustrating. So the best strategy is to keep it very simple and tell them what you want to accomplish and why it would be good for the manager to meet with you. If you do that, you will differentiate yourself from over half the idiots who are lying and making up stupid stories to get on the boss's calendar. It's very simple. If it still doesn't work, you need to find a more creative way to persuade the admin. If the admin shuts you down, you have to find a way to go around that person. At that point, it won't matter if he or she gets irritated at you for doing that.

Some admins are so numb to the constant barrage of people trying to get access that they shut everyone down. Usually these admins are rude or sound mad on the phone. You will encounter these types. Don't expect them to be helpful. The only way to deal with it is to go around them for access. But if you're really good, you may find a way to reach them.

If you are lucky enough to have administrative people working for you at your company, treat them very well. Reward them for extra effort. You may even give them presents at certain holiday occasions or buy them (and their spouse or friend) a dinner for two at a nice restaurant. If you share someone with other people, differentiating yourself with the administrative person will ensure you get special attention. This comes in handy when you need favors like something for a customer near the end of the day.

At one time I had field salespeople and a staff of two administrative people. It was amusing to watch how one of the salespeople never did anything for the administrative people while the other salespeople treated them far better. Whenever the first guy needed something, it was low priority for the staff. He got what he needed, but it was done after everyone else got what they wanted. Favors he asked for were done reluctantly and sometimes never finished. As a sales manager I looked the other way while this was going on. I did that because salespeople should be good to everybody. If this sales guy couldn't treat his people well, he wouldn't get what he needed. Also, if he treated his staff like this, he probably treated the customer's staff like this too. I figured salespeople like this eventually fail. Though I did mention this issue with him in his reviews, he ignored it. His inability to rally his support staff eventually was part of his undoing on the team. Eventually he moved on, and we were all thankful.

Treat admins like friends. If you're lucky, some will befriend you and become allies. This can be an incredibly valuable asset to your success. They can share inside information, let you know what your competitor is doing, and maybe even notify you if a decision is being made in your favor. It's up to you how well you maintain relationships with the admins, whether inside your own company or the customer's. Both are equally important.

Now that you have some great relationships with administrative people, you're on your way to dominating your competition. Some may become close allies, giving you a huge edge. Administrative people will be positioned all over your factory and the customer. Some will have more important positions and others may be lower in the organization, but all yield tremendous power because of the department they're in. In larger companies, one of these areas where the administrative people can be very powerful is purchasing.

Procurement and Purchasing

Your job as a salesperson is to generate revenue. The final phase of your sales cycle is taking orders or having the customer provide a purchase order. These are physical confirmations the customer will pay the invoice for the goods or services stated. Somewhere within that company is a person who will provide the purchase-order documentation and/or has the authority to place orders (which is a commitment to pay the invoice). In small companies, one person may handle all the transactions. It could even be an administrative person doing it as an additional responsibility. In larger companies, it can be a group of hundreds of people.

The job of discovering who is responsible for providing orders is simple with a small customer. If the customer is large, the task can be daunting. If your company has established business with a large customer, you are probably not the only salesperson handling it. There may even be an inside staff handling daily transactions. In this case, the sales responsibilities are split up. Some salespeople exclusively handle purchasing while others are responsible for creating demand for new and existing products.

If your company uses indirect channels, they will handle the order-fulfillment process for you. They will manage the purchasing part of your business. This doesn't mean you can leave all work with your customer's purchasing organization to the channel partner. You will still need to manage the relationship with the customer's purchasing department, but you won't spend as much time on it. If the channel partners are ineffective (which can happen), you may find they create more work for you than if you didn't use them. Theoretically, channel partners are supposed to expand your coverage and augment the sales function. In reality, if not managed properly, they can be a real pain to deal with.

Purchasing/procurement can be easy to deal with or very difficult. There is no standard way purchasing people deal with their vendors. Some are heavy-handed and others are more concerned with relationships. How your customer's procurement people behave will have much to do with their company's culture. Heavy-handed purchasing people are only concerned about price and delivery, nothing else. Sometimes these people are abusive and rude. Relationship-oriented purchasing people are concerned about what they get by treating their vendors with respect and in turn expect extra favors that can help their company be more competitive.

Salespeople and procurement people have a codependent relationship. No matter how it is painted, your customers need you as much as you need them. The relationship can be shallow or deep. If it's shallow, either the salesperson or the customer doesn't much care about anything other than price and delivery. If it's deeper, each side gains more benefit.

Shallow relationships are based on the strategy of keeping the salespeople from getting strategic information they can use as leverage in negotiating. You will be kept at arm's length. This type of strategy can work in certain commodity environments when the products or services are widely available and there is no advantage to exposing any information to the vendors. In some cases, purchasing may be the only way to interface with your customer. The purchasing people will have informed the rest of the employees they can only work with vendors if purchasing approves it. Usually this happens when

1. purchasing is very powerful politically, and
2. salespeople are making it difficult for purchasing people to do their job.

The procurement people within a company have various goals, but mainly they want to keep costs of products and services as low as possible. This can include margin gain, holding costs low, and meeting targeted reductions in pricing. They also have to work with manufacturing to keep the flow of products into the production line smooth so that inventory doesn't build up or have a shortage.

Vendor salespeople care for none of that and will try to maximize the number of products or services they can get the customer to use. If the vendor has proprietary products or services, this will be a priority to get into the customer's product because it is sole-sourced, so pricing can't be negotiated. Also, the product only comes from one supplier, so if there is a shortage, the manufacturing line will stop, which means revenue stops. These products will be used to leverage the customer's procurement people during negotiations. Sole-sourced products are the bane of procurement organizations, but they can make a customer's product or service highly competitive in their marketplace.

Sole-sourced products, like most one-of-a-kind things, are highly specialized. If it is a good product and well made, it will provide very competitive features not found in commodity goods. The engineers or people who evaluate the merits of vendors' products will favor these proprietary goods because they make the final product more competitive.

Procurement wants to micromanage the vendor sales process, and the vendor salesperson wants to convince the customer's engineers or product-evaluation people to use as many sole-sourced devices as possible. Akin to the sales funnel, salespeople have to maintain a steady flow of their products being adopted by the customer's product-evaluation people. This is demand creation, which is a continuous process. Without it, the customer's revenues will taper down to nothing.

You can imagine what happens when procurement is powerful and heavy-handed. The vendors are tightly controlled, and there are limits on who the vendor salesperson can talk to within the company. When the power is too far weighted to procurement, the company suffers and lags behind its competitors. Manufacturing can sometimes make up for this if there aren't many proprietary products for the application. This happens because procurement people are the ones to decide whether the new technology presented by a vendor will be adopted by engineering. Also, they filter or restrict what engineering sees from the vendors. Vendors are told they can't expose a type of product to the engineers.

In this situation, procurement people are making the choice of what technology is "allowed" into their company. This should be the job of engineering people, as they are far more technical and understand the deeper benefits to their company's products. In some cases, vendors may choose to restrict what new technology the customer sees (not showing roadmaps) so customers fall even farther behind their competitors. During your career, you will encounter this type of customer.

When the procurement people are weak and powerless (as in an engineering-driven company), the vendors design in everything and create havoc by getting the customer to use many sole-sourced products and take too many risks. Costs are too high, manufacturing frequently shuts down because of shortages in proprietary products, inventories are all over the place, and the end product looks like an exotic car sold in a low-priced car marketplace.

In healthy companies, there is a balance between how much freedom the vendor people have to design in their product or service and how much purchasing is involved with the demand-creation process. Proprietary products can make the customer's product more competitive, but pricing can be artificially set to excessive levels if the vendor wishes to do it because there is no competition. Also, if the vendor stops shipping the product, the customer's manufacturing can be halted, restricting revenue. On the other hand, if vendors are happy about their relationship with their customer, they will do extra things to help out. Some of those could be expediting the proprietary product for the customer when it's in short supply, or keeping procurement informed as to how the demand-creation process is proceeding. The pros and cons have to be carefully evaluated. Most sophisticated companies realize a healthy balance makes them more competitive.

No matter what department you call on, you should be calling "high and low." Each requires a specific method. One of the more challenging and perceptually intimidating people you will call on is the senior manager, or the CEO.

What Do I Say to the CEO?

Meeting with the CEO is very intimidating for some people, especially a new salesperson. Encountering a senior manager in a hallway or trying to set up a meeting with one can be a daunting experience. You have to be able to get to them despite the barriers to access. There are ridiculous demands on a CEO's time, so getting in front of one can be a challenge. In small companies, CEOs may be easier to access.

There are a few things you should do before you have your encounter. Make sure you know all about the CEO's company before you speak. Do some research. What do I mean by "know all about the company"?

- number of employees
- annual revenue
- whether the company is making money, and why or why not
- what products the company builds
- the contents of the latest annual report, in which the CEO will probably be quoted
- the latest business news on the company, and anything the CEO may have said to the analysts or tabloids that is a key strategy or interest
- any predictions or opinions freely stated by the CEO

These things can give you ideas of what to talk about. The basic rule is that CEOs want to find out something they don't know related to their business. You need to do some research to discover the company's unarticulated needs. Talk to people around the CEO. Find out what he or she is like. Maybe an internal ally will counsel you on what to say.

You may not have a chance to do research. Sometimes you just bump into these guys when you're not expecting it. I can tell you that eventually this will happen to you. This is the perfect opportunity to close a deal, get some advice on the company, or get your foot in the door. It's a good idea to think of something to say now and keep it stashed in the back of your head so if you have a spontaneous encounter, you can retrieve it.

It all depends on what you need to do with your customer. If you haven't penetrated the customer yet, you can introduce yourself and find a way to get a follow-up meeting. To do that, you will have to come up with a reason this is a good idea, which is why you need to do research on your prospects to discover their needs.

What are CEOs like? Well, they're all over the map in personality types. Some of them are dreadful people, others are downright nice guys. In larger companies, they tend to be very polished and sophisticated. Some are more approachable than others. Most are sharp as a tack. After you meet them, you will look back and say that some of them were the smartest people you ever knew. Some will really try to help you; others won't care.

One time I ran into the CEO of one of my biggest customers while I was Christmas shopping. He was Christmas shopping too (during business hours ... hmmm). I had never met him and knew very little about him. He was reclusive within the company and hard to reach. I knew a lot about his company. After getting past my shock at seeing him in the department store, I began to quietly stalk him while I thought about what to say. We needed to meet with him because he was always getting involved in decisions that involved our products, and he never was available to meet with my managers.

I knew this guy was very unapproachable. That is, he wasn't friendly with anybody who talked to him. I walked up to him and introduced myself. No response. I told him about how excited our company was that we were engaged in a strategic project with his engineering team. I asked him if he was involved in it, and he said he knew about the project. I told him about some new market his product could be sold in, and he became interested. (I had done some research with my factory people on this.) I closed by getting him to agree to meet with one of my senior vice-presidents to discuss working together to get his company into the new market. A few weeks later, we had the meeting and began a collaboration with the company.

Don't be intimidated by CEOs. They put their pants on just like you do. Some develop a thick skin because so many people are trying to get access to them and take up their time. You have to differentiate yourself by bringing some interesting information. It can be about how your company can help their company grow revenue or solve an issue, or you can alert them to something they didn't know was happening in the market. The point is, bone up on your prospects, understand their business, and get creative on how you tell CEOs something they haven't heard before.

CHAPTER SIX

NECESSARY BUSY WORK

Lead Generation

Generating leads is a fundamental part of sales. Every salesperson has to generate leads. This keeps the front of your sales funnel full. There are many ways to do this. Cold-calling is one way. Networking and research are two more. If you work in a larger company, there could be marketing departments that will forward you leads generated by various methods. These can be shows, webinars, press releases, calls into help lines, or just a simple call into the main number of your company requesting information. Your company should be pushing information out into the market constantly to generate interest in your products or services. Every time there is a hit, the contact information should be forwarded to sales for follow-up.

If your company is very small, with only a few salespeople, the burden of lead generation will be more on the salespeople because there just aren't as many resources to generate leads. Your management should be keenly aware of this and, when the opportunity presents itself, invest in ways to help augment the lead-generation process. The more leads generated, the more opportunities the salespeople will have to close deals.

As a company grows, the salespeople will concentrate on closing larger and larger deals. When the company was very small, a $5,000 deal might have been a huge win. After successful growth, the salespeople might be routinely closing $500,000 deals. Your salespeople should prioritize their activities to close larger and larger deals. In doing this, they become more and more valuable to the company. Their time is worth much more, being in front of prospects and customers.

At some point, lead generation should be delegated to less-critical individuals. An example is cold-calling. If your salespeople are closing huge deals, you don't want them to spend much of their time doing cold-calling. That activity can be delegated to inside salespeople or contract organizations. Management should be continually studying how lead generation is being done. If it isn't done correctly, out of necessity, your salespeople will do it. If their sales-funnel pipeline isn't full, the prospect of them meeting or exceeding quota in the future is slim. When the system is unbalanced, usually management will hear the salespeople complaining about it.

Lead generation is a critical activity and, to be effective, all departments should be aware of the strategy and how leads are to be handled. Leads can come into any part of a company. Any one of your departments that receives phone calls or e-mails from the outside may get an inquiry. They have to know how to identify and ask questions and how to route the prospect to the right people. An inquiry may be direct—someone asking for information—or could even be a complaint or product return. Any interaction should be viewed as a potential lead, no matter what the reason for it. Every department should have awareness and be ready to qualify a lead.

There is no fixed way to generate leads. It can be fun to create a new way to get people interested enough to ask for more information. The sky is the limit on how you do it. No matter how small your company, there should be multiple methods running in parallel to generate leads. All these processes need to reviewed on a regular schedule and evaluated on how effective they are. Many different internal departments should be involved. At a minimum, your sales and marketing departments should be represented. Here are some things to think about:

1. Should you continue using your present method?
2. Has it been productive?
3. Does the process need to be modified based on feedback?
4. Is it time to add new programs?
5. Should you use outsourcing?
6. Do you need more resources?
7. What do your salespeople think of it?

Leads are the lifeblood of any company that sells something. Having a robust lead-generation program will insure revenue growth. How you manage a lead-generation program should be considered a vital process and involve your entire company.

Lead generation is another form of must-do busy work that seems productive some days and on other days, you ask yourself why you ever decided to do it. Like chores around the house, it's something that has to be done. Another chore your factory will encumber you with is excessive paperwork. From forms on web pages to expense reports and sale forecasts, these take up a lot of time you could be spending in front of a customer.

Paperwork

Paperwork is the bane of salespeople. I don't know a single salesperson who thinks paperwork is a good thing. The reason is simple. A salesperson's job is a never-ending chain of one action item after another, with no hope of ever completing the list. No matter how many hours in the day salespeople work, it is never enough. To be effective, salespeople must be as efficient as possible to maximize revenue and meet quota. Any activity that extends the time it takes for them to complete action items is a barrier to productivity. People experienced in sales understand this.

Too much paperwork is an indication of problems with upper management. They may be totally clueless that their job is to remove as many barriers to selling as possible so the salespeople spend most of their time generating revenue, not reports. It also could be an imbalance of power within senior management where the sales vice-president is dominated by a different department, such as marketing.

Salespeople's ideal world is being left unencumbered to manage their business as they see fit—prioritizing action items, strategizing, and getting in front of customers to close orders. You would think any organization they work for would do as much as possible to help the salespeople work efficiently. Unfortunately, it doesn't work out that way. Unless you work alone, you are working for a company. Whether the company is small or large, there are always people who think they know what is right for salespeople. If they happen to be in a position of power, they can make the salespeople happy or very, very angry and demotivated.

Usually one or more people will institute rules the salespeople need to follow. Don't get me wrong—if you don't lay down rules for salespeople, you'll end up with a bunch of mercenaries holding your company hostage. In any company, rules and accountability are important. But the rules should strike a balance between too much accountability and not enough. The more rules, the more documentation and paperwork is required.

Documentation is always left to the salesperson to manage—quarterly reviews, monthly reviews, weekly reports, managing a CRM, etc. Additionally, salespeople need to fill out expense reports, create presentations, and compose reports for customers. These and other bureaucratic tasks keep them away from interacting with the customer.

Paperwork does have an advantage. Properly executed, it can force salespeople to plan more thoroughly by having them focus on what they do. At times, a salesperson's job is akin to being in the center of a tornado, completely disoriented. It's good to get your head above water now and then. So having to do reports and paperwork can be a good thing, depending on who's calling the shots. If you have managers who understand what a salesperson needs to be effective, they will put systems in place to make things run efficiently. Problems happen when the people designing the criteria have no sales experience—or have issues with power and exert rigid control over the salespeople.

In every healthy company, there is a yin-yang tension between opposing forces. It can be sales and marketing, sales and manufacturing, even the CEO versus the salespeople. One is always trying to institute heavy-handed rules over the other to gain control. How they implement a strategy of control can be blatant or subtle. When these forces are in an imbalance, it can compromise how effective the salespeople are.

A classic example is when marketing exerts too much control over sales. This is why you should beware when one of the top senior managers in the company has a title of vice president of sales and marketing. Look at that person's resume. You will find an emphasis on sales experience or marketing experience, not both. If it's marketing, the salespeople will be miserable. If it's sales, the salespeople will be happy.

When things are running correctly and there are separate VPs for marketing and sales, they engage in a healthy push and shove for control. If the power is unbalanced, the salespeople have too much paperwork, and they are miserable. Too many people get involved in "helping" the salespeople, and the result is "report creep." Over time, the amount of paperwork increases. At some point, the salespeople complain to management that there is too much (they will always be complaining there is too much, but now they will ratchet it up). Management addresses it, but if they have too many battles in progress, they may choose to ignore it rather than squandering their resources on fights.

A job at a company may look great from the outside, but the amount of paperwork and accountability may make it difficult to do your job. Such a huge amount of useless work can be a substantial barrier to your success. Some managers simply don't understand that salespeople should be selling, not writing reports—which is why it's important when you interview to find out if the company will leave you alone or bury you under mounds of paperwork. There is a balance of too much paperwork and too little. With luck, you can find a job where management supports salespeople in a healthy way, which means your paperwork will be minimal. If you spend any money for your sales job, though, there's one type of paperwork you can't escape: the expense report.

Expense Reports

If you have a company expense account, periodically you will need to fill out personal expense-reimbursement forms. Your company will have some specific hard-copy or web-based form. Get to know how to fill them out. If you are spending money on a regular basis, fill them out regularly. Don't wait too long. Over the years, I have worked with people who waited until the last minute to submit expense reports. One or two people I know never did them, yet spent their personal money on company activities. One had almost $10,000 spent on company business one year and never got paid for it. Filling out expense reports can be painful, but you need to submit them regularly. If you spend money weekly, submit a monthly report. If you don't do it, you'll never see the money.

Having expense privileges as a salesperson comes with a degree of responsibility. Some people abuse it by expensing money on themselves, friends, or even family. One company I was at had a liberal expense policy regarding cash transactions. As long as you had a cash chit as a receipt, you could claim up to $100 on it. There was one guy in our office who was adding an additional $12,000 a year to his income by submitting phony cash chits. He had a whole shoebox full of cash chits he'd dip into every week. What encouraged him to keep doing it was that his manager was clueless and didn't bother to check his reports.

Other salespeople write off a dinner every now and then. Some don't dare do it. If you are starting out in a new sales job, the best advice will be to not abuse this privilege. Some companies "allow" a few personal expenses now and then, like dinners with friends or family, or sports tickets. This is called a *perk* or *perquisite*. There is a very fine line between what is perceived as okay and abuse. Most companies will immediately terminate salespeople who are caught abusing expense reports. If in doubt, don't do it. You will find out your peers are doing it, but that doesn't mean it's accepted. They may work for a manager who doesn't care. Your manager may be very strict about it.

Every now and then, your manager may tell you to have dinner on the company. Just be careful with this. One sales office in one of my companies had a senior manager who let his people write lots of extra expenses. He got fired for doing it. Upon review, some of the salespeople who worked for him were let go along with him. Not to confuse you more, but be aware that even if your manager condones padding your expense account, that doesn't make it the right thing to do. You may find your peers want you to do it so they feel better about what they are doing. Let your conscience be your guide. You will probably figure out the correct thing to do after you've been on the job for a while.

A friend of mine told me of expense-report abuse inside a Fortune 100 company that had a huge sales force. Among the things he did was monitor the cost of sales. One day he noticed a big spike in car rentals. Over a two-month period, car-rental expenses more than doubled, even though the travel never changed. Considering how many salespeople they had traveling, this was a huge amount of money. He did an analysis of the expense reports and noticed salespeople were going against the company policy of renting midsize cars and renting luxury sedans instead. Aghast at this flagrant abuse, he checked with the people who were responsible for approving the expense reports. He was told the salespeople were having trouble renting standard cars, so they were getting whatever was available, which turned out to be luxury cars.

Smelling a rat, my friend drilled down further and noticed a trend. The company had a contract with only one car-rental company, so salespeople had only one company to choose from when they rented a car. One time a sales guy went to the only rental company he was allowed to rent from and, indeed, this time they happened to be out of cars, including the one he had reserved. In haste, he took what they had, a Jaguar convertible. When he submitted his expense report, it was rejected because of the expense for the Jag. He called up and told the expense person the story and told her to call the rental agency to confirm it. She verified his story and approved the report. A week or so later, a few more expense reports came in with more luxury-car rentals. They all had notes on them that no other cars were available. These reports were approved.

Eventually more and more salespeople submitted similar expense reports with luxury-car rentals accompanied by tender notes on how they looked and looked but couldn't find a single midsize car. The approval people became used to these excuses and just rubber stamped the reports. Management put down their foot on this and stopped it. Nobody got into trouble. Secretly, management was impressed their salespeople communicated so efficiently. Today, many companies strictly control this. Just remember not to push any expense system to or beyond its acceptable limits.

Companies vary in how long it takes to issue a reimbursement check. The time can vary with a remarkable correlation to how well business is doing. The worse business is, the longer it takes to get a check. I have seen it take checks over eight weeks to get to a salesperson. If you are entertaining customers frequently, this can add up to thousands of dollars out of your pocket.

Most companies reimburse in a reasonable time, especially if you are physically close to the people who write the checks. If you work in a remote office, it might be good to get to know these people and befriend them. In the case of long delays in getting paid back, make sure you can cover the cash-flow issue it will create for you. Keep a buffer amount of money in your bank account to cover an extended delay in reimbursement. Definitely take direct deposit if the company offers it. Your money will be returned to you faster.

For situations where you spend cash without getting a receipt, like tipping valets, you will need to get the money back somehow. Some companies allow salespeople to claim a cash amount without a receipt, up to a maximum number. Discuss the right way to do this with your manager or expense people. They should understand this and work out an agreed-upon method for getting your money back. Some companies will let you take your girlfriend or family to dinner on the company once a quarter if your cash expenses are approximately the cost of a modest dinner. Or you can make up cash chits from a restaurant and submit that. There should be some accepted protocol to help you out.

Make copies of your expense reports if you submit hard copies. Some companies require hard copies because they need the original receipts. If this is your company's policy, make copies of the entire expense report, even the receipts, before you send it in. Your report could get lost along the way or misplaced after it gets to the person receiving it.

Many companies use electronic forms for expense reports. You will still need to show a receipt—you'll have to scan it in or take a picture with a smartphone to provide an image. There are even cell-phone apps that will automatically submit the receipt for you. Even for online submissions, you'll still want to make a copy in case something happens. It's just insurance to protect yourself in case things get lost.

Expense accounts and entertaining are great relationship-builders in the salesperson's toolbox. One of your largest expenses is travel. Your company may pay for the tickets or you may have to pay out of pocket. Either way, there is a lot detail that goes into having a pleasant experience traveling.

Organizing Your Travel

Your job may require you to travel away from your area. Usually this means getting on a jet and flying somewhere. There are some basics to traveling these post-9/11 days that are important to know if you want to make it there on time. Also, there are some basic things you need to bring with you. The basic rule of travel is to bring, at a fundamental minimum, your driver's license, charge card, and cell phone. Everything else is extra.

First off, you need a bag to put your clothes and toiletries in. I recommend a rollaway that can fit in the overhead bin of most major aircraft. If you are going to travel a lot, you should get a brand of bag that is high quality. These aren't cheap and can cost more than $500. There are several brands. If you know which one you want, you should buy it online. Otherwise, you should go to a store that specializes in baggage. Once you get a bag, mark it so you can easily identify it in case you need to check it for a flight. Marking your bag in some unique way will prevent someone from accidentally taking it. I have a friend who tied a huge red scarf to his bag. He's never had a problem.

Carry-on is the way to go. Bring your briefcase and rollaway with you on board. If you fly in coach, try to get to the front of the boarding line. Everyone is trying to use carry-on these days, and despite the efforts of the carriers to provide larger overhead capacity, a booked-up flight will run out of overhead space. Even though your intention is to carry it on, there will be situations beyond your control where you'll be forced to check your bag at the last minute. It's first come, first served when it comes to claiming overhead space. Also, if you travel on short flights that use business-size jets with no overhead space, you are only allowed one carry-on no bigger than a briefcase. You will have to check your bag in the Jetway and pick it up at the Jetway of your destination. If you fly first class, your chances are better that they will accommodate you even if they are full.

Your briefcase should have enough things in it to keep you occupied for the length of your flight. Most first-class seats have power sockets. There are websites that actually tell you all about what is going on with your seat on most types of planes. One such site is seatguru.com. You can check legroom, power outlets, even if a seat gets a cold draft.

Entertainment varies from airline to airline, so it may be good to bring a book and other devices to watch movies or listen to music. (You'll need some type of headphone or earphones too.) Other things you might bring are books and magazines. This is a good time to read that motivational book you've seen in the airline terminal bookstore. If your flight is long you may get tired of doing work the whole way. I know a CEO who told me he doesn't use a power adapter. He works until the battery gets low and then he does other things, like watch the in-flight movie, read, or sleep.

One other very popular travel accessory is noise-canceling headphones. Bose, Sony, and other companies make them. They are expensive, ranging from $100 to $300-plus. I have a pair of Bose headphones. The inside of a jet cabin has a lot of noise from the engines and wind. These headphones eliminate almost all this noise, which can be very relaxing.

Join the frequent-flier programs for all the airlines, rental cars, and hotels you will be using. If you don't sign on from home or the office, you can sign up onsite. Airlines will even sign you up while you're in flight. These programs are full of all sorts of perks. Even if you don't think you'll be traveling much, you should still sign up. Things can change for you very quickly, and it's better to be ready. It won't cost you anything outside of getting on their e-mail list.

Most everyone today uses an e-ticket. E-tickets are issued online or through ticket agents. Many carriers also allow you to check your seat online. If you join their frequent-flier program, you can do things like change seats and even print out your boarding pass at home. You can put your boarding pass on your smartphone, but beware that not all airports have smartphone scanners, usually smaller airports. To be safe, print your boarding pass.

If you collect frequent-flier points, you may be able to upgrade to first class online. If you plan to upgrade, do it as soon as you get your itinerary. Other people will be trying to upgrade, and it's first come, first served. You will notice what is called a "record locator" somewhere on the itinerary. Usually this is a six-digit alpha/number that the airline uses to find your reservation. Use this to tell the computer which flight you are trying to find.

Allow plenty of time to get to your gate. Don't assume you will cruise your way through unimpeded. If you drive to the airport, you will need to park. Parking at some airports is horrendous. You may find when you reach the garage that it is full and they're rerouting you to some outdoor parking lot two or three miles from the outside of the airport and then busing you back. Nothing like being late and finding out you need to go to Neverland to park. Another delay can be construction. If you have a rental car, you have to return it and then take the bus or monorail back to the terminal. This all takes time.

Print out your itinerary before you go to the airport. You may be asked for it by security. It has things like confirmation numbers for the airline, rental car, and hotel. Several times I have arrived at the rental-car agency or hotel only to find they didn't have my reservation. I showed them the printout with the confirmation number and then my reservation magically turned up. I really don't understand that, but it happens.

Security at airports these days is very tight, which means it can be a big bottleneck. There will be single or multiple metal detectors and X-ray machines used to screen the passengers. Read the signs as you move toward the machines. They tell you what the rules are for that airport. Different airports have different rules, so be prepared for variations in how you are screened. Crew members are allowed to cut in front.

I am very conservative and try to arrive at the airport well before my flight for domestic and more than two hours before for international flights. Security check-through times vary all over the place. Don't assume that if the first time you go through in a minimum time it will always be that way. I have found, traveling on a weekly basis on the same day and time, that the lines one week will be nothing, the next week jammed. A long, long line can take almost an hour to go through. Usually lines move reasonably well.

Don't be stupid and put things in your briefcase that will trigger a search, like nail clippers or sharp instruments. Don't joke or make light of the situation. If you forget to remove an object that violates the rules, be prepared to let the security agents confiscate it. Be courteous and do exactly what they say. If they tell you to do something, do it. This may sound obvious, but these workers can make your life miserable very quickly over a small incident. I know people who came close to being seriously delayed because they tried to be funny and made a borderline joke. Others get mad because they can't hold their temper. This will surely get you supervised by the police.

If you are really late and fear you will miss your flight, you can politely tell one of the TSA (Transportation Security Administration) people that you are late for your flight. Sometimes they will let you cut to the front of the line.

Bring cash with you and make sure you have room on your personal credit cards for emergency charges. Most of the companies I worked for issued me corporate charge cards. One night I arrived at my hotel to discover that my corporate card was denied use. It was past one in the morning, and I would have been screwed if I hadn't been able to use my own card. The next day I found out there was an accounting error, which was fixed after a few days. I have personally experienced this situation several times.

Put all your receipts in a safe place. If your company reimburses you for expenses on your personal charge card, it's your responsibility to keep all your receipts until you have time to write up an expense report. The receipts can add up to a lot of money, so keep them in one consistent place where you can find them and won't lose them.

While in flight, don't wait until the last minute to use the bathroom. Turbulence can suddenly force everyone to stay seated, including you and your rapidly expanding bladder. Coach bathrooms can be crowded all the time, especially on large jumbo jets for foreign flights. Some people seemingly take hours and hours in the bathroom. I timed one guy more than twenty minutes in the bathroom; he changed his clothes, shaved, and brushed his teeth. This showed a blatant disregard for the scarcity of bathrooms on planes. First-class bathrooms can be crowded too, but usually they're more available.

Travel within the USA

The "equipment" you fly on may be a wide-body or a tiny business-size jet that seats only about fifteen or twenty people. The wide-bodied planes are nice because they have a lot more room. Also, the seats are more comfortable. When you make your reservation, find out what type of plane your carrier will be using. Check out your seat selection online to make sure you have a good one. Some carriers like JetBlue are all business class. The seats are larger and more comfortable. They also have free in-flight video screens.

If you fly regionally, or "puddle-jump," your plane may be a turboprop. Turboprops vibrate like crazy. Once I was using my laptop, and the vibration from the props was so bad that the disk drive on my notebook began to fail. I had to hold it in the air while I shut it down. I almost lost everything on my notebook. The seats in turboprops are tiny, and there isn't any headroom. Many carriers have replaced turboprops with business-class jets for regional service. These planes are more quiet and comfortable.

Larger jets use a Jetway to board passengers directly from the terminal gate. Smaller planes will board with a metal staircase from the ground level. You'll have to go outside and walk to the jet. Sometimes passengers board a bus and ride to the plane in some remote location on the airfield. If the weather is bad, you'll regret not wearing a warmer coat or bringing an umbrella. I have had to walk through a raging blizzard about five hundred feet in six inches of snow to board a small business-class jet. This is a really nice way to ruin a pair of expensive shoes.

If you fly domestic coach, there are some basic rules to make your flight easier. On a larger jet, get an aisle or window seat and avoid the middle at all costs. If you are issued tickets automatically by your business or travel agent, double-check the seat location. You can change it right up to the time you board. The earlier you change it, the more likely you'll get the selection you desire. Try to get a seat by the emergency exit. There is more legroom in these seats. The "bulkhead" seats are those directly behind partitions. You can't and won't be allowed to store anything in front of you, even a laptop. The crew will make you store anything you are carrying in the overhead compartment. There is a storage pocket on the bulkhead wall you can use, but they don't like people stuffing notebook computers in them.

Book your flight early and check in early. Remember that all the other passengers on the flight know checking in early will give them an advantage too. Lines at check-in can be incredibly huge, with over an hour-and-a-half wait. Don't think that getting there early means no line, or that if it's very early in the morning nobody will be there. I have seen huge lines at six in the morning.

Hotels

If you will be staying at hotels frequently, get a frequent-stay card. This way you can accumulate points for personal use. If you stay at the chain often, you can bump up to a better room automatically. Check out various hotel chains and choose one to stay in that allows you to do this. The person handling registration has a large degree of discretionary power and can put you wherever he or she wants. You can ask for a particular floor level or inside or outside room, whatever your preference. If you don't ask, it won't happen. Some hotels have "concierge" floors that are more luxurious. They can have perks too.

You should be aware of safety procedures in the hotel. Acquaint yourself with how to escape if there's a fire. Many fire departments can't extend ladders beyond seven floors, if that. Fire is a danger that really isn't talked about much. Years ago, most of the senior executives of a large distributor of components lost their lives in a fire because the fire-truck ladders couldn't reach them. The company was devastated. Planning an escape route is easy and takes just a minute to visualize. On the back of your hotel door (in US hotels) is a map of the best escape route. Look at it, and then go out in the hallway and walk to the stairwell it tells you to go to. Try to imagine you are crawling to the egress. What markings on the floor can you follow to the door?

If you work out in the morning, you should locate the fitness room and check it out. Some hotels have really nice fitness rooms with attendants who hand you towels and water. Others have tiny rooms with a couple of machines. These days many people are exercising, and there can be a long wait to get a machine to work out on. The early bird gets the worm here. Get there when the fitness room opens or very early, and you'll be able to get your workout done first thing.

Keep in mind what is around the location of the hotel within the city. There are "cool" spots and not-so-cool spots. Find out which hotel is better for your needs. Some are located in vibrant sections of the city that have local shopping and restaurants all within walking distance in safe places. Others may be located in more remote areas, and you'll need a taxi or rental car to get anywhere.

Renting a Car

Your company may have strict rules on what you can and can't rent. Get acquainted with the rules before you travel. You don't want to find out your expense report was rejected because the car you rented was out of policy. As with flying and hotels, getting a frequent-renter card will qualify you for perks with the company. Each rental company has its own separate procedures for renting. Find a company you like and use it as often as you can. The smaller companies may have cheaper rates, but you get what you pay for. Your driver's license is absolutely necessary to have with you; otherwise, you'll be stranded. No company will rent you a car without a license.

Sending Packages

If you have a really important package to send to your customer and it has to get there overnight, make sure you use a top-notch carrier you can trust. Don't be cheap when everything is riding on a critical delivery. Saving a few bucks when your job or your company's credibility is on the line is absurd. If you don't understand this, you are clueless. Some companies have strict policies on which carrier to use; if the one they've chosen is undependable, consider using a better one and paying for it yourself.

For packages that need to get where they're going in hours, not overnight, you can do the delivery personally, use a hand-carrier service, or, if the distance is far, put it on a jet and have someone pick it up on the other end. This works great. Most major airlines have programs that allow you to send packages on passenger flights. The only problem is that someone has to go to the airport and pick up the package at the baggage carousel or the special pick-up area. I have used the passenger-flight method several times when a customer production line was held up because they didn't order enough of our product.

Most carriers provide tracking numbers that allow you to follow the progress of your package as it travels to its destination. You get the tracking number with the paperwork when you finish your transaction with the carrier. Always send the tracking number to your customer or whoever is expecting the package. If it's a very important delivery, specify "signature required." This way, if the package gets lost, you have a person identified who signed for it. You know where to start trying to find it.

Carriers have various options for sending packages. Make sure you understand what each option means. Sometimes carriers aren't that clear on, say, what the latest delivery time will be. Some don't commit to a time and just say they can deliver any time of the day.

Some large companies have very strict requirements on how they receive packages. Sometimes these receiving areas are huge and not managed well. I have had critical shipments go into these receiving areas and get lost. If there is a lot of pressure to get the shipment delivered, this is a good way to make everyone upset. In your dialogue with those who are receiving shipments, make sure they are clear on how they will pick it up.

Shipping to another country can be a complicated process. You have to deal with customs workers who are not usually motivated to speed anything through. My advice is, don't try to do it yourself. The paperwork is daunting and full of weird terminology. Should you make a mistake on the form, you may not find out for days. Your package may end up in limbo somewhere or worse, lost forever. You can hire a customs agent to carry your package through customs. Agents are companies who have relationships with the customs people and know how to slip something through legally. They are expensive, but can cut days into minutes. They know the paperwork and how to get around the barriers.

If your company is big enough, you may have logistics resource people who know all about shipping. Get to know them and treat them well. They can be an invaluable resource to help you get something shipped quickly.

When there is a lot of pressure to get the package somewhere as quickly as possible, you have to manage the expectation of the customer carefully. Review how you will send the package to make sure the process is acceptable. Tell the customer when to expect the package to be delivered. Remember, you can only commit to what the carrier will commit to, nothing more. Send the customer the tracking number.

You have to decide who is going pay for the shipment. Depending on the size, overnight shipments can be very expensive. Your company or your customer's company may have specific policies on who is supposed to pay or even the particular carrier that has to be used. If your company is at fault in a situation but the policy is to have the customer always pay, you will need to get your management to understand this may be rubbing salt into a wound so they agree to override the policy. The problem with this is it may take a lot of time to get management approval. This delay may infuriate the customer, who is expecting word on the shipment. It isn't wise to expose your internal political issues and blind policies within your company. So if you have to go through an override process, push it hard and fast. Hopefully, your manager will understand.

CHAPTER SEVEN

PRODUCTIVITY

Information

Information is all around us. It is everywhere, and we are constantly immersed in it. It takes on many forms, which can be straightforward or sublime. Sometimes it needs to be decoded or interpreted before we can understand it. All of our five senses can be used to convey information.

Information can be right in front of us, but we may not see it. When we receive information, it is taken in through our senses. We can *sense* things, but to get the information processed, we have to *perceive* them. So we may sense something but not perceive it. Saying it another way, something may be right in front of you, but you may not see it. Extracting information from your senses can be difficult.

What compounds this is that your brain can color your perception, so even though you perceive a thing, you may "get it wrong" or not even know it is there. This is when the unconscious mechanisms of your brain are trying to protect you from what you're really seeing. All of this also applies when you send or convey information. As a salesperson, getting information and using it productively is one of the most overwhelming things.

To develop a strategy, you need information. There is so much information in our lives, it can be difficult to sort through the volume of data at our fingertips. Mixed in with all this information is false information. To be successful in any undertaking, you have to know how to efficiently sift through information, extract what is correct, and then know what to do with it. Today, there are a huge number of sources for getting information:

- TV
- radio

- the web
- stock tickers
- news tickers
- periodicals like newspapers, trade rags, magazines
- social networks
- rumors
- friends
- peers
- managers
- customers
- competitors
- analysts
- stockbrokers
- government liaisons

The list goes on and on. You need to develop a keen eye and ear for qualifying good sources so you don't waste time. The way you do this is to be methodical about what you do and note, as you go from source to source, which ones you think are the richest in quality of their information. I have used many of the above sources and find that they all have their uses. But there are some things you need to do to get basic information.

Since you are in business, you should know what is going on in the world. If you spend time in a car, spend your "window time" efficiently. Your car radio, smartphone, and tablet are key factors. The radio can give you information on what is going on in the world and business. Listen to world and local news, plus take in a business station. If you have satellite radio, there are even more stations to listen to. Experiment at first. Scan around until you find stations that you think provide the richest data for you. Podcast feed services can make good use of car time. Make sure that you listen each time you are in your car. Allocate a certain amount of time for each one. Eventually, you will develop a routine when you drive. Even if you don't drive a car much, you can still use portable devices to connect you with feeds that keep you informed.

Salespeople usually have more information about what is going on within a customer's company than its employees do. Customers are always fascinated to hear what is going on in other parts of the company. This is powerful information and puts you in a position to provide valuable information. This is a good way to build relationships. By giving customers information about what is going on in their company, you are providing them power within their peer group. This makes you valuable to them.

Internal information can be used to help you get orders. I had a competitor who was an outstanding salesperson. This guy knew everything about the customer's company. When I first took over this customer, I was astounded how much my competitor knew about the customer. When I called on the purchasing people, they would rave about this guy to me. It was humiliating. So I began to steadily get information about him from the purchasing people and directly from the sales guy. Turns out he had a very big ego and didn't mind telling me the way he did some of his business.

What he did was cultivate key relationships with the managers on the manufacturing floor. These managers would pass him production information about what was being built. Then he figured out which of the customer's products used his parts and how many each used. Once he had the production information, he knew exactly how many of his company's parts they were going to order. The key here is that the production floor would fudge their numbers to purchasing. This was because the relationship between purchasing and production was poor. They withheld information from each other and were always trying to get advantage over each other.

By having the correct information, the salesman got to be in a consultive position with the buyers. He would get the production information before they would, and the information would be more accurate than what the buyers got from the production floor. The salesman even had the information before it was entered into their system. The buyers became dependent on the salesperson because they could perform better with his information than what they got from production. He had the purchasing guys locked up.

It took me close to a year of hard work to get into a consultive position with the buyers, but I did it. I even stole some of his business away. Though we never talked much or even saw each other at the customer, we could sense each other's presence and respected it. Information is the key to controlling an account.

Every day, we emit information in various ways. In this complex world, what you try to communicate using information can be interpreted in many ways. A salesperson has to be careful to release only enough information and not too much. Too much information can alter an expected outcome, especially when you are trying to execute a sales strategy.

There are many vehicles for relaying information. Social networks are the mainstream method for work and personal means. The problem is that the line between personal and work-related information is blurred. It is just as easy to get information on someone's personal life as it is with his or her work. In fact, many people mix them. They will post personal information on work-related sites like LinkedIn and post work-related information on personal sites like Facebook. Also, these sites all have subgroups for both work and personal information. How much information you choose to expose is up to you, but you have to be careful that the party picture of you making a fool out of yourself doesn't make its way to a business site.

This goes back to the rule that you release the minimum amount of information about yourself. There is no upside to releasing huge amounts of detail on your private or work life. Once it's posted, anybody can access it, including the company you are interviewing for, your competitor, or your customer. Anything you post may be used against you at some point. Posted information is permanent, no matter what the site tells you. Once it's posted, assume it's irretrievable.

Expert use of information can make a salesperson very effective. How you obtain it, manage it, and release it is a learned skill. Many people in our culture are familiar with the many vehicles available to receive and promulgate information. Not many salespeople know how to use it effectively. Never expose more information than you need to. Exposing too much information may lead to a distracting situation, possibly one in which you lose business. Why risk it? Only tell people what is necessary and refrain from blabbing too much.

The more experience you get handling information in sales environments, the more expert you will become. If you can, ride with peers or other salespeople and listen to how they give people, like customers, information. Wondering why they did or did not mention something? Ask them later, after the meeting, when you're alone. Every piece of information a salesperson divulges should be backed by a reason for releasing it.

One of the ways people release too much information is in e-mails. E-mailing is an art and not a very hard one to master if you just follow a few simple rules, mostly based on how to use information.

E-mail vs. Voice

These days, everyone is using e-mail and texting. You can bet that everyone on your address list has at least one e-mail address, sometimes two or three. But when should e-mail or voice be used? One time, I was trying to set up an important meeting with a customer. We had recently penetrated management of an important account and were looking forward to making our pitch to the decision makers. These guys were pretty important, high-level managers. Though this company was a start-up, they were on a fast track to being successful. (Can you smell success when you walk in the door?) They were so hot, everyone wanted to be in front of them. So it was really hard to get in there, let alone get time with the decision makers.

At the time, I was in a start-up too. Since we didn't have many salespeople, we used reps to get more feet on the street. The rep company had all these salespeople calling on the customers in the region. There was a salesperson assigned to this important account. So this one sales guy was responsible for managing this major customer for us.

I have a rule I always use with reps and people who report to me: I let them manage the account up to a point. I work in the background like a coach, discussing strategy and strategizing on the best thing to do. We mutually agree on what needs to be done, and then I expect them to do it. If they don't, I remind them about it and give them another chance. If they still don't act, I step on them and do it myself. I apprise them of what I am doing, but only after I step in. If they get mad, I ignore it. They should know better.

I had spoken to this sales guy about setting up a meeting with one of the key managers. He said no problem, he could do it. We both agreed that this was very important for us. A day later, I called him and asked if he had set up the meeting yet. He sent me an e-mail that he had tried to set up the meeting and hadn't heard from the manager but would let me know as soon as he heard. Another day later, I called and got him on the phone. I asked if he had talked to the manager yet. He hadn't. At that point, I noticed he didn't really say whether he had left the manager a voicemail or he couldn't get the man on the phone. I asked him right then if he had called the manager. He said no, he sent an e-mail about the meeting. He didn't call the manager at all.

To get the picture right, you have to understand that this guy had no relationship with the manager. I am sure the manager looked at his e-mail and thought, *Here's another jerk trying to get my time, too lazy to call me.* I was furious. But I contained my anger. I asked the salesperson to call this guy as soon as he could. The salesperson was taken aback by my orders, but at this point, all I wanted was the meeting. If this salesperson didn't understand how to set up a meeting with a senior manager, then I would do it. All I was asking was this guy to call the manager. Why is this so complicated? Finally he called the manager and got the meeting scheduled.

What was brutally exposed was the fact that this sales guy had been relying on e-mail so much that he had virtually stopped using his phone for anything. This is the trait of a mediocre salesperson. It's too easy to use e-mail. It's also easy to ignore e-mails. It's much harder to ignore someone if you pick up the phone after it rings and say hello.

Phone is voice. Voice exposes far more information than an e-mail can. The additional information can be extremely useful. In a conversation one thing can lead to another. E-mail can't do this. Voice is more difficult because people can be hard to reach. E-mail is far easier to use because when you hit send, it goes to the recipient. On the other hand, you really don't know if (1) they received it or (2) they read it; do you?

Asking someone for an answer in an e-mail is risky. It's easy to shoot you down; he or she replies, "Sorry, can't do it." When they do that, you don't have options. Your job is to persuade, and e-mail doesn't give you much room to do that. Voice is very different because you can try to persuade someone to change his or her mind if you are in a conversation. E-mail is not conversation though many people think it is. Someone can just stop responding to your e-mails and there is no way for you to know what happened. Is that the way a conversation goes? Knowing when to use e-mail or voice should be carefully considered. Don't rationalize using e-mail when it's far more effective calling someone up. Sure, you can get results on e-mail, but voice is clearly definitive.

E-mail has its place but not without cost. Composing an e-mail can take a long time. Write one too short and you may not convey what you meant. Compose a long e-mail and it will probably be ignored. Make a mistake and write the wrong thing, spell a name wrong, it's done for all time. There are very good uses for e-mail. It is a permanent record, is undisputable, and can help you in confirming many types of business deals. It really is "putting it in writing." Despite good intentions, it can be misinterpreted negatively. E-mail has a downside when you write something you wish you hadn't. Everybody can see it and even pass it around for others to laugh at—a permanent record of something stupid you said.

E-mail is a very powerful tool, as the phone is. When you need a permanent record or you need to send brochures or just confirm a meeting, e-mail is beautiful for this. More complex subjects, including making critical decisions or trying to reach an important prospect, require a phone call. Use good judgment in deciding which to use. Just choose carefully and don't get mediocre.

While you're trying to decide whether to e-mail or call someone, you might spend some time figuring out what your business looks like. Do you have enough prospects identified? Will you close enough business this quarter to make quota? The funnel is a great tool for getting a quick look at the current state of your business.

The Funnel

This is one of the most basic tools for a salesperson who has responsibility for multiple accounts. A funnel is a listing of all your prospects and customers categorized by stage of closure. You should always maintain a funnel to manage your progress. Management may ask you to keep a funnel. If they haven't asked you for one, make one up and show it to them. In one glance, they have a status of your account responsibility. You also will use it to track how well your entire program is going. Below is a typical funnel.

The Sales Funnel

Expenses, Inc. ABC Company Acme Scientific Generic Products Long Drive, Inc. Lotsa Money, Inc. Target Market, Inc. Prospect Corp. PO For U, Inc. Orders Be Us, Inc. Waste Of Time Corp. Mucho Dollars, Inc. Big Company, Inc. Play Golf, Inc.	Call Me, Inc. On The Road, Inc. Coastal Products Inc. Big Cheese Corp. Hard To Reach, Inc. Galactic Prospect, Inc. Order Maybe, Corp. Cold Call Me, Inc. Rock Fetch, Inc.	Canned Air, Inc. Need It Now, Inc. Slow Boat, Corp. Huge Org, Inc. Product Stuff, Inc.	Decision Maker, Inc. Lowest Price, Inc. Want It Now, Corp.
Prospects Who Need First Call	**Qualified Prospects In Dialog To Discover Needs**	**Prospects Doing Evaluation**	**Prospects Likely To Make Decision To Buy Soon**

You can see why it's called a funnel. There are many more prospects on the left side than on the right. This makes sense. As prospects move from left to the right over time, the "real" prospects make it to the next step while others who won't buy your goods or services (at this time) drop out or move back. Obviously, you don't really need to draw a funnel like this—the point is to have an orderly way to categorize your opportunities and monitor your progress visually over time. Your categories can be different too, just as long as they can be partitioned to match your sales progress from mining prospects to closing them. It is a continuous process. Sometimes sales organizations have only two or three stages, the last being customers who will buy in the current quarter.

Many companies use a CRM, or customer relationship manager tool. They use this to monitor all the activity with customers, including booking and billing. Expect to see a method for entering customer data to provide a sales funnel for management. The format is very flexible, so it varies from company to company.

Funnels are only as good as how often you update them. That, in turn, depends on how frequently things change and how much they change. If you have many irons in the fire at once, a funnel is a great way to take a high-level snapshot of your status.

You should always be filling the funnel on the left and moving customers to the right. Problems in selling show up immediately and can be addressed before they become serious issues. An added feature could be a weighting component to each prospect. You can add a subjective percentage to each prospect that indicates your feelings about how well things are going. Another piece of data to add is an estimated forecast of potential revenue multiplied by the subjective percentage.

Knowing the revenue potential at each stage will give you (and management) a good indication of the likelihood of you making your quota. Most quotas are paid quarterly. More rigorous companies enforce funnel reviews regularly, especially at the end of the quarter. Both revenue potential and funnel "health" are reviewed. If your manager is a good one, he or she will push you to keep your funnel full and make sure you have enough end-stage prospects that will place orders before the end of the quarter to make your "number." Smaller companies aren't usually that organized. You may be the only person who is responsible for the funnel. Still, you need to be disciplined enough to keep some kind of funnel going, especially if you have many accounts.

Your company may be a stickler for funnel management, so much so that it becomes paperwork. You spend too much time adhering to management's obsession with the funnel. This usually happens when a CRM is involved. Usually this activity is around managing the funnel status.

The state of the funnel should constantly change. Prospects will move from left to right or up to down, depending on how you structure it. At the end of the quarter (or quota period), prospects should be moved from one stage to the next. Some may be dropped, as nothing will happen in the near future. If you have a funnel for each quarter, you will move each prospect to the new quarter's funnel and make changes as you review the state of each opportunity.

The funnel is an absolute necessity for salespeople. You can make up almost any categories that reflect what is important in the way you run your business. There is no right way to do this. Just keep it as simple as possible, resisting the temptation to add too many categories. Too many categories will make it too difficult to manage; if it's too much work, you won't keep it up.

A spreadsheet works well as a start. If your company has a CRM, get to know it. There will probably be canned reports. If the reports don't fit your needs, you can always make a funnel up in it that suits you.

Now that you have a funnel, you have a good idea how your business looks for the near and far term. Some of the companies in your funnel may be large. If your boss sees your funnel, the next question out of his or her mouth will be, "What are you forecasting for this funnel, and what do you think you can commit to?"

Forecasting

Sales is never a straight line.—Old sales proverb

A forecast is a way of looking ahead to how much business you could achieve. This has several important functions. It helps you estimate how healthy your business will be in the future, forces you to think about what you might not be doing, and possibly warns you to change your strategy. There should be a direct correlation between your forecast and your sales funnel. Everything in your funnel should be represented in your forecast.

Your forecast may be used by other people in your company to plan building products. It takes time to build stuff. If the lead time to build products is long enough, having a forecast of business to come will help manufacturing have enough inventory to sell when the time comes. It also will keep manufacturing from building too little or too much inventory. Both situations can hurt your company.

Management will use your forecast to determine the health of the business and make plans for the future, including assessing the need to hire more people. Marketing and operations will use it to determine if products are getting old, whether they need new ones, and when to introduce them. A forecast can even tell your people that your products are being used in ways they never thought about. Forecasting has a lot of terminology associated with it. You can have a top-down forecast or a bottom-up forecast.

Top-down means some numbers-crunchers create a theoretical model of how much sales the company should do. For example, they took market data that the total available market (TAM) was, say, $50 million. Then they calculated based on how much total production capacity you had plus how much penetration of customers and prospects the company could achieve in the time period, added that up, and derived what is called the SAM, or share of available market. The SAM represents the maximum theoretical sales your company could achieve if everything in the model worked out.

So, if the TAM was $50 million, a SAM would be some percentage of that, say $25 million. That would mean your company could get 50 percent of the total market. A very good number. They take the $25 million and divide it up among an estimation of which products you sell and roll that into a theoretical forecast. Sometimes they add new products that haven't been introduced yet. This can be an accurate way to forecast if your data is very good and you have lots of it. That is top-down.

Bottom-up is when you estimate what each customer or prospect will or could buy over the period of time in question. Usually, salespeople are asked to do this. An example of bottom-up forecasting is when management asks all the salespeople in the company to forecast every product they sell over a set time interval. So the salespeople estimate their total sales based on what every customer will buy now and over a future time period, usually two to four quarters out. Sometimes it's two to five years. When the salespeople do their forecast, if it's a long period, like a year or more, they add in an assumption that the company will add new products.

As you can see, assumptions are a big deal in forecasting. They can make or break the credibility of the data. If you are asked to forecast, make sure you understand what the rules and assumptions are. Most of the time, you will be doing a bottom-up forecast. Other departments like marketing and manufacturing will do top-down forecasts, and management will evaluate both. Your funnel should closely match your forecast.

How the forecast ends up is rather complicated. The departments doing the forecasting can be sales, operations, manufacturing, and marketing. All departments have distinct methods by which their performance is measured. Because of that, each forecast is biased to conform to how the measurement is taken. If manufacturing is in part measured on how little excess inventory is left at the end of the quarter, they will build fewer items than sales tells them to. Sales, on the other hand, isn't measured on inventory, so salespeople don't care how much is left over at the end of the quarter. In fact, they want to ship as much as possible at the end of the quarter (to make quota), so they want lots of inventory to be available. The sales forecast may be excessively bloated for the end of the quarter in the hope that manufacturing will have tons of inventory to ship. Everyone puts a spin on the forecast as it makes its way to senior management for review.

Forecasting is something that all salespeople should learn to do. You would think the data should be presented as objectively as possible, but it doesn't always work out that way because of the spin doctors and politics. Here are some general unwritten rules that go along with forecasting:

- Salespeople will try to be accurate in the near term, optimistic in the long term. In reality, the little secret is that nobody can really do an accurate bottom-up forecast looking beyond two quarters. But you will still be asked to do it. Also, a top-down forecast is so idealistic it's only good for qualification of a business case. (Some people will disagree with that.)
- When marketing people receive the sales forecast, they figure no salesperson wants to turn in bad news, so they assume the forecast is weighted too far to the optimistic. They ignore it and apply their own spin to it. They think they know exactly what the needs of the customer are even though they have no idea. So the final forecast may not look anything like the bottom-up forecast you submitted.
- Manufacturing people always make a top-down forecast. Since they get measured on having as little excess inventory as possible, they always err on the side of caution. Manufacturing knows what the order rates are, so they predict future volumes based on history, not new information. They have no idea what is going on with future demand. They are in a vacuum and blind, but confident they are going in the right direction.

- Senior managers will develop various methods of counteracting the forces that bias the forecast data. Sometimes they will create wild mechanisms, such as making the salespeople "own" what is built in manufacturing. No matter what, various other counterproductive by-products of the rules negate their efforts. Nobody openly admits it, but since each department is measured differently, the forecasts will always be slanted.

- Your sales managers will take your forecast and run it through their "politically correct data manipulator" before letting their bosses see it. So the end result will look nothing like what you submitted. Remember, it's not that they don't believe you; it has to do with what they are dealing with upstairs. Their motivation is to protect you from the beasts of management.

- Actually, I lied. Your management really won't believe your forecast anyway, even though you are the closest person they have to the account. With that in mind, you are probably asking yourself, *If they think this way, why do they bother to have me do a forecast?* To explain this further, we need a deep understanding of motivational psychology and chaos theory.

- If business is bad for the company, the number of forecasts salespeople are asked to do goes up indirectly proportional to how much revenue declined. So does the amount of detail they ask you for. I know a story of a sales guy in our company (when business was very bad) who tore a hundred-dollar bill in half and put one half in the middle of his twenty-five page forecast with a note that said, "Call me at (this number) and I'll give you the other half." No one ever called.

- In a down market, when sales are poor, salespeople will generate the classic "hockey stick" forecast illustrated below for meetings where management is attending and the salespeople are presenting their business. No salesperson wants to forecast bad news. Your sales management will laugh at this graph because they've seen it so much. Unfortunately, you're in a trap. If business is really bad, you don't want to look at the future pessimistically, even if the market outlook is bleak. On the other hand, a hockey-stick forecast is an amateur move. However, if you are good at what you do, your management will understand the predicament you're in if you present them with the ol' hockey stick. The hockey-stick forecast graph should be a message to management that politics is far more important than accurate information. Every company is different.

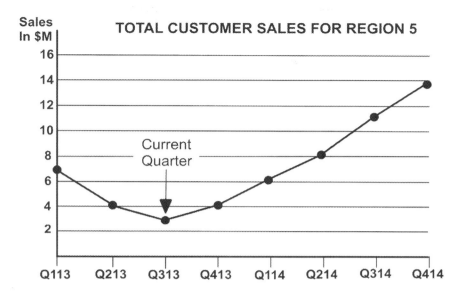

The Ever Classic Hockey Stick Forecast Graph

There is a fine line between being brutally honest with your forecast and outright lying. You need to be in the middle somewhere. Which side (truth or lie) depends on the politics within your company. Talk to your manager and your peers about it. The larger the company, the more complex the politics of forecasting will be. Your manager may give you a subtle or not so subtle indication if he or she wants you to "influence" it. Overall, if you lack data about the future, be as reasonably optimistic about your forecast as possible. Try to get planning data from purchasing or manufacturing. Salespeople often spend little time with the customer's manufacturing people, who can offer a wealth of information about near-term activity. Always ask your customers about the future. Nobody can argue with you about your forecast if you get your data directly from them.

If you're lucky, there could be many salespeople presenting before you do. You can watch their presentations and tune yours after seeing how management reacts. Every company has a particular way to forecast. Get to know your company's method and use it. After you get more comfortable with the culture, you can buck a trend if you feel like it. Sometimes management is desperate for someone to break through all the forecast BS.

No matter how small your company is, you have to forecast. There is no more powerful tool to assist you in contemplating the future of your business. Deep insights, surprises, and solid strategies can all come out of it. Next time your manager asks you to do a forecast, understand that no matter how the data is interpreted, it still is providing valuable information that helps your company stay healthy.

There are many tools for forecasting. How productive you are at forecasting may be dictated by how well you utilize technology. In fact, how productive you are these days is directly proportional to how well you have mastered the use of technology.

Technology

We have so much technology and so many gadgets. Some of these can give you an edge. Both hardware and software products are available to help salespeople do their job. These days, if you don't embrace technology you are doomed to fall behind. Social networking, enabled by cheap and powerful technology, is something you must harness.

There are some holdouts, but if you can't master all the tricks of a smartphone or cloud computing, you'll be lost. If you aren't so adept at technology, I'm sure you know someone who is. Go to that person to figure out what might help you. Technology and people who understand it are pervasive, so it isn't hard to find someone to help you.

There are people who are very good at the "bleeding edge" stuff. I am fairly technical, but some of these people blow me away in how they adapt technology to increase their productivity. I learn a lot from them. Find at least one of these people to hang with.

Many people get frustrated by how fast technology advances. I always encounter a friend who says something like, "Every time I go to buy the latest smartphone, I hear another one that is better is coming out."

I always reply with a very famous line that characterizes the march of technology very well: "If you are going to wait for the next great high-tech gadget to be introduced, you will always be waiting for it."

There is always another one coming out. Technology always advances. If you buy that great smartphone, in two months another will come out that makes your phone look like junk. Always expect technology to advance at a rapid pace.

Gordon Moore at Intel noticed a trend in the development of microprocessors: every eighteen months, the number of transistors would double. Nowadays, people cite Moore's Law in reference to the expected steady growth of technology. In fact, you should expect technology to just keep going.

The company you work for should be aggressively exploiting technology. If it isn't, there may be problems ahead in being competitive. Even low-tech companies are now using advanced technologies to improve business. Companies even use "compute clusters" to optimize the size and curve of potato chips or design a cardboard box that won't crush when shipped by rail. Does your company have someone who drives the technology? Are they "allowed" to implement their ideas and improvements, or is their position a token one? The culture of a company will determine whether or not it uses technology. I know companies that make very advanced products yet are encumbered with very old processes internally that hold them back. Just because a company has a high-tech product doesn't mean it uses technology for operations or has a roadmap that leverages the newest technology. It all can be very deceptive.

Get used to technology. Love it. Use it carefully and be smart how you apply it. Add a bit of creativity if you can. Take some risk with it. Keep current on it. If you look away too long, you will fall behind, and it will take a long time to catch up. Technology enables us to build things we never imagined possible. You and your company should be doing this. If you don't, you might as well check out.

One way to use technology is to keep track of a large customer. If you're going to call on a company with more than a hundred employees, knowing who's who in the organization can help you focus on spending time with the right people. You obviously can't call on everyone. Mapping out who is in the company helps you visualize which people you should call on. With larger companies, having a handy map that shows who's who makes you more efficient in worming your way through an organization successfully. The organizational chart—or "org chart," for short—is a fantastic tool that's like a roadmap to quickly get you to your destination.

Organizational Charts

If the number of employees at your customer is above a certain size, it can get difficult to keep track of where everybody fits who is making the decisions. A good way to visualize it is to draw up an organizational chart or "org chart". Org charts are like a map of your customer's structure. At a glance, they will show you where everybody fits in, but more importantly, where the decision makers and decision influencers are. Here is a sample org chart:

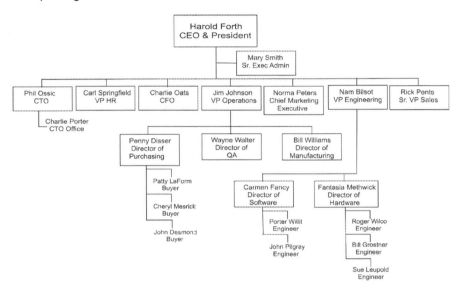

You can use any method to draw these charts. I have used Microsoft Visio or PowerPoint to do them. The format doesn't matter. What's important is to have a way of visualizing an entire organization.

The information in an org chart is perishable, so it needs to be updated regularly. People quit, are transferred, get moved, or are victims of a reorganization. Stuff happens every day that affects the organization, and the larger the company, the more stuff changes. Your management will probably ask for a chart. If the request doesn't come, show your manager what you've done.

Don't count on your customer giving you one. They may or may not know how to access it or more usually, the org chart is considered proprietary information which cannot be shared outside the company. Many companies only keep org charts with the senior managers, and nobody lower knows they exist. Some companies keep them online so people can find them. It all depends on how big or small the company is. When companies grow beyond fifty or more employees, someone will create at org chart.

You should know something about each person you put on the chart. When you start building an org chart, you can get data from various sources. One source is the customer. Whenever you visit a customer, you should take a moment to make sure you write down the names and titles of the people you're meeting with, who they report to, who reports to them, and who their peers are. You have to be sensitive about extracting too much information from someone. Nobody likes a lot questions. You may have to pace yourself asking the same person, depending on how he or she reacts to your inquiries. Looking like a data vacuum cleaner will only make you look bad and hurt your long-term relationship.

If you have built some good relationships with a customer, you might show him or her your org chart and ask for comments on it. I find that customers are fascinated seeing the organization laid out in front of them. Many times these people have no idea about the structure of their organization but would love to see it. When you show it to customers, they may even help you edit it. I give them a pencil and let them make changes.

Make sure you correlate the information customers give you about their organization. They may be a bit fuzzy on the more unrelated parts of a company they tell you about. Never take one person's word. Always substantiate data.

Other sources of org-chart information are salespeople who previously called on the account (they may have an old org chart), your manager, annual reports, and other public statements like trade-rag articles. If you have an online brokerage account, you may be able to get organizational information from the analysis tools provided. Brokers and analysts have really good organizational information.

If you have an ally in the customer's organization, he or she may provide you with the corporate org chart. This is the best way to begin an org chart: get it from the customer! Remember, the information in it may be slightly outdated. You'll need to review it to make sure it's up to date. I have been handed org charts that the company claimed to be current, but after I looked at it I realized it was outdated. Be careful, as this information may be controlled by the company and may not be allowed to go outside or be seen by outsiders. You and your ally could get into trouble handling this hot information.

If you have time, make two org charts for every customer. Mark up one chart show who is involved with the decision—label them as DMs and DIs. This will give you a better perspective on how to accomplish your goal of closing the customer. Keep a second org chart unmarked to show your customers when you want to update it. I would not recommend showing the DI/DM org chart to customers unless your relationship is strong.

Keeping org charts updated takes a lot of time. If you have a lot of accounts, they may not be practical, or you might just sketch a quick one for each account. But if your account is large, an organizational chart can be very handy to help you focus on where to best spend your time. Just making one forces you to concentrate on each department you call on and reflect on the state of your business. Think of it like an artist who paints a picture of a subject—to capture the true elements, he or she has to study the subject before the work can be finished.

Maybe you'll get lucky and the salesperson who left the account gave you an existing chart or you found it in your desk. Looking at the org chart, you can see who reports to who. Good. Knowing the information is perishable, you can use this org chart as a starting point, but won't count on it as law.

At this point, you are very organized and in control. You are the nexus of information and can use it to execute a solid sales strategy. Many companies manage the huge amount of information with a customer-relationship manager. This is database software that keeps track of what is going on with every customer, in excruciating detail.

CRMs

To most salespeople, these tools can be like a virus that infects your company and creates an excessive amount of paperwork, which becomes a barrier to reaching your quota. Management loves Customer Relationship Manager software (CRM). Salesforce.com is one of the more popular ones. The "sell" of a CRM is fantastic. Management can monitor in whatever detail they need the progress and state of their sales at any time. With one click, they can see what the total business picture is, in real time. Salespeople report everything they do, every activity, down to the single molecule of every keystroke in the CRM. The more detail management can get real-time, the better and more accurate their understanding of how to manage the business. The CRM allows them to get far more information than they ever could with spreadsheets. It generates reports in any format you want, arranging the data in an unlimited number of ways. Manufacturing can build to real-time forecasts instead of guessing with top-down forecasts. The sell of these tools is easy. However, implementation and management are a different story.

Senior management can become overly obsessed with watching the numbers. More detail means more questions as to why this is happening or that is happening. Sometimes that is a good thing and sometimes it isn't. Lower-level management is barraged by an incessant stream of questions about micro-niche pieces of information. All this rolls down the hill to the salespeople. Rules can get very strict on the necessity of entering data in the CRM. You many even hear the famous CRM-based quote, "If it isn't in [the CRM], it isn't real." The CRM, not the outside world, becomes reality. This means if you forget to enter an order that books and bills, you don't get credit for it, even though your management knows you won it. At this point you realize the CRM has substituted reality with a weird abstraction something akin to a bad dream.

If you find you are spending more time with your CRM than your customers, you may need to think about whether this is what a sales job should be. There is a delicate balance between how much information is required and how much management expects the salespeople to provide. What and how much information management requires directly correlates to how much information salespeople need to input. Some salespeople will work at their desks all day entering data into the CRM. It's more difficult for people in the field to enter data, so if the expectation is that they enter as much as inside people, it can be a problem. Sometimes this is overcome by having inside people enter the data for the field people. If it is managed well, it can be a powerful tool. If not, it turns the salespeople into note takers, not order takers.

The CRM can help create discipline in a large organization, which it may need. As a company grows in size, the amount of information grows to huge proportions. Management needs information to make decisions, and if there is too much in too many different places, they can't be effective at their job. A CRM can organize all that information into concise reports, coalescing it into usable chunks to make decisions with. The CRM can force salespeople to be more organized about the way they think about their business. Many well-organized salespeople have systems they use to evaluate where they stand. A CRM can do this too. Having all the salespeople standardize the forms they use can help them be more productive.

If a CRM isn't managed well, though, it can be a nightmare for everyone, salespeople and management alike. There are many things that can make it unruly. For example, if many people are allowed to access and modify the database, it becomes corrupted by repeated updates by those with less information than the original ones who entered it. Reports will randomly change or even disappear for no reason. Data a salesperson enters can be modified by people who have no idea what is going on with the customer. Part numbers have multiple variations that no one understands. You enter something, and then a while later you discover someone changed it so it's wrong. It gets harder and harder to find information because there is too much, it's changing too frequently, and it's too fragmented. I have seen people stop using the CRM and go back to spreadsheets—a signal that this high-tech tool is not working.

The factory people running the CRM may lack insight into the needs of the users. This only makes the CRM more dysfunctional. Instead of creating it in a vacuum, each department, down to the individual, needs the ability to give feedback on a regular basis. Otherwise, the CRM will take on a life of its own, which may or may not have any usefulness for the people depending on it.

If your company uses a CRM, there is probably a guru somewhere in your organization. Find and get to know that person. He or she will be your key to using the CRM in a productive manner. The larger your company, the more intimidating the CRM will look. This guru can help you get going and will be available to you whenever you call.

The CRM can be a very powerful productivity tool for a salesperson as long as it's managed well. If your company can't manage the CRM, it will sap the productivity out of everyone, especially the salespeople. Like fire, it can be your friend or foe.

CHAPTER EIGHT

GETTING BETTER AT SELLING

The Stages of a Salesperson

There are all different levels a salesperson can attain. Some sales jobs don't require you to develop a very sophisticated level to make good money, only good basic selling skills. But like any other profession, there can be very refined, powerful salespeople. Depending on your type of product and what DMs you call on, your success will depend on how strong your relationships are and how well you command your business. Below is a table that is a crude measure you can use to evaluate what level you are at with customers and/or your factory. Sometimes this is referred to as a "stage 1" salesperson or "stage 3." I have come up with some crude definitions as a guideline.

Minimal	Professional	Strategic	Consultive	Confidant

Minimal—Stage 1

This is the lowest level and the easiest type of relationship to attain. In reality, it doesn't have much going for it. At this level, you contact the customers by e-mail and receive e-mail replies. You go by the seat of your pants. You have a good sales instinct, but that's about it. You don't know the fundamentals yet. You have little, if any, product knowledge. You don't know many people in the factory, so you can't and don't know how to get resources to help you with customer issues.

You call customers but have trouble getting meetings set up. Your day is pretty much driven by the ring of a phone. You go from customer to customer with no priority, much like a bee going from flower to flower. When the phone rings, you have something to do. Planning how to meet quota isn't on your to-do list until it's too late to do something about it. You have little or no value to the customer other than filling out an order. Some salespeople I know think this level is a great achievement. I feel sorry for them. If asked, the customer may or may not even remember who you are or that he responded to your e-mail. The only positive thing is that you have the customer s phone number or e-mail address, so at least you have a place to start.

You should have done some research on the customer to understand some areas where you might be able to provide a solution to a need. You have a lot to learn. Hopefully, you won't stay at this level very long. You should strive to achieve something greater rather than being a cork on the water.

Professional—Stage 2

Here, you have meaningful conversations on the phone and can set up your first meeting with customers. You can cold-call pretty well. You can get to the ground floor of a meaningful relationship with customers by providing good value. You know your company's products pretty well. You know the sales cycle and the fundamentals. You know how to use factory resources to help your customer. You figure out how to fulfill needs and can close. When you phone customers, they will remember who you are but may or may not take your call. Your best place is order fulfillment—transactional selling.

You are viewed as a good, solid salesperson who can meet quota in most cases and can be depended on. Professional salespeople at this level can make very good money, but they don't make deeper relationships. Rather, they are very good for transactional selling, like lower touch environments, where deep relationships are necessary. Professional salespeople are solid performers.

Strategic—Stage 3

You can meet with customers, discover needs (especially unarticulated ones), cleverly construct a powerful solution, and close. You have deep product knowledge and win extra business because of it. You have a good network. You drive very good business for your company and may receive awards for your work. You can put together a decent sales plan and plot a clever strategy to win difficult deals. You are good at high-touch selling. The customer thinks you are very good. Your company may have you call on larger accounts; you get promoted regularly. You may have allies.

Congratulations, you are doing a great job. Because of your hard work, the customer believes you help solve issues and have a command of your factory's resources. They answer your phone calls. For many reasons, most successful senior salespeople stay at this stage. You can be very successful at this level and make a lot of money.

Consultive—Stage 4

Consultive salespeople are very valuable to the customer. You have mastered how to get and use information. Your extensive product knowledge coupled with a thorough understanding of how the customer shops for, buys, uses, and disposes of your product allows you to discover unarticulated needs and create new business other salespeople have no idea how to do. Your network is large and has some very influential people in it. You can solve many problems with just one phone call. Customers will actually believe you know more about their business than they do. So much so, they may consult with you on important business decisions. You are known throughout the customer's company and are sought after to be seen with. You have many allies, some in powerful positions. You may have the same level of influential relationships outside of work in the public community.

You work best with top management and help with strategy and other projects at the customer and factory. Factory people have tremendous respect for you, and you frequently get inside information from the customer about delicate issues plus first and last looks at opportunities. Business will be directed to your company based on the value of your relationship and less on pricing. The customer may make a statement like, "I wish our salespeople were as good as you." In some cases, they may even try to hire you into their company.

The Confidant—Stage 5

At this level, you have become personal friends with one or more people at high level positions at your customers' companies. Ironically, this may make you less effective, because the relationships are personal. This can compromise your ability to distinguish who you really work for—are you doing all the things my company asks or protecting your friends? On the plus side, you can usually get any information you want, no matter how delicate or confidential, and immediate access anytime. You might also divulge your own company's very confidential inside information, though, to protect your friends or possibly land a large deal. It can get very, very complicated.

At the confidant level, your own people may not trust you enough to discuss delicate internal information if your relationships are known. It's a two-edged sword. I have been in this position, and it's tough but worth it. It's nice to have friends in high places. You really can get things done. I want to say here that most salespeople in these positions are very effective and use their powerful status wisely.

As a confidant salesperson, you will rule over your accounts and squash most if not all of your competition. You will have senior managers as allies who will want you to win. You will be connected in a vast network that may include not only businesspeople but politicians, university figures, and other powerful individuals.

Nothing lasts forever, and most people move on to other positions. This is a good thing. At one company I was at, many of the customers I built friendships with went to other companies into high-level positions. I realized all these people I was pals with left and went to all these new companies, and I could waltz right in and close business with all of them. I was worth more to a different company than the one I was with. So I quit, found a new job, and landed a large amount of business right away.

Attaining a confidant level of sales is very interesting and rewarding. The people who become friends with you will always remember you. If you keep your relationships current, you will always be able to call and do business but also have fun. They will probably call you to get advice, offer you a job, or just talk about the weather.

Strong salespeople have relationships from all five categories going at once. Like a sales funnel, as you go from left to right, the number of customers goes from many to few. Not all levels are right for everybody. You can have fun at any level. Just be good at what you do, recognize and leverage your strengths, seize opportunity, and do what is right.

One of the key people in your life at a company is your manager. You will always have a manager. This is a person you will have to coexist with and be dependent on to make or break your career. Make sure you know how to work with this very important person.

Managing Your Manager

Rule #1: Your job is to keep your manager happy. It's that simple.

Managers have all different types and styles. Some are easygoing and others can be heavy-handed. They may be very detail oriented and ask you for lots of status reports. Others are more hands-off and just want a verbal status at the end of the week. Some may not even talk to you. One manager may review your priorities and another won't. There are so many different managing styles, it's amazing anything gets done. Your manager will either be secure or insecure. These are some basic things to watch for.

If you are lucky, you will have a great relationship with your manager. You will quickly find the common ground of a productive relationship. However, it doesn't always work this way. Most times, you have to work at keeping your relationship a healthy one. This is all part of working for someone—having to put energy into keeping things running smoothly. It's work, which is in addition to what you have to do with your customers.

Theoretically, your manager's job is to find ways of maximizing your time spent with customers while minimizing the amount of busy work. This means your manager works to insulate you from upper management, keep bureaucratic tasks to a minimum, vigorously defend you from political attacks, and keep the amount of energy spent on your relationship to a very low level. Some managers are very talented at doing this. Unfortunately, some are not. In fact, some are completely clueless.

One of the ways to improve your relationship with your manager is to understand more detail about his or her world. A manager's job can be very complex and challenging, in a completely different way than a salesperson's. The more you know about what your manager has to deal with, the higher-quality relationship you will have. Managers have various ways of coping with their issues. They are stuck between demanding, sometimes heavy-handed senior managers with unreasonable expectations and a group of salespeople who behave like unruly schoolchildren. They have to please upper management while trying to keep their kids on track to a sales-revenue goal.

Depending on how crazy the environment is, a manager will develop a defense mechanism to cope with it. Intellectual rationalization is one way he or she does it. Another word for this can be *denial*. Everyone does it, and managers are expert at it. You may notice your manager seems completely oblivious to what seems to be an obvious problem in his or her territory. Remember the rule: managers know more than we think they do. If the problem is obvious, the manager probably knows about it and chooses to ignore it. If it is a conscious act, he or she has decided there's just not enough in the day to deal with it and chosen to fight other battles.

If you think your manager should be helping to solve a problem he or she consciously wants to avoid, make sure you have a solid argument why the manager should drop other things and make this a priority. If you can't make a good argument, you are wasting the manager's time. Not a good situation for you. If the manager is unconsciously ignoring a problem, there is a very good chance he or she doesn't consciously know it exists. If you think the problem is important to bring to the manager's attention, you may get a response like, "What problem?" The manager may disagree with you that it exists and possibly get angry with you for bringing it up. This indicates he or she really doesn't want to talk about it. It's your call whether to push, but you'd better be prepared with lots of supporting data, because it can get ugly for you. I am not saying to never bring problems up with your manager. I am saying to understand there are two distinct types you may encounter: one listens for a persuasive argument and the other may think you are trying to argue that the world is flat.

Managers who are secure will be nonintrusive and pretty much let you do your thing within certain guidelines. They may take responsibility for your professional growth and work to make you a star. Other secure managers will let you alone to fend for yourself. This isn't negative, but it isn't positive either. A secure manager who spends (what you think is) a lot of time with you is an indication that he or she may perceive an issue.

Insecure managers can be trouble for strong salespeople. Their interest is in protecting themselves from any perceived threat from above (their management) or below (you or your peers). If you are good at what you do and confident, they may actually try to keep you from succeeding. Depending on how severe their issues are, you may be forced to find another position. Usually their behavior can be tolerated, but to a successful salesperson, it is frustrating and should be dealt with.

Read more about the different kinds of managers and their strengths and weaknesses.

The Dictator

- unapproachable
- consciously competent
- commands, doesn't ask
- seems devoid of any feelings
- can be paranoid
- hated by subordinates
- does very little to motivate
- good at managing up, poor at managing down
- good at buffering subordinates from upper management
- easily throws people under a bus
- always gives poor reviews
- can be a headache to HR
- customer visits can be very good or very bad
- can be strong ally or terrible adversary for vendor
- untrustworthy

The Manipulator

- mildly unapproachable
- unconsciously competent
- insecure, possible serious personality issues

- takes credit for work done by subordinates
- enjoys having his or her worshippers fight his or her detractors
- easily throws people under bus
- uses vendors for personal gain
- untrustworthy
- always gives poor reviews to feared people even if they are good
- hated by subordinates
- will expose his people to upper management to get them in trouble
- good in customer visits but may resist scripting
- good managing up, poor managing down

The Hippie

- approachable
- consciously incompetent
- in another world
- has no idea what you do and doesn't care
- wants to talk about anything except work
- poor managing up and poor managing down
- useless for follow-through
- can be good in customer visits but needs scripting
- very poor conflict skills
- willingly exposes (no idea what he or she is doing) people to upper management
- may be impossible to reach
- always gives good reviews
- vendors or partners find them useless
- sell stock in this one

The Responsible Manager

- approachable
- consciously competent
- mostly on top of what is going on
- cares about subordinates and fights for them
- okay at managing up, better at managing down
- mildly strong in political clout
- good at customer visits

- can handle confrontation okay but not extended big fights
- good political skills
- can be good at keeping upper management from messing with their people
- good at managing conflict
- can be reached
- good at managing vendors or partners
- reviews employees fairly

The Peter Principle Manager

- way over his or her head
- unconsciously incompetent
- may actually think self well suited for position (clueless) or may be freaking out over saving job
- approachable
- knows should help subordinates but too consumed trying to save self
- poor at managing up and down
- unwittingly exposes subordinates to upper management
- poor political clout
- mostly in this position because of blind spot or some other unusual mistake
- may be able to do customer visits well
- can't handle conflict as the people he or she deals with are more talented
- if too distracted, may be difficult to reach
- a joke to vendors or partners
- avoided by employees
- reviews employees unfairly, having no have skill set for it

The Good Manager

- approachable
- consciously competent
- leaves senior employees alone—only spends time with those who need it
- cares and fights vigorously for subordinates
- very good at managing up and down

- good at buffering upper management from subordinates
- good political clout—has credibility
- does a good job with customers and can stand in for their people well
- reviews employees very well—rewards for good work
- makes sure key salespeople are well paid
- good with vendors or partners
- no mystery who he or she is—he or she reveals himself or herself

The Absentee Manager

- never around or available
- consciously incompetent
- approachable (when present)
- may or may not fight for people, but needs to be there to do it
- poor managing down and okay managing up
- poor at buffering employees from senior management
- can manage conflict
- may have some political clout
- can do a good job with customers if available
- reviews of employees will be based on little, if any, reality
- good with vendors and partners

Managers are constantly looking at their subordinates and unconsciously evaluating whether or not they are effective. It is a natural process and is very much below their conscious awareness. They do this with their most effective people.

This gets exposed when the report engages the manager about an issue. When first presented with a problem, the manager will go over the facts and data. As the data builds up in the manager's head, it reaches a critical mass when he or she has enough information to determine if this is a real problem; if he or she really needs to be involved or if the employee can do it; and if the employee created the problem in the first place. As the manager gets more involved in it, even more data may come out, like whether the employee is in this position because of a skill problem—he or she is unorganized or didn't prepare for the meeting with the manager. If it gets to this point, the manager will become conscious of a problem with the employee and will now concentrate on evaluating whether or not the employee has the skills to fix the problem.

Once in this stage, an employee has a problem with the manager that will take more work to fix. Some managers will go beyond this step, and some may even ignore it, choosing denial. As you can see, you want to only meet with your manager when you absolutely have to because it can make more work for the both of you. Most managers hate being in the position of having to suddenly evaluate an undiscovered problem with an employee.

How you perceive your manager and how your manager perceives you is key to managing the relationship. He or she may not have sophisticated skills in perception. This is where many relationships have difficulties. It is your responsibility to make sure you have a good relationship with your manager. It's key to your success. Adjusting your behavior so your relationship works out is just one of the things you have to reckon with. The better you understand how your manager thinks and acts, the better your relationship will be. Getting data on your manager from other people who have interacted with him or her is a great way to get objective insights that may not be as colored as yours. Talk to peers and other people in your company. Keep conversations about your manager neutral. You may be surprised at what you hear.

Recognize if your manager has a perception problem with you. Does he or she ask you a lot of questions that make you think, *I already know that* or *You asked me to do that already and I did it.* Does your manager's questions irritate you or make you think you are thought of as a rookie? These could be symptoms that your manager perceives a problem either unconsciously or consciously, that he or she has a weak skill set, or that the manager is just too overwhelmed in his or her job and doesn't have enough time to get to know the employees and what they are doing.

How you address this is complicated and all depends on whether it's a manageable problem and worth spending time to fix. Unconscious problems are way too complicated and deep to try to rectify. One such problem would be called *transference*. Transference is when the person you are dealing with has similar issues you do. When this happens, it can illicit unconscious behavior problems in you that may not be obvious. It can be something like "I don't know why I don't like this guy". Conscious problems mean your manager is quite aware he or she is asking you rookie-type questions, which indicates he or she indeed has a problem with you and is directly trying to make you feel uncomfortable. Lacking a skill set means there is no hope of fixing this situation, and you have to ask yourself if you can live with it. If your manager is overwhelmed with the job, one strategy is to make an effort to help out. Otherwise, it's another situation where you have to evaluate if it's worth it to ride it out.

Your manager will have a style of communication. He or she may be dictatorial. This isn't necessarily bad, but it takes a lot of work to manage. This type of manager may not even seem to listen to you. This can be frustrating. But don't mistake this style of communication for not wanting to talk to you. This is why understanding how the manager works and communicates is key to you not worrying about your manager and your job. It's all in the perception.

If you think you have a lot of issues with your manager, chances are the manager feels the same way about you. It could be that you aren't getting along with your manager and anything he or she says may make you feel ill. If you reach that point, it may be time to find another job. I had a manager who never seemed to listen to me. Trying to engage in a basic discussion was a lot of work. I spent a lot of energy to make it work out. Despite this, he would make patronizing remarks and move on to the next subject. He didn't want to listen to me or try. I ended up quitting because of a blind spot and his lack of attention and his apparent disinterest in putting any effort into working with me.

Good managers who have professional people working for them leave those people alone to do their work. They keep communication at a minimum because they know it takes work to interact and prefer that you work on your customer, not them. I had a manager who never ever sent e-mails with more than five words. At first it seemed he didn't want to make any effort to communicate. But I found out he did this with everyone. So I adapted and, when sending him an e-mail, only used a few words. We ended up sharing a lot of success in landing some very big deals.

Talk to your manager only when you have to. The subject should be pertinent and have substance. Don't engage in idle banter. This is a waste of time and doesn't endear you to someone with a busy schedule. People who waste other people's time are insecure and need attention. Managers hate salespeople who talk too much and waste time (unless the manager too is chatty—but that is rare). If you feel you have to go into your manager's office all the time, you will be viewed as too needy.

That is considered a weakness. Avoid the urge to make frequent office visits unless your manager asks you to.

Listen carefully when your manager speaks to you. How he or she speaks to you tells you exactly how you are perceived. Does your manager listen to you? Does your manager hear what you are saying? Does your manager talk up to you or down? After a conversation, do you have a feeling you aren't communicating? When you leave your manager's office, do you feel it didn't go as you expected? It gets complicated. You may be misinterpreting how you are perceived, or you may be correct. Either way, this is a sign you need to find a better way to communicate.

Miscommunication between a manager and subordinates is a common issue. Most salespeople have strong communication skills, but that doesn't mean they can figure it out. It can be complicated by personality traits.

Some managers will interpret a verbal status report as a request to give you advice or tell you what to do. I had a manager who would ask me for a status on a particular customer and when I gave it, he would tell me what to do even though I already knew it. Usually the advice was so obvious a simpleton could've figured it out. Oftentimes I left his office wondering if he thought I needed a lot of help. Since these situations happened whenever we were together, I chose to avoid him. It worked. I got raises and high performance reviews, so I assumed he was like this with everyone.

If your manager seems to always be telling you what to do, even with simple things, make sure you find out if he or she does this with everyone or just with you. You have to be careful, because managers may develop an unconscious perception you always need their advice. This can make them feel you are inadequate in a way they can't articulate. They feel it. Overall, their impression of you will be diminished, even if you are doing a good job. It's important for you to find out if they do this with everyone. Remember, perception is reality.

Some managers are just plain difficult to deal with. Be careful in this situation. If you think your manager is hard to deal with, it's a good bet that he thinks the same thing about you. Try to work it out as best you can. The problem might be bad chemistry. If it is, then you either have to manage it or get out of the situation.

After you work at a job for a while, you will notice things that need changing. You will undoubtedly accrue a list of things you think your manager should do. Be careful what you pick to fight for. Fight with your manager as little as possible. Every manager knows you will eventually fight over something. This is healthy. But you can't fight for every little thing. If you really need to push as far as you can—it's called falling on your sword—the subject better be worth it. Before you fight with your manager, prepare for it. Nobody should know your managers as well as you do. Put yourself in his or her shoes and role-play. What will the manager's arguments be? What counterarguments will be persuasive? Keep cool. If you lose, learn from your encounter and get over it.

Most managers don't like the review process. It makes them uncomfortable because they have to give feedback and rank people. When you get a review or feedback, keep your cool. Be positive and objective. Your manager is probably as uncomfortable as you are, so make the best of it. If you disagree, make counterpoints with real data, not opinions. If the dark clouds of a fight loom over your head, back off and make your point without emotion. Don't fight over small stuff. It's not worth it. Should you be in disagreement with your manager's judgment, ask for a review. Do this carefully, as this means you want his or her superior to get involved. An insecure manager may react negatively. Choose wisely in this situation.

A manager will tell you to do things, and you will be expected to do them. So do them, and do them before your manager expects it done. If you don't like that, then there are issues with your relationship or your job.

Some managers are hands off and others will micromanage you. Some people thrive on micromanagement and others don't. It takes a lot of work and energy to deal with a micromanager. If you are detail oriented, this may be an environment where you flourish. But if you aren't, your life could be hell. Micromanagers need to know every step you take and why you took it. Some managers do this because they are very insecure. Unconsciously, the message is lack of trust of their people. On the other hand, some managers may be forced to do it because their sales plan doesn't work. The manager fails to make quota because the system failed. This manager has two choices: figure out what failed and fix it, or become excessively intrusive into what the salespeople are doing. The manager dictates what the salespeople should do almost every day, making them submit reports daily on their activities and progress. As you can see, this way of managing salespeople can be very stressful and demotivating and may force people to quit.

Managers may have a few reports or many. If they have many direct reports, they are probably very busy handling all their people and don't have much time for each person. You shouldn't be a person they are forced to babysit. Some are only good at "managing up" and others are only good at "managing down." Your boss should be a healthy combination of both. Recognize your manager's unique strengths and weaknesses. The better you know him or her, the better your job will be.

Managers hate bickering among their subordinates. To them, it's like children arguing over a stuffed toy. They prefer to have arguments sort out by themselves and are loathe having to mediate. Avoid going to a manager to complain about someone. This will only make you look like a whiner. Without a doubt, your manager will know exactly what is going on. Just because your manager chooses not to do anything about it should tell you something. Don't ignore the obvious. This may frustrate you, but it's your issue. Managers may choose to ignore personality issues among their subordinates and assume their people will adapt to it. They will assume everybody is grown up and will work out issues themselves; if they don't or can't, too bad for you.

This attitude is important for managers so they can get their work done without being a mommy to everyone. Usually, it's a manageable situation despite what some people think. Occasionally it isn't. You are an adult. Take responsibility in sorting out your own problems. If there are a lot of personality issues within your group, your manager may not care and is choosing to be in denial. If this is the case, it may be time to move on.

Most managers are smarter and more perceptive than you think. But there are exceptions. If your manager does show favoritism to someone else over you, it's something you'll have to work around. You can quit if it bothers you too much.

Managers want results above all. The best thing for them is when one or more of their people produce results without much intervention or need for attention. In a busy environment, the manager has too much to deal with, managing up and down. So anything that relieves managers of extra work is a welcome thing. They appreciate this so much that most managers are willing to look the other way if an employee is somewhat disruptive or causing issues with his or her team. As long as their salespeople produce results, they won't care about other things they may do, which could be a problem for other people in the company up to a point. If you want to make your manager really happy, get results and don't be needy.

There are a lot of books on dealing with managers. Read up on the subject. The more you know about dealing with your manager, the easier it will be to succeed in your career.

Like a manager, a salesperson always has too much to do. Always. So you never can finish everything you want to. Unfortunately, your company will expect you to do it alone. Everything. Almost everything you need to get done, you have to do it alone.

You Are the Cook and Bottle-Washer

As a salesperson, you have an unusually large number of things to accomplish and not enough time to do them all. You prioritize as best you can but keep wishing your factory would provide resources to assist you. How much support you get depends on how much money your company can afford or what your manager perceives you need.

Salespeople who are lucky enough to work in a sales office may have support dedicated to them. Even then, it's probably shared. No matter how much access you have to administrative support, it's never enough. This is one of the more subtle and unappreciated aspects of being a salesperson. The buck stops with you, so if something has to get done and nobody is around to do it, you may have to do it yourself.

If your manager is good, he or she will have a quiet appreciation for the frustrations salespeople face in getting things done. But that is simply the way things are. Instead of griping about it, you must get over it.

There are situations where there are so many administrative things going on they really keep you from dealing with the customer and making money. One example of this is when a company is growing so fast that there aren't enough systems in place to handle all the work. Your concerns about being overwhelmed should be presented to your manager. Avoid making general comments without data. This sounds like complaining and will get you nowhere. Come up with a justification that has details on what the problem is. More than likely, if your manager agrees with you, your data will be used to convince your manager's manager that you need relief. If you have a hard time convincing your manager, another tactic would be to bring him or her along with you to experience the problems firsthand.

Having to do everything from arranging travel, filling out expense reports, keeping up with weekly/monthly reports, setting up meetings, entertaining, paying fees, managing PCs, cars, and office expenses—it can be overwhelming. This is one aspect of sales that not many people understand.

With all the things you have to do for work, what you don't need is a bad surprise. Nothing is worse than a customer telling you he or she discovered a serious problem with one of your products and wants to return all one hundred thousand of them. Many salespeople think they ship the product to the customer and everything just works out. That isn't how it works. Without telling the salespeople, your factory may do a bit of "innocent" deception and allow a crap product to ship to customers. Over time, this will happen to you. This is another job for the salesperson, to make sure the customer stays with your company after shipping of the merchandise.

Product Warts

Don't expect selling your product or service to be a cakewalk. There will be bugs in the product or issues in delivery of service. This is one of those things that you usually discover at the customer. Your peers will discuss product problems among themselves. If you have technical field people or field support people, they will have stories about product issues. Some are well known, some only the factory knows (not the field), and some are yet to be discovered. Your job is to sell the product, even if it has warts all over it. If your senior management has allowed products to go to production, then it's your job to sell them, warts and all. If your customer has problems with the product, it's your job to find the company resources to make it work and keep the customer happy. If you find yourself complaining about every little wart you see, the issue may be more about with you. You could have burnout or have gotten mediocre.

Product problems can reach a threshold of pain. Also, they can hurt your credibility. If product problems are very bad and your company ships an endless stream of poor products into the marketplace, they will quickly get a reputation for that. If you aren't careful, you can be contaminated by your association with poor products. This is a fine line. Part of any sales job is supporting weaknesses in a product, but this can go too far. Should your company be shipping bad products as a standard procedure, business will suffer. This means it will be harder for you to achieve quota. If it gets really painful, you might think of leaving this company and finding a job with someone who ships something half-decent.

Product warts are commonplace. Salespeople usually can smooth over the issues and get the business back. It happens all the time. Being creative and resourceful really helps you be better at handling the harder aspects of your job.

Being Resourceful

Implementing creative solutions to problems is being resourceful. As a salesperson, this is one way you can be more competitive and work around difficult situations. If you are good at this, you can get just about anything done. Here is a personal example.

I had been working at my first high-tech job for about a year. I was working for a California company, but I was based in a regional sales office outside Boston. My manager had recently given me my first high-profile account. I was calling on engineers and their managers and was at the point where I was trying to build relationships. I was making good progress.

One day, a manager at this account informed me they wanted to visit my corporate headquarters for a new program—quarterly reviews with all the vendors. The visit would encompass several days. I set up the meetings with the corporate people and made flight reservations. Because of scheduling issues, I had to fly out alone. My timing was tight. I would fly in and have only a short amount of time before I had to meet them for dinner with some of the factory people. I had flown out to California a couple of times before and figured I knew the drill. I made flight reservations, rented a car, and booked my hotel. Everything was all set.

I confirmed with my management and the customer just before I left that everyone had the schedule and was committed to it. Good.

I flew out to sunny California, eager to show everyone I could handle this customer. After I arrived at the airport, I went to the car-rental place. I walked up to the woman behind the counter and began talking about the car. The woman asked me for my driver's license. I pulled out my wallet and discovered the license was missing. I am usually very good about keeping important things like a license in only one spot, so I freaked out. How could my license be missing? I never take it out of my wallet. But then I remembered I went swimming and put the license in my bathing suit, which was unusual for me. I knew my bathing suit was back in Boston, with the license still in it. I told the woman I didn't have my license. She gave me the bad news that I couldn't get a car unless I had a license. I was in trouble.

The meeting was going to be at six o'clock at a local restaurant, and I needed the car to pick up the customers. It was already two thirty in the afternoon. I didn't have much time. I figured I had only one option: rent a limousine. To rent a limousine for the entire stay would be a terribly expensive alternative. Then I had an idea. I wondered if I could get a temporary driver's license. Who knows? I figured it was worth a try. I found out the nearest DMV was only a few miles away, so I got a cab and rushed over there.

I had the cab wait. I went in and had to wait about thirty minutes to get the front of the line. I walked up and told the woman behind the counter my predicament. She told me they indeed had a temporary driver license, but it was only for people with a California license. However, they did have an option where I could take a written test (no ID required?) and get a temporary license for thirty days. So I went in and took the test without reading the manual. Let me tell you, this test had been simplified to the lowest common denominator, so you didn't need to read very well. I took the test, passed, and got my license. I jumped back in the cab, went back to the airport, and got my rental car. Whew! I made it to the dinner meeting, and the rest of the visit worked out really well.

This is just an example. You have to remember that when you get in a tight situation, you've got to believe there is an alternative. Being resourceful is having the energy, drive, will, and creativity to knock down barriers. You can't look at a situation as hopeless. You have to find a solution. That is what can help differentiate you from the rest. Find a new way to look at a problem Barriers are just that: barriers. Your job is monkeying your way around them. Look, if I can pull off stunts like the above, you can do this. I'm no special person. I just think being resourceful is lots of fun.

To really draw on your resources, you have to feel good about yourself and what you're capable of. If you have a strong will and are on a firm footing, there isn't anything you can't do.

Confidence and Decision Making

> *All you need in this life is ignorance and confidence; then success is sure.—Mark Twain (Samuel Clemens), humorist and author*

> *I think I can, I think I can …—The Little Engine That Could*

Confidence is the ability to believe that you can succeed at something when there is nothing around you that indicates you are doing the right thing. It is a belief in yourself that you can do the right thing and know your decision to do it is the right one. Too many times, people fall short of an attainable goal because they give up. They lack the ability to convince themselves they are doing the right thing because they don't have the confidence. Life is about making decisions because life is choice.

You can't get away from making choices. Making decisions is something people have to do in order to get along in life. An inability to make decisions will hamper your growth, career, and life. How do you get confidence? How do people seem to make decisions without problems? How do you do this?

It's because these people have an abundance of confidence. They understand that life is about making choices, so you might as well make them, right or wrong. If you have some common sense about things, making decisions isn't all that hard. Before you can do this, you have to have confidence in yourself. If you feel weak about your confidence, you have to find a way fix it before you can make decisions.

Two things can impede you: you may fear the outcome of a bad decision, or you may feel you make poor decisions. These issues can be either conscious or unconscious. You may know exactly why you fear decision making (conscious) or you may not be able to articulate it (unconscious). If you know why you feel uncomfortable making decisions, it's important to discuss your issues with people you know who make decisions. The more you talk about it, the more confident you will become. Talking about it will help you resolve your issues and discover the confidence in yourself to step up.

I am sure you know people who you appreciate because they look like they have confidence in what they do. Confidence is not something that you get from other people. It is a state of mind in which you develop a belief in yourself. It requires you to believe that what you do is the right thing without letting the fear of making a bad decision cause you to falter.

We are our own worst enemies when it comes to building confidence. Many times the people who lack confidence are the ones who need constant feedback from others that they are doing the right thing. You have to believe in yourself. Everyone has the potential for an abundance of confidence. It's about feeling good about yourself and that you can do the right thing. You need to divorce yourself from what others think of you. Spending energy comparing any action to what people will say is destructive and will inhibit you from doing anything creative. Some people need approval before they do anything important. How can these people accomplish anything?

In some cases, you may know you can't make decisions but can't put your finger on why. More than likely, your unconscious self is prohibiting you from making decisions. In this situation, there are conflicting issues that you may be in denial about that consciously you are unaware of. This is a more complicated situation, but it can be managed. If you think you have issues that make it difficult to make decisions, you'd benefit from therapy. Therapy is useful for solving complicated unconscious issues. Sometimes friends can help, but it takes a lot of work to uncover, identify, and acknowledge unconscious issues. It all comes down to how much you desire a solution.

Honing your decision-making skills is an important thing to do. Being confident in how you feel about yourself is key. If you can get in touch with how you make decisions, you can get better at it. One part of making good decisions is knowing when you are beyond your capability. You have to push yourself to the very edge of your limitations, sometimes exceeding them, to really understand where that line is.

Know Your Limitations

One strong characteristic of a professional is a clear understanding of the limits of what you can do. While this may sound rather simple, many people get into trouble with customers because they wander into a territory where they are clearly unskilled. This may be something like trying to answer a customer on a subject about which you know nothing. You do this because you want to show the customer how smart you are. We all want to please, but wandering into unfamiliar terrain without knowledge will only make you look like a fool.

A simple rule is to know what you know and what you don't know. Believe it or not, because of personality issues, some people just can't distinguish between the two. If you are in sales, one of the most profound things you can say is, "I don't know, but I will get you an answer." If you are mature and confident, you can make that statement without any issues. If you can't resist trying to answer any question no matter how little you know, your credibility will be destroyed and you will be viewed as a useless salesperson.

Professional salespeople know their weaknesses and compensate for them. The result is a strong, viable presence that is greater than the individual. If you are going into a meeting and parts of your discussion will be details you aren't comfortable with, bring someone from your team who knows the subject cold, or arrange for that person to be on a speakerphone during the meeting to answer the questions. Customers don't care how you get them the information. They just want simple, accurate answers to their questions. What is remarkable is that many salespeople can't distinguish between what they know and don't know. Customers will view them as idiots. Don't be an idiot.

It's all about knowing where you limits really are. Some are obvious, others are vague. Getting experience in pushing your limits hones your skill in knowing where the boundaries are. Screwing up isn't necessarily bad. Every now and then, you need to push past your limitations so you know where they are.

This rule isn't just for sales. It's for your life. Knowing what you can do and what you can't establishes credibility and trust in yourself. Make sure you understand your weaknesses, compensate for them, and lead a well-balanced life.

Speaking of limits, there are those who don't push themselves. A malady that infects even the best salespeople is lapsing into a soft routine. At some time, every one of us will be tempted to kick back and milk our gig. This very tempting idea has corrupted many salespeople. I know several people right now who are cruising through their job, not pushing, only taking low-hanging fruit. The problem with this is eventually the low-hanging fruit disappears.

The Comfort Zone

This is one of the most prevalent debilitating diseases of great salespeople as they accrue time on a stale account package. An objective observer can easily see it. The salesperson with the problem can't.

One company I was working at had a reorganization of the sales force. Suddenly, I had a new boss. This guy replaced the manager who had been running the whole region for many years. Knowing the situation, this new guy was a hit man put in place to purge the office. Our office had salespeople—including me—who had been hanging around for years and had gotten mediocre. His job was to clean house and bring in new blood.

He came in and spent a lot of time observing. I knew this was the calm before the storm. Eventually, we started talking. I began to think that this guy might not be so bad, even if he shot me in the head along with everyone else. The factory had been going through major reorganizations, and the new managers were coming in and pushing the field very hard. So I kind of woke up and felt like this was going to push me somewhere I didn't know, but it was better than being mediocre.

One day the new boss asked me to go with him on a series of field visits to watch salespeople introduce him to their customers. I knew that this was actually an exercise in seeing who was going to stay and who was going to go. We traveled around the region, and for the first time

I saw how many of the salespeople like me were comfy and doing our weekly routine because nobody was pushing us. We had lost the fire in the belly. Oh, we made the moves and talked the talk, but you could see it everywhere you looked. We watched these salespeople give presentations, and you could even smell how everyone was real comfy.

As the presentations continued, I got the feeling our whole region was infected. It would start when the salesperson put up the presentation. First the org chart would go up. This is where the problems began to be illuminated. They would show an org chart that would look complete. But then you would notice large parts were missing. When asked where this business unit is (with a big company), the salesperson would gloss over about how unimportant this unit was. Of course, this would be a lightning rod for the new manager to take out his drill and begin to go deep. The questions would be asked for the salesperson to explain why this business unit was unimportant. Every time the manager went a little deeper, the salesperson would begin to speculate more and more about what was going on there. The manager was very clever and reached a point where he stopped and changed the topic. Completely unaware of what just happened, the salesperson would be convinced that he had answered the questions right and was on his game. In reality, he was worm food. Sometimes it isn't so subtle.

I know another high-level worldwide director for a large multinational corporation who basically flies around the world to visit all the locations that report to him. He is responsible for sales and operational management of the company's field offices. This guy can't sit in one place for very long before he is on a plane again. I asked him once how he handles accountability and salespeople who stagnate. He said it's simple: every time he travels through, he gives his managers tasks to do. They mutually agree to what will be done. The next time he travels through, he asks them if they got those things done. If they didn't, he fires them on the spot. He complained that many times the problem was good salespeople succumbing to being too comfortable and getting lazy.

One reason salespeople get into a comfort zone is just because of the way they are made. Since salespeople are good at manipulating a system, they know how to cut through red tape easily. This talent also makes them good at knowing the minimum amount of work to get a job done. I mean, who wants to do more than they have to? Take the quota. The quota is the goal. Salespeople have a knack for figuring out the shortest path to the quota. I mean the absolute shortest path. They don't waste energy on this. So when a company doesn't push their salespeople too hard, the salespeople react accordingly. If there is an easy path to a quota, they will take it.

I am not saying salespeople need to be beat on. What they need is constant and regular accountability to make sure they do what they're supposed to. If the company makes it too easy to make quota or has very nebulous rules for making it, the salespeople will discover the easiest way to do it. If this path isn't challenging, they will slide into a comfort zone and just do the job. Some salespeople can't do this, others can. A comfort zone can be very boring and some people can't take that. These people are true performers.

Comfort zones may be related to personality issues. When you are in denial about something, you will feel more comfortable about avoiding it than facing it. Sometimes the forces of denial are so cleverly hidden by your unconscious, you aren't even aware that you are avoiding anything. This could be problems with your personal life, a customer who you don't get along with, or a manager at your company who you feel uncomfortable with.

The comfort zone is the downfall of many salespeople. To fix it, you need to do two very hard things. The first is to be able to honestly admit to yourself there is a problem. The second is to do something about it. If you are strong and determined to help yourself grow, you need a method of recognizing when you are drifting into a comfort zone. This requires you to be able to see beyond your denial and defensive forces. Many people can do this but only lack the training. You can assume there are aspects of your life that you avoid by rationalizing that all is under control and things are just right the way they are now. One way to deal with it is to assume you are drifting in a comfort zone.

Challenge yourself. Embrace the potential to change and grow. Try to look at yourself as another person would. Then ask the tough questions. *Am I doing everything I could with my customer?* Think like your competitor. How would he or she work against you? Do you have an exposed flank? Do you actually think your competitors aren't interested in besting you? If you do, you should quit sales and become a short-order cook. That way, you could still take orders and not have to worry about competition.

I have a friend who was in the National Guard. After years of service, he had the military way instilled in him. Of all the things he learned at the Guard, one was how to look at a situation in an objective way, carefully take it apart piece by piece, observe, and find a solution—even when you do the same thing every day. He was very methodical, and I learned a lot from him about this. If you think about this from a military viewpoint, it makes sense. You train every day for something. You train by doing the same thing over and over. As you train you get used to it, even comfortable doing it. Then it comes time for war, and now your life depends on doing this routine the right way.

Think how concerned you would be about what you're doing if your life depended on it. During war, would you gloss over some routine? Or would your eyes look at it as if you were seeing it for the first time? This is what you need to do. Look back at what you are doing as if you are experiencing it for the first time.

One day, we were in a boat cruising down the Charles River in Boston. It was nighttime, which presented more of a risk than going in daylight. Even though the boat wasn't his, he was very conscious of boat safety (which many people take for granted and then suffer the consequences). Suddenly he announced we were going to play a game. The game was that something was wrong with the boat and we had to find it. Though we all were pretty experienced boaters, his point was that even we overlook things, and at night in a boat a situation can develop that could be very unforgiving. It's a good time to be cautious.

So we played this game of thinking that something was wrong but we didn't know what it was and we had to find it. We found a few things wrong but fortunately nothing serious. We had done a good job of getting the boat ready properly. The point here is that he was able to get us out of our comfort zone by playing a game and opening our eyes so we were able to "see" differently. Then we could look for the problems and be more objective about analyzing them. You need to figure out a way to motivate yourself to see what you could be doing better and then do it. It can be a game, or you can use friends or peers to help find chinks in your armor. Perhaps your friends or peers are already telling you something, but you are choosing to ignore it.

The comfort zone is like a drug. Not everyone wants to get out of it. I can guarantee that all salespeople have some sort of comfort zone they're living with. Some are challenging themselves to push their limits and go where it's uncomfortable. Others sit around thinking that everything is great with them. I feel sorry for those people.

Recognize the danger signs of too much comfort. If you're good, you'll know you should be doing more and have this sick feeling of being held back. Eventually you'll have to push yourself to break free. Once you do, you'll be very happy and know you defeated one of the oldest enemies of the salesperson.

The relationships mediocre salespeople have are superficial because shallow relationships are easy to manage. But to be really influential requires deep relationships with people at your customer and factory.

Do You Have an Ally?

An ally is a teammate who is either a customer or someone within your factory who wants you to win. Allies will offer advice, give you valuable data, and tell you what your competition is doing. Allies do not need to be a decision makers or decision influencers. All they need is access to data within the organization and a willingness to take the risk of sharing information with you that could be confidential.

A successful salesperson will court ally relationships within accounts and the factory. These relationships often turn into longtime friendships. Anybody can be an ally. You need the ability to tell when someone is a potential ally and develop that relationship. You can't pick allies; like customers, they pick you.

There are constraints to developing an ally within an organization. Salespeople can be perceived as powerful and influential. People who are weak in the customer's organization may want to become your ally. They do this as a way to make themselves look more powerful. These people will unconsciously or consciously expose their relationship with you to others within the organization to make themselves look more important. Aligning yourself with a very weak person can hurt your image and possibly attenuate your ability to reach the high-level decision makers.

Consider it a good sign of your influence when weak individuals try to offer data to cozy up to you. But be warned that spending time with these people can hurt your overall efficacy as a salesperson. You can't rebuff them completely, as this will get them mad at you. You need to have some finesse at making it look internally as if you are keeping him or her at arm's length while making this person feel as though you are being friendly.

When a salesperson develops an ally, the more perceptive people within an organization may guess that this person has a disproportionably favorable view to you. This is not necessarily bad. It can work for you. Many senior managers understand high-level salespeople develop deep relationships with their people and can understand more about their organization than they do. But it can backfire if a senior manager isn't favorable to your company or products, or is an ally to your competitor. Either way, you should develop as many allies as you can. The more powerful an ally, the clearer the information is about what is going on with a decision and the company. But just because an ally is in a low-level position doesn't mean he or she can't help you.

Once I had an account that was the majority of my number. It was my first big account. They had a big lobby with lots of room to make phone calls and do e-mails. I decided instead of hanging in the sales office, I would hang in the lobby all day if I wasn't at appointments. After a while, I "claimed" a place in the lobby. This lobby was the nexus of people coming and going for the company, including my competition. I observed that almost everyone in the company passed through it, including the senior managers. I got to know the receptionist. Her name was Janet. She and I hit it off. After a while, we got to be good pals. One day she called me over. She told me my competition was meeting with a senior manager and I should be too. Janet became my ally and watchdog. She actually began advising me of many things I was unaware were happening with my competitors. (For whatever reason my biggest competitor was arrogant to her—big mistake.) She wanted me to win. We had a great relationship that lasted a few years until I was transferred to a large account. To this day, I will never forget how she helped me keep track of my competition. This is a great example of how powerful administrators can be.

Allies will find you. Your challenge is to recognize the signs that a customer wants to build a stronger relationship. You have to determine if you want to keep it at arm's length or encourage it. Allies can happen at any time and at any level of a corporation. They can be a custodian or a senior vice president. The more allies a salesperson has, the more effective he or she will be.

Your ally may alert you either directly or inadvertently to an opportunity. Perhaps a new project just got funded, or the president mandated a new product be built. Maybe you get a piece of information that allows you to suddenly realize a group within your customer who you never knew before could greatly benefit from your product or service. Opportunity is all around you. The only thing you have to do is recognize it when it presents itself.

Seizing Opportunities

Recognizing an opportunity is a very important talent. Many people aren't even capable of recognizing one even when it drops on their lap. Sometimes it's presented to you right in your face so you can't ignore it. Other times the presentation is more subtle and takes insight to recognize it. Then there is the opportunity that is right under your nose but you can't see for some reason.

Opportunities can show up at the weirdest times. Count on it. We hear about them all the time. Especially when friends say something like, "You should have taken that job" or "Why didn't you talk more with that VP when he asked you about our company?" Even though we see it, we may not perceive it as an opportunity. We aren't conscious of it.

There is a kind of blissful ignorance associated with missing an opportunity. Most of the time, we choose to unconsciously ignore an opportunity if it creates a conflict with another. People who are risk-averse will take fewer chances and may be less inclined to be put in a position to choose. Opting for a new opportunity may create a lot of issues, including the risk of making the wrong decision and living with the pain that follows.

In some cases, you may not even be consciously aware that a very good opportunity is right in front of you because your unconscious self is trying to protect you. This is when others around you comment about your bad decision. They can see the opportunity while you cannot. Take heart, it's easy to be critical of people who make decisions and live vicariously through them. Hindsight is really 20/20. So even if you feel you've made the right decision on an opportunity, your friends may have chosen differently. Still, there will be times you are reminded by them and your gut will tell you they are right.

The most successful people have a talent for seeing an opportunity that is worth the risk. You can do that too. The way to sharpen your talent for recognizing an opportunity is to review it with peers, friends, and family. If your unconscious is blocking your ability to see an opportunity, you may feel it in your gut, which will manifest itself as an uncomfortable feeling. This is a good time to discuss the situation with someone else who can be an objective evaluator.

Some of us do this without even thinking about it. An opportunity makes us not feel right, so we discuss it. If you don't take the step of discussing it, you will never know whether or not it was an opportunity. Sometimes friends will push you to face it. "You are crazy not to do it!" So one good step in the right direction is to understand how you view risk and behave when something is presented to you. If you can dig into that a bit, you might come up with a set of fixes that open your eyes wide enough to recognize an opportunity when it presents itself. Here are a few obvious examples:

- Your manager has to leave unexpectedly on a trip. He asks you to watch over things while he is gone. That's all he leaves you with.
- You are making idle conversation with one of your support people. He is describing some recent events his group had to take care of. One in particular was a serious problem with an account in your area. You recall that you had trouble finding high-level decision makers there. Your support friend tells you one of the high-level managers was very upset and the problem hasn't been fixed yet.
- You're food shopping on a Saturday at a local supermarket. As you cruise the aisles with your cart, you happen to notice the CEO of your largest customer shopping alone in the next aisle. You have never met him before but want to.
- You are walking to your car in the parking lot of a customer when you spy a decision maker going to her car.

- You have just started with a company. You are asked if you want to go with a manager to a meeting at corporate headquarters where the senior people for the company will be in attendance.
- Your CEO is visiting your remote sales office. He is going to speak to your sales team.
- You are a volunteer at a local emergency support center. During a regional meeting, you notice one of your best customer's companies is a sponsor.
- Your factory people are presenting to a large audience that has key decision makers in it. You notice the highest level vice-president getting up to leave. You know he is the one person who has to hear the final conclusion of the value proposition. If he leaves now, he will never hear it.
- You are in town to meet with a customer. Your VP of sales calls and asks if you are in the town you are in. You answer yes. He asks if you could stand in for a sick salesperson at a key account.
- You are at a show in Las Vegas doing booth duty for your company. You take a break and go to lunch at the show cafeteria. As you are eating, you notice someone near you whose badge identifies him or her as a prospect you have been trying to get to.
- You are at a customer site visiting with a high-level manager. Your conversation gets interesting as your customer begins to talk about outside activities with you. After a few minutes, you realize you are hitting it off pretty well. Soon you are talking about restaurants, and he mentions one he really likes.

As a salesperson, you will meet a lot of people. People make opportunities happen. So it stands to reason that the more people you meet, the more opportunities will be presented to you. This makes life fun because of the mystery of what and when the next opportunity will happen. Opportunities will come and come often. It's up to you to be on the lookout for when it is sitting there in front of you. Not all will be obvious. Very significant opportunities can be buried just beneath the obvious. Every day when you rise, you should be thinking there is one there today. Think of it as a daily treasure hunt.

It's all too easy to categorize sales, but in the end, it means nothing. That's because no matter how you brag about your talents and expertise, only one thing matters: results.

Results Are What It's All About

Your job is to create revenue for the company. You do this by getting a quota and maxing it out. Results are the purchase orders that come flooding into the company because you closed the orders.

A good company will reward salespeople who produce results and not care about the method. Companies who tie their salespeople's hands with strictly enforced rules and guidelines will find they have a group of mediocre performers. Fortunately, most companies allow salespeople a certain leeway as long as they are performing.

I've been in conversations with salespeople and asked them what they think a salesperson should do. Sometimes I get convoluted answers about customer satisfaction and making sure the backlog is maintained or responding quickly to e-mails. That doesn't really matter. The process doesn't matter. How you get results is your business. If wearing a clown suit and walking on your hands gets an order, then so be it. Get it in that head of yours not to be concerned with the method but the results.

It's so funny to see mediocre salespeople make snide comments about how one salesperson doesn't follow all the rules the company dictates. When I hear this going on, I know they are jealous because the salesperson is breaking rules, like not showing up to "mandatory" meetings or being absent from an internal conference call. Deep inside, they know it's really their problem. This achiever is probably at a customer and let his manager know he had something important to do.

Egos should be left behind. If you are trying to reach a goal and someone on your team dunks the ball, then you have succeeded. Just because you didn't do the final close doesn't mean you weren't part of it. Let someone else bask in the light of success. If you are really producing all the time, your management will know it. If they know it, they will quickly figure out that the deal was in part a success thanks to your back-room efforts. You should have an abundance of confidence in yourself. You know you're good. So someone else getting the deal is good because you got the results.

Always concentrate on the results you're trying to get. There will be distractions. Many people fail at sales because they get too caught up in needless complexity over how to reach a goal. They are so caught up in the barriers or other issues they lose sight of it the goal. Keep it simple. Don't let other people's opinions and wild ideas sidetrack you. It's okay to get a peer to review your strategy, but in the end, you're the one calling the shots. Your peers don't have skin in the game, you do. So you make the decision on the quickest way to the order.

> *The world is divided into people who do things and people*
> *who get the credit. Try, if you can, to belong to the first class.*
> *There's far less competition.—Dwight Morrow*

The most destructive disease in sales is mediocrity. This problem ravages many salespeople's careers and leaves a wake of lost business, ruined careers, and lackluster lives in its wake. Many salespeople are mediocre. It's so easy, and many companies tolerate it. Recognize the danger signs.

The Mediocre Salesperson

It's easy to be mediocre. This doesn't mean failure. This means that salespeople go day after day under the delusion they are on their game and have the customer under complete control when they are actually on a plateau of low performance. Sure, they may have worked for the company for eight or ten years. They may have called on a high-profile account for more than five years. They have lots of allies in the organization. They know what is going on to the fiber of the customer. In their minds, they know the customer better than the customer does. These people are wallowing in their comfort zone and are in denial about how they stopped pushing.

I worked for a long time in one sales organization where I worked my way up the ladder and eventually won awards for sales and was recognized for penetrating and controlling my customer. I started to believe that I was in the driver's seat. I was one of the top performers in the company. I was a big shot. Then there were big reorganizations. The senior managers who were my pals went away. My power base eroded. Still, I thought I was a big shot. When I went in front of the new management, they asked me questions I couldn't answer about my customer. They wanted me to get things from my customer I thought were unreasonable, but in hindsight, I was just making excuses and rationalizing my problem. What happened?

In my self-revelry, I believed I was really good. While I was feeling so good about myself, the organization stagnated. It lost the ability to challenge its salespeople. What do I mean by challenge? How about your manager asking you to get an order from your customer that you know will be very difficult, if not impossible, to get. Then your manager reminds you in a not-so-nice way that your job is on the line for this order. This is extreme, but the problem is that many salespeople get into comfort zones which are very dangerous.

Here are some of the deadly signs of sales mediocrity or sales impotence. Some of these situations can be debated, but I don't care what you say. They can be indications.

- You think you are in total control over your customer.
- Your boss thinks you are in total control over your customer (he should be fired or soon will be).
- You believe your company is ignorant and doesn't know how hard you work.
- You think your competitors are incompetent.
- You think you know your competitors, but deep down, you really don't know what they are doing or what they think of you (consciously or unconsciously).
- You give the impression you know all your competitors, but in reality you don't.
- You're not sure what the customer would say about you if asked.
- You're calling on only a fraction of your customer's organization. You've convinced yourself that the other guys aren't important.
- You never get more than one data point when presented with important data or when trying to locate a "key" person.
- You have relationships with junior-level people and few relationships with management or senior managers within your customer.
- The days in which you called on someone new every week are long gone.
- You can't remember the last time you did an organizational chart of your customer.
- Your management begins to ask about your most important customer. They ask about a department that you haven't called on in months (or years). You tell them nothing is going on there though you know your data is very old.

- Your management comes in your office with news that your customer announced a new product that uses a competitor's device. He asks you why you didn't tell him about it. You knew nothing about it but make up some excuse about why you couldn't have won the business anyway.
- Your contact database hasn't had a major update in six months
- You start work late and end early. Doesn't mean you have to report to the office early or leave early, it just means working.
- You get bored at work and are in massive denial about it.
- When you make out your expense report, it is a stretch to show you're really entertaining. You might even think when you fill it out that there really isn't much going on here.
- You send more and more e-mails to customers and shun using the phone and face-to-face meetings.
- You spend more time in the office or at your home office than at the customer, and you tell yourself you are getting more work done.
- You think you're a top-level sales person and in complete control.
- You boast to others about how good you are or how others think you are so good.
- Work is boring, but it's a job.
- You never notice salespeople who work harder than you (or you do but ignore the comparison to you).
- What you call allies are actually impotent people in the organization who need attention.
- You spend your time with people who are easy to access and not the ones who challenge you.
- Work sucks, but you live with it.
- When you forward an e-mail attachment to a customer that someone sent you, you don't inspect it and just forward it along instead of making sure the document is the right one and there isn't anything the customer shouldn't see in it.
- You've never taken the time to learn who the administrative assistants of all the high-level managers of your accounts are.
- You've never met the senior managers of your account, or even know what they look like.
- You never spent the time to find out personal details of your most important customers, let alone their birthdays and important events of their lives.
- You play golf with your coworkers or friends more than you play with customers.

- You can't correctly spell the names of the decision makers in your most important accounts.
- You choose not to be too visible in your company. You actually believe it's too politically dangerous to do that. Better to meld into the background.
- You avoid the thought of what your peers would say about you if asked.
- When a customer tells you something can't happen and you don't really know, you hang up the phone and rationalize why it can't happen.
- Every barrier that needs work, you pass on.
- You stop taking risks.
- You dwell hopelessly in your comfort zone, whiling away your time thinking how cool of a salesperson you are.
- You begin to dress down for selling, convincing yourself that everybody else is doing it or you notice your competitors doing it so you say you can.
- You get great tickets to a sporting event you know one of your key customers would kill for, but you take someone else instead.
- If asked, your factory people would say you are lazy, never call with questions, and don't challenge them—or they simply don't know who you are.
- You let the phone drive your schedule for the day.

There are other reasons you could be performing at a mediocre level. You could be depressed. You may or may not be aware of this. If you are, then do something about it. Seek professional help, at least from your doctor. If you blame the world for your problems, you're screwed anyway. You have some kind of personality disorder or other inability to take responsibility for your issues. You'll never improve or grow.

If you are not aware of being depressed, consider it. Talk to friends or your doctor. The point is, if you want to stop being mediocre and don't know what to do about it, you may be unaware that you are depressed. Your issue may be you don't have the skill set to understand it. But if you are frustrated about where you are, then do something about it.

You may be completely aware of your situation and living in it. You may hate your job but think there isn't anything in the market for you. This could simply be a fear of change. This is normal. But you have to look at your situation. If you are going day to day and not really happy, you have to face it. Don't look the other way. This is important for you both personally and professionally. You have to be able to manage change in your life. Life is about choices and recognizing when you should make them. If you continue to deny a choice you have to make, then you will always be unhappy. Being unhappy leads to depression. Some of these beliefs may be deterring you:

- There are no jobs out there.
- The job you choose may not pay as well.
- The job you choose may not work out.
- Your boss may find out.
- They are paying you really well, and you need the money.
- You don't know anybody where you can find a job.

These are some of the excuses people use to avoid making a decision. All of the above can be dealt with. You have to realize you are a powerful instrument of change and can make anything happen. The first thing you have to do is make the decision to do something. If you can make the decision to change, you are halfway there. I know many salespeople who can't take that first important step. Taking that step is a good test of your strength. When you make the decision, don't just quit. Use your network. Find out what you should do. You may be unhappy because this isn't the right type of job, or you may need a career change. Talk to your mentor.

Being trapped in a job that you aren't happy with is terrible. If you are the type who can tolerate this situation, good luck. You are doomed to be there until they let you go. Be warned that if the company is doing reasonably well, there may be a time when they aren't. At that point, management will look at the salespeople and clean house.

Whether you realize it or not, your management knows about your performance. Eventually they will look at how much return on investment they are getting from you. Salespeople are very expensive. If you've been there awhile, you are probably paid more than others with less time on the job. When money is tight, this is one area that goes under the microscope. You can be replaced by a cheaper person with less experience who is fired up and more motivated than you are. There is always someone better than you. Unless the company is completely mediocre or your uncle is the CEO, eventually, you will be let go.

The lure of being mediocre is in all salespeople's blood. It is a drug that hooks you, especially when management is mediocre. I have worked in organizations where I wasn't challenged or the manager didn't make sure I was doing my job. Salespeople have a tendency to move to their comfort zone. This is okay and normal. Some salespeople can't live in their comfort zones and naturally challenge themselves. A good manager will be pleasant to deal with but firm in driving his or her people out of their comfort zones. This is how a salesperson grows.

You should always be wary of being mediocre. You can wake up one day and suddenly realize you are drifting in that direction. Slap yourself in the face and fix it. Salespeople are very resourceful and can help themselves. You don't need a manager to kick you in the pants. Many sales managers want to be nice to their people. It's hard to drive people when it might make them hate you. Make sure you understand your situation. You should be the instrument of your change. The best salespeople are.

CHAPTER NINE

MORE TIPS ON SOCIAL INTERACTION

Three Types of Learners

Before you walk through the door on your first customer visit, be aware you must be fluent in communicating three different ways. Using the wrong method can be very frustrating for you. This isn't a language like French, Chinese, or English. It's more about how people learn.

People learn in one of three ways:

1. Audio
2. Visual
3. Kinesthetic

People learn best by listening, seeing, or touching. It's important to understand this before you get into your sales pitch. If you have time, you can observe nonverbal cues that will reveal how a particular person learns.

Kinesthetic learners will need to touch something to get it into their head, so give them something to touch. I carry some samples with me to help a k-learner get it. It doesn't have to be a sample; it can be a spreadsheet or data sheet describing your product. But a 3-D sample works best here.

Audio learners have to hear it to know it. All you have to do is describe in detail what you are talking about with them. Maybe have them listen to something like one of your product managers who is talking at a conference. Be creative. Sometimes I send e-mails with a short audio to the a-learner.

Visual learners need to see it to learn about it. That's true of most of us. Presentations, documents, anything that has pictures and words will work. The more you can show them, the faster and better they will understand what you are talking about.

When I have meetings at a customer where I present, I try to cover all the bases. The presentation is shown through a project for the v-learners, the circulation of physical samples of our product for the k-learners, and a walk around the room talking and making eye contact for the a-learners.

If you get perplexed because a customer or prospect doesn't seem to get what you are talking about, consider that you may be presenting using the wrong method to help that individual learn. A k-learner may not understand e-mails, no matter how well you can write. Showing a v-learner a sample of your product will be lost on them. It's difficult to categorize every single customer you know, so try to cover all your bases by using all three ways to reach people.

Once you know how to recognize the three types of learners, you are on your way to being a masterful communicator. There are many formats for communication. None has been more significant than the web and its social vehicles for getting your word out. How you use it requires some finesse if you want to be successful in your sales job.

Social Networking

Most everybody is using the web to network. There are very compelling reasons to use it and very compelling reasons to be wary of it. It gets your story out to millions of people, and that's a huge advantage. The downside is any negative information associated with you will also be available to millions of people—and worse, will be available forever. You give up a portion of your privacy when you use these tools. How much you give up is up to you.

Not everybody is smart about this. It amazes me how some people post information about themselves that is embarrassing, immature, radical, and sometimes even criminal. Also, people like to tell their whereabouts: "We are going to Europe for two weeks and can't wait!" They might as well put up a sign that says, "Hey, our home will be vacant for two weeks. Feel free to break in." The rule for social websites is pretty simple: anything you post can and will be used against you. A corollary of this rule is: anything you post, especially embarrassing pictures, will turn up twenty years from now at the most inopportune time. Information on the Internet is very, very sticky.

Also, the way the Internet works, when you send information, copies are made along the way. These copies are archived in various servers. Also, many social websites have EULA—end user license agreements—that state somewhere that the service actually owns the information or has access to it and can use as they wish the information you post there. Everything you send—including e-mails, pictures, music, and any file—is probably copied somewhere and stored in an archive. These archives are run by people. Sometimes people like to peruse the archive information when bored. In more devious situations, they may intentionally dig into it for money. You may say that's against the law, but it doesn't matter. If something gets out, the damage is done. Don't trust these systems. Use common sense when you release information.

Many of the most popular websites like Facebook, Twitter, and LinkedIn offer great services. I know many people who use them with a lot of success. Be careful of becoming too reliant on them, though, and having an expectation that everything will be solved online. This is mediocrity beckoning to you. Yes, you can score a great job online, but the very best ones are landed not by websites but by telephone and your network. There is a healthy balance between online and face-to-face. You should use all resources available to you, but remember to have a good, clear understanding of the strengths and weaknesses of each.

Social-networking sites want as much information about you as they can get. You should only supply what you are comfortable with releasing to the public. Maybe you don't want to put everything online so someone who peruses your page will be forced to engage you with questions to ask you. This will make face-to-face more interesting. You always want a face-to-face meeting, so don't put your entire life on the page. Keep your page neutral and positive. Show successes and try to telegraph you are a hard worker, talented, and have healthy relationships—but again, keep it simple. Are all your friends mostly normal, or do they post radical thinking or behavior? This is all information that will be gathered about you.

When managing your public information, think how someone who doesn't know you will get an impression of you and your friends' websites. It's okay to omit information. When in doubt, leave it out. Social networking is intertwined with our daily living. Overdependence on it will make you one-dimensional and less interesting. Use all your resources available and don't discount how powerful meeting face-to-face really is.

A sales job is a very social position. Depending on your type of business, it can be compelling to use social-networking sites. Some companies actually require their employees to post on social sites. When you are posting something, think of how it will read in two or five years.

Using anything like this is a balance of what you can get vs. what you give up for it. Social networking is very powerful and can work wonders for your career. But just like fire, it can be a benefit or burn you badly if misused. Use common sense and don't be careless. Social networking is becoming more intertwined in our society. Five years from now, it may be absolutely essential for your success to maintain daily activity on several different sites. Like any productivity tool, it can be a powerful asset if used appropriately.

Your network should be extensive, with both personal and professional contacts. Some of these relationships will be close and others superficial. Nothing is more rewarding and powerful than having friends who can offer counsel and tell you the truth.

Friends and Asking for Advice

Friends are very helpful in life and can be invaluable in making decisions about your career. One of the things (besides trust) a friend offers is objective advice. Advice from a trusted source can help you evaluate difficult decisions. He or she does this by giving you feedback on your thoughts.

We all use people for feedback when we have to make a decision. Friends are absolutely key in understanding if a decision you are about to make is the right one. A new job, relationship, purchasing something, or feedback on a thought train are just some of the valuable things friends can help you with. Friends can be very understanding when you are having problems with other people, including customers. Also, a good friend will value the advice you give to him too. This reciprocity in exchanging information allows each friend to grow and become a better person.

There is a limit on how much you should depend on a friend's advice, however. You have to admit that the feedback you get from a friend is only as good as the information you provide. If you leave out certain facts, you will influence the advice you get. There are some things we can't tell a friend. It could be some intimate piece of data we don't want to tell anybody, or it could be that we just don't want them to know. Also, the people you know have various levels of comfort with risk taking. Talking to a friend who is risk averse about a risky opportunity may not be the right thing to do. On the other hand, you know you'll get an opposing viewpoint.

This is why you have to go to at least two friends for advice: a risk taker and one who is risk averse. This way, you get point and counterpoint to broaden the scope of the advice. By doing this, you will know the spectrum of risk in your decision, and you also may pick up new ideas that you didn't think of. The more people you speak with, the more information you will get. The more information you get, the better prepared you will be to make a decision. This works with any two or more people you talk to. Just make sure you know if they are risk averse or risk takers.

Also, it helps if you know whether they are detail oriented or not. People who are detail oriented tend to pick up on minuscule things you might overlook. On the other hand, they may completely miss a galactic strategy idea that is right in front of them.

Never be a taker in relationships with friends. Get to know how you satisfy their needs and make sure you fulfill that with them. I can't stress enough how important friends are. They are so important to a happy life. If you're in sales, you probably already have a lot of friends. Maybe lots or maybe a few very special ones. Hopefully some of these friends will be very special for you. Treat them well, and they will treat you well. Get to understand them and help them when they need it. Don't "count chits" or play games like, "I will do something for you if you do something for me." That isn't friendship. Cherish your friends and do almost anything to help them. They are one of the most important things you can have in life.

Someone who has great friends is a very successful person. In sales, it's absolutely indispensable.

Promise me you'll always remember: You're braver than you believe, and stronger than you seem, and smarter than you think.—Christopher Robin to Winnie the Pooh, written by A. A. Milne

Having close friends makes life far more enjoyable. Friends come in all shapes and sizes. Some are very close while others are less so. If you look at the universe of the people you know, there is a continuous spectrum from who is very close to you to who is a remote acquaintance. The ones who are close are friends. The ones who are not are just contacts. This universe is your network, a labyrinth of connections and influence. Understanding what your network of contacts is and how to leverage it directly affects how well you can perform as a salesperson. It all comes down to who you know.

Networking and Contacts

Everybody has a network of people. A salesperson should have a large but, more importantly, a high-quality network. A high-quality network is one in which, with a phone call or two, you can meet a need—arrange a high-level meeting on short notice, ask for a purchase order to speed through the system, get tickets to a sold-out sports game, arrange access to politicians and other important people, find someone a job, and of course, find yourself a job.

Many people begin to cultivate a network when they need a job. That isn't the time to develop a network because it takes a long time to develop one. Nothing is more sobering than losing your job and realizing you don't have anybody to call. Don't be the person who calls people you don't know well and asks for a favor. You get what you put into it. If you don't bother to put something into relationships with people, don't expect to get anything out of them.

High-quality networks are hard to cultivate. It's easy for a salesperson to have a large network but not a quality one. I know many who go through their careers without spending a lot of time taking care that their network is diverse and deep. They have a LinkedIn account with 450 people, but they have no idea who all those names are. They end up with a long list of people who really can't do much for them. If you are successful, your network will grow with people who can help you. You will help these people too. When there is a back and forth in your network, it is healthy and will grow strong. If you tap it all the time for favors, you deplete it. If you genuinely care for others and spend time meeting new people, chances are your network will thrive.

LinkedIn is a good way to do social networking for business. You should have an account and link to people you know well. Some people think just linking up makes for a good relationship. That isn't so. Just because you've linked to someone on LinkedIn doesn't mean that person will do something for you. In fact, the more influential a person is, the harder it will be to get them to do something for you unless you have a close relationship. LinkedIn works the same way that real life does. If you ask a favor from someone you hardly know, don't expect much to happen. On the other hand, sites like LinkedIn offer a much faster way to access lots of people. You can get to know people there, but it takes effort—just like real life.

As you work as a salesperson, your network of contacts will grow. As it grows, you will have opportunities to touch people's lives and make a difference here and there. Be on the lookout for opportunities to help someone or meet someone new, and you'll do fine.

To expand your network beyond work people, you'll need to find other ways to branch out. Try joining professional organizations. You never know who you will meet. But if you really want to develop key relationships, you have to be creative. Everyone is using a professional organization. To distinguish yourself in a big organization will take time. You will need to take a leadership position. If you don't, you won't stand out. You won't be influential. When you lead, people will look up to you. Just make sure you join the right committee.

Try volunteering at an organization that has relevance to your job. If that's not possible, see if there are organizations that leaders in your field belong to. Other types of organizations are museums of technology (use your sales talent to raise money), political groups, special university-sponsored groups like start-up management training that is open to the public in an open format (these exist at business schools), job-creation groups, high-tech lobbying organizations, and ad hoc business consulting groups. The more people you meet, the more likely you are to hear about something.

Be creative. Every organization has a need. Your expertise is discovering a need and filling it. Do something that differentiates you. If you are driven to make yourself better this will come naturally to you. Don't be afraid to ask a senior manager about joining organizations. Use your network to develop your network.

If you are young and new to sales, just keep listening to people. You will eventually hear about something that sounds interesting to you. Don't be afraid to join an organization and then leave it. If it doesn't do anything for you, don't force yourself to keep attending meetings. Eventually you will find something that fits.

Make sure you deliver on any commitments you make. Surprisingly, many people can't deliver. If people are able to count on you to follow through on what you say, you will build a strong reputation and garner respect. This leads to people wanting to do things with you. This is how your network expands. Keep at it. Always be building your network. Put substance into it, and you will get substance out of your relationships. Do it enough, and soon you will be influential because of your network.

Your network will be dynamic and always changing. Some contacts will get stale while new ones will be added. Some links will be forgotten and then suddenly reconnect. Networks are absolutely fascinating and make life fun. Every time you meet a new person, you are potentially adding to your network. Not everyone you meet will be someone to add to your network. Many times we overlook adding someone because of issues with personality or perceived compatibility. You meet someone for the first time and don't hit it off. You shouldn't immediately discount an encounter just because of your first impression. People who have issues with others before even finding out about them will write it off to bad chemistry.

Chemistry

Chemistry is a metaphor used to describe how well (or poorly) people interact. "There is good chemistry between those two," people will say. While the concept is somewhat overused, this is a very good way to describe the complex interaction between two or more people. Others will understand right away what you are talking about if you use it correctly in a sentence.

More deeply, the chemistry between people is something a salesperson not only has to clearly perceive but manage. Take, for example, a meeting you arrange with a customer. You bring in one of your senior VPs to talk about a grand strategy or possibly to tender a proposal for a business deal. Since the meeting is between the VP and the customer (who is probably another high-level person), they do most of the talking. You sit back, take notes, record action items, and facilitate the meeting. More importantly, you carefully observe the chemistry between them and any subtle opportunities that may emerge from the conversation. What you should look for is whether they have good, bad, or indifferent chemistry. Nonverbal communication will tell all.

If the chemistry is good, the two executives will be friendly with each other. Their body language will show relaxation and interest. Their speech will be energetic and engaging. The meeting will begin to feel good. Sometimes, the meeting can feel *too* good, and the managers will deviate off the subject, jeopardizing your goal for the close of the meeting. If this happens, you need to slow it down and keep the managers on track. You may need to interrupt them to do this. Don't worry about it; if they are good, concerned managers they will appreciate you keeping the meeting focused. Ideally, your manager will try to close when things are feeling good. If he doesn't, make sure you do at the wrap-up. When you are alone with your manager, ask how he or she felt the meeting went. Ask if he or she liked the other manager. If the two got along really well, you might want to facilitate more interactions between them. It could benefit you and your company if your manager is able to develop a good relationship with one of your customers. This is part of your job, developing peer-to-peer relationships.

Sometimes the chemistry is bad, and you need to find a way to get out of the meeting quickly before any damage is done. Afterward, review your manager's feelings about the meeting and the people. You need to make sure this manager doesn't go back to the factory and spread hate and destructive stories about your customer. This won't help you. It's your job to nip this before it can propagate. You have to review your manager's feelings. He or she will probably be in a bad mood, and talking about it will help the manager get over it. Reinforce how well your customer is doing overall and try to minimize this bad experience as stuff happening sometimes with customers. Not all customers are good people, but they still have money.

Indifferent chemistry is neutral. This just means that the two or more people get along well enough and no emotional interplay is apparent in the meeting. This doesn't mean there isn't chemistry. It just means it's being effectively managed by everyone. Your meeting should go on without you having to manage high-energy emotions. After the meeting, as part of your normal debriefing, you should ask your people what they thought of your customer. You may be surprised about what you hear. Your manager may be very perceptive and behave well during meetings, but inside, he has other notions about the meeting he isn't revealing. Note any issues and try to get him to talk about it right then and there. Remember, your customers have feelings too. You should make an appointment as "feedback" from the meeting. During your follow-up, find out what they thought of your people.

Bad chemistry or feelings a customer has with one of your factory people can also be very damaging to your overall business, especially if the customer is a high-level decision maker. You need to get to the customer, if you can, and make sure you hear all the complaints about your factory person. It's important to look like the person in the middle. If you are doing your job right, your customer will view you as such. If you have a good relationship with your customers, they will tell you their true feelings. Note what they tell you and take action accordingly.

It would be great if you could know the chemistry of people before they meet. Sometimes you can predict it. If you think the chemistry could be bad, you might consider not having the meeting at all. Bad chemistry has no upside.

Outside of meetings, you, as a salesperson, need to have good chemistry with the people you interact with. It's *your* job, not the job of the people you interact with, to take responsibility to make sure the chemistry is good. Don't expect everyone to cooperate with you. Many of these people aren't making money by having relationships. Also, they can be completely uninformed on how to conduct a relationship and have a lack of interpersonal skills. You need to be able to interact positively with this kind of person.

Bellyaching about a customer you deal with who is a jerk is inexcusable. One of the reasons salespeople get paid so much is they can make good chemistry when there isn't any. Being an alchemist at making good chemistry in relationships and making them work between you and others is an important and necessary asset of the successful salesperson. As you get more experienced in managing interactions between yourself and others, you will become a master at this important skill.

When you interview for a job, the chemistry can be good, bad, or indifferent. There are many factors in this, but you should be able to test the air and have a gut feeling for how you all are getting along. The feeling you have interviewing with these people is probably the one you will have if you work for them. Is this what you want to feel every day on the job? Of course, you may not meet everyone you will work with during your interview. You may encounter people later where the chemistry is bad. This is something you can't avoid, and it is due to chance.

After you accept a position, you eventually will meet everyone you're supposed to work with. The total chemistry will emerge, and you will get a gut feeling about how well you like (or dislike) the job. This is where it gets interesting. I really believe chemistry has a profound effect on how someone performs in the job, no matter how much talent the individual has. A highly talented person will perform badly if the chemistry is bad.

When I say "the chemistry is bad," I don't just mean the person doesn't get along with somebody or some people. It goes much deeper. It is the entire environment:

- people
- culture
- geography
- time zone
- technology
- market space
- individual products
- color of the office
- windows or no windows
- cubicles or offices
- modern equipment vs. outdated equipment
- micromanagement vs. hands-off management

- tight-money vs. loose-money policy
- hubris
- personal situation

The list goes on and on. The lesson is, you put a salesperson in one environment and he'll perform a particular way. Put him in a different one and he'll perform differently. This is key to understanding that it isn't always your fault that things just can't seem to work out. On the contrary, it is also why, given the right environment, the chemistry will be very good and the same salesperson will excel.

Being in sales, you probably have a good sense about chemistry and using it to make yourself more effective at your job. One way of improving your chemistry with people is to get to know them better. If your company allows you an expense account, nothing can build relationships faster than entertaining.

Entertaining

Entertaining and sales go hand in hand. Building influence is building relationships. One way to build relationships with customers is to meet with them away from the work environment. This is why entertaining is so important to selling. Any company whose product success depends on a strong sales relationship will provide expense accounts to their people who work with customers. Contrary to what seems like common sense, some companies refuse to allow salespeople to spend money on customers, highly regulate the amount they can spend, or create a myriad of rules on how money can be spent for entertaining. Try to stay away from companies like this. It is a good indication that senior management doesn't trust salespeople to make good decisions, or the intention is to hire very low-level salespeople and churn them. Neither of these environments is healthy for a good, talented salesperson. This is why it's important to ask about the rules for entertaining before you take a sales job.

With expense privileges, your management will expect you to spend a certain amount of money every week. Companies can vary on this. Some give you a stipend (a fixed amount of cash up front every week or so), others will give you a budget you can't exceed, some will have no limit on what you can spend, and some will give you nothing. My opinion on this is if you work for a good company, they will let you expense whatever amount you spend as long as you deliver results. This includes $2,000 dinners with senior executives or even a cross-country ten-day excursion in an RV with your best customer (one salesperson I know did this).

If you don't spend the money, it will be noticed. If you don't spend enough, don't be surprised if a manager asks why you aren't spending time with customers. Management will view your spending as a way to monitor how engaged you are in your job. How much to spend per week depends on the company and the sales culture. If you are new, start by taking people to lunch. If there isn't a mandated amount per week you're expected to spend, talk to your peers about how much they spend. Another way is to spend more every week until you're told it's too much. (Better to ask forgiveness than permission.) As long as you're spending money on legitimate customers, it doesn't matter—you know you're doing the right thing.

Usually, entertaining rules are explained to you before you begin your sales job. Ask your manager how to cover expenses you can't have a receipt for. This all depends on how communicative your manager is. Some expect you to learn by the deep-water method.

Tipping

When you tip, tip well. In the USA, an average service tip is 15 percent. For great service, tip 20 percent. Other countries have different customs for tipping. Make sure you clearly understand them before you go. If you frequent an establishment a lot, always tip the people well. If you go to a high-end restaurant for dinner, tip the maître d' twenty to fifty-plus dollars for a good table. Special functions require some creativity.

At one point in my career, I was in the city a lot, as my senior factory people would stay in the higher-end hotels. Since I was picking them up all the time, I would tip the doorman twenty or thirty dollars to park my car out front. When you look at it, having the hotel park my car was going to cost me twelve to fifteen dollars anyway. After I did this a few times, the doormen would always remember me and treat me like a king when I arrived. They would greet me by name and ask me if I wanted the car out front. This created quite an impression with people I would be with, including customers. I did this with several hotels in the area. Years later, there is a doorman working at one of these hotels who still treats me like a king when I arrive. I still give him a good tip, and my car goes in the "limo" spot. Of course, if your territory is more rural, your choices on entertaining may be more limited, but the overall methods still apply.

Your life in sales may get complicated when your manager is cheap and his manager isn't. This gets very interesting when they both go to a lunch or dinner you are organizing with a customer. While it may not seem fair, however you handle the first dinner you arrange with a customer and your senior manager will be remembered by them. If your manager is a cheapskate and his boss is polished and extravagant, I would say you better be polished and extravagant and screw what your immediate boss thinks. Somehow I don't think your boss will be around long.

Special Functions

If you need to arrange a big customer dinner with your factory people, depending on your corporate culture, you may need to secure a high-end restaurant for the evening. If you have more than four people, you should book a private room. This will allow you talk about confidential things you wouldn't want to be heard in a restaurant and also lessens distractions. Preview the room to make sure it's suitable for what you want to accomplish with the dinner. Seating should be arranged so that people who need to talk to each other are seated together. You can do this with little signs or just tell people where to sit.

I had to arrange a dinner for my CEO and some big shots from my most important customer. The CEO was very particular about where he ate, and I knew that if this didn't go right, my job was on the line. I selected a restaurant I knew the CEO would like (this can be complicated, as you need to understand his expectations and what he likes in general). I drove in there a week before the dinner and made the reservation personally, not over the phone. It was a remodeled bank, and the vault in the basement had been turned into a very private dining room the restaurant was famous for. I knew this restaurant would be in high demand because there was a big high-tech show in town and all the restaurants would be booked up. When I talked to the maître d', he told me the room was already booked. There were other restaurants in the city, but I knew this would be perfect. So I took out a crisp hundred-dollar bill, handed it to him, and asked if he was sure of the reservation. He took the bill, walked away for a minute, and came back. Turns out the room was now available. (Someone had booked it over the phone—too bad for them.)

A few days before the dinner, I made sure everyone knew how to get there. The night of the dinner, I drove in early. They had valet parking, so I tipped all the valets well and told them who was arriving and to treat them like kings. I gave them each an additional twenty dollars to park all the cars directly in front of the restaurant. Everything went well, and we even got a deal out of the dinner. I tipped the maître d' another hundred dollars after the dinner and gave the waiter a good 20 percent, as he worked flawlessly with the customers.

This all worked perfectly for my situation. Your situation could be very different. I know some CEOs who would view this kind of pompousness as too extravagant. You need to adapt to the situation and work your creativity.

Dinners and other entertainment opportunities require the same level of internal planning as presentations in an office. Conduct a conference call or meeting with all the people from your company who will be there to set the strategy and expectations for the outcome of the event. If someone can't get on the call, contact him or her individually and rehearse what he or she is supposed to do and say. Everyone should be on the same page. This is a very fundamental part of being a good salesperson: preparing for any contact between your company and your customer.

That said, entertaining should be fun. Do it as frequently as you can. Your customers will appreciate it, and don't be surprised to find yourself with stronger relationships than your competition.

CHAPTER TEN

CHARACTER

Do You Have an Abundant Reservoir of Confidence?

Many of us are insecure. Others are not. Are you confident you are doing a good job? Before you go out into the world every day, do you reflect on how good you are? Or do you think about what could have been?

Right after you get up every morning, think about how good you really are. Your confidence in yourself is key to how successful you will be. If you can't muster confidence in yourself, you will always doubt how much you can achieve. If that's the way you feel, you will be mediocre at best. Good salespeople have a strong perception of their ability to reach lofty goals. If you don't have that, sales may not be the career for you. Don't worry—many beginners stumble around for a while, but after some successes realize they're very good at what they do. If you can get there, others will notice.

You are the best, and you should think of yourself that way. What you do is the right thing, and you make good choices. Think like that and not much will bother you. In sales, you will be bombarded with distractions. Some of them will challenge your belief structure. A good salesperson will deflect distractions that can erode self-confidence. The way you do that is to believe in yourself. You are good at what you do in all aspects of life. Even when you fail at something, you will see some good in it.

There will be times you will fail. Failure is a good thing. Learn from it. Pick yourself up and reenergize yourself. Look at it as an opportunity. Don't let it bring you down. Even if you get fired from your job, it doesn't matter. Be smart. Figure out a plan. You are good; everyone is. It's all in the attitude. If you are convinced you are good and doing the right thing, there's no reason to doubt yourself, is there? Just move on and get over it.

Read inspirational books. Go to seminars. Strive to make yourself better every day. Find the true you inside and make it a solid foundation of unshakeable confidence. You can do it. If you can find this reservoir of abundant confidence in yourself, you will become a fantastic salesperson and look at every new day as an adventure.

Something that will help you feel better about yourself is people trusting you with confidential information. If people do this with you, consider it a compliment to your character. People who share delicate information with you are telling you they trust you and are possibly asking you (indirectly) for advice. This doesn't happen because you announce to everyone you are receptive to personal information. It is through what you do and how people perceive you as a leader and confidant.

Being Discreet

There's not much that's more important for a salesperson than being discreet with personal information. I can't tell you how many people I know who I can't trust with private information because they have a tendency to blab. There is a sense of betrayal when someone takes your private information and treats it casually. Some people really don't know how to treat personal information. Others do. You need to be able to tell one from the other. This applies to people in your private and business life.

Most people of solid character will respect your confidential information. You should respect theirs in return. Over your career, you will notice that people who can't be trusted with confidential information won't go very far. They get a reputation for being indiscreet. Indiscretion is the same as being untrustworthy. Your management should be very aware of who and who isn't discreet on a team. You will see that the indiscreet people are treated differently and usually overlooked for promotion. You absolutely need to understand that if people share private information with you, there is an expectation that you aren't going to betray them by sharing it with others. If you can't understand how important this topic is, I feel sorry for you.

During your career, your discretion will be tested to its limits. Eventually, some high-level businessperson will share with you a piece of information that could make the nightly news. When you hear it, you won't believe you are being trusted with this information. After you hear it, you may feel like you absolutely have to tell someone. The information could have come from one of your customers. This person could be a high-level senior manager. You know that if one of the senior managers at your company hears this information, it will be very strategic. Also, you will look very, very good to your management for having access to the deepest depths of your customer's most private information.

Here's where your dilemma begins. Do you share the information and risk being exposed as indiscreet? That will undoubtedly shut you down at your customer and make your life miserable there. Can you trust that your manager will care enough not to expose it? These are the stakes of high-level strategic sales. If you aren't sure the information will be used appropriately, consider not telling anyone about it. But if you are good at selling, you should know the limitations of the management of your company. Some of them you will be able to trust and others will be untrustworthy and would readily sacrifice you for their personal gain. Make sure you know the difference.

If you are a discreet person, you have learned that people need to grow, and to do that they sometimes have to ask for advice about a situation that is very personal and shouldn't be exposed publically. Distinguishing between what is confidential and not to be shared and what can be takes some intelligence. You don't have to be a genius to do this. It takes some learning and following what your gut tells you. Figuring this out is one way you get smarter.

Being Smart

Go back in time to when you were in school. Think about the smartest kids in your class. What was it about them that made you think they were so smart? Did you notice how they asked questions? How they figured out answers? How they took tests? What I noticed and admired was how they attacked a problem. Instead of asking a series of questions that got them the answer, they first tried to figure it out themselves. Only after tackling the problem from many angles did they ask questions, and those questions were well thought out.

I noticed in college, professors liked the students who were more independent and liked exploring and solving problems. Some students didn't think about their questions and just blurted them out. They didn't want to think of how to solve the problem or use creativity in finding the answer. Many college-level courses are taught assuming that most of the work to find the answer is left as an exercise for the student. This is done for a reason. Professors want you to try to solve the problem and exhaust all possible methods. It is a skill. Some people do it naturally and others learn it.

Exceptional students look at a problem differently than others. They answer most of the questions themselves. This is how they learn and become smarter. In doing this, they build the skills to tackle problems efficiently. This is how salespeople get smarter too. You think hard about solving problems and don't stop when you get your first solution. You keep going, wondering if that is the best one or there's another way to look at it. It's the process of solving a problem. Patience and tenacity are how you become smart.

In sales, like in class, you have competition all around you. Exceeding your quota is like getting an A. Beating the competition is what it's all about. Looking at the way you solve problems and improving on it gives you a powerful edge. Developing your problem-solving skills helps you work smarter and get smarter. Evaluating how you solve problems and trying new methods helps you get smarter. Analyzing how people you admire solve problems can give you insight into better methods. Reading motivational books and studying them on the web are other ways to glean key information.

Don't be lazy and think you're smart. There is always someone smarter than you, but that doesn't mean you can't beat that person to an order. It's the method of how you go about your business. Be better at it. Be smarter. Thinking you are smart means you are comparing yourself to people around you. What if they are all dumb? It only means you are less dumb. Be paranoid and always think you have to keep growing and sharpening the way you attack problems. If you stand still, you are just mediocre. Clean it up and always ask yourself when you come to a solution, "Is there a better way to do it?"

Being smarter doesn't always get you to the finish line. It takes work. Lots of work. When tackling a sales problem, there are times when the road to winning seems way too long. It is then that doubt creeps into your thoughts. Doubt can deceive you into giving up before you get to your goal. A good salesperson knows the warning signs of doubt and can overcome those feelings that lead to quitting. Sometimes just staying in the game longer than everyone else makes you a winner. This is true when dealing with a prospect who keeps putting you off. If you keep trying over and over, you can wear down the strongest resistance.

Persistence

Persistence is a strong characteristic for a salesperson. It allows you to keep going even when things don't look good. I think it's obvious that if you are rejected, you need to look beyond it and keep coming back until you win or get told to go away. If you can't do this, don't go into sales.

You have to keep trying until the customer tells you to stop. I have been told many times that my persistence is what won the deal. Others have told me they wished the salespeople at their company were like me. Customers value salespeople who keep trying. Persistence will win over time. Sometimes it takes a long time. But this is one trait you have to get good at. Push hard, and keep pushing. If you can do that, you are going to win. It's all about who can last the longest and wear people down. No matter what customers say about very persistent salespeople, they will be admired for keeping at it.

Being persistent doesn't mean everyone you encounter has to be worn down. Choosing which opportunity to push hard on takes some common sense. When you couple being smart with persistence, knowing what a good decision looks like helps you to be efficient at what you do. Not everyone gets this.

Good Judgment and Common Sense

Common sense is the knack of seeing things as they are, and doing things as they ought to be done.—C. E. Stowe, biblical scholar and early advocate for the development of public schools

Common sense is the collection of prejudices acquired by age eighteen.—Albert Einstein, physicist and one of the greatest minds of the twentieth century

Good judgment comes from experience, and experience—well,
that comes from poor judgment.—Cousin Woodman

Rule #1: Use your good judgment in all situations.

There will be no additional rules.—Nordstrom Employee Manual

In principle, this is a very simple concept to understand but very difficult for some people to execute. Why is that? Much of the reason people can't make good decisions or lack judgment is that they don't have the skill set or they don't want to face looking at potential issues. Of the people aware of some problem, the ones who know they could improve are willing to do something about it. Others feel they can't do anything about it or are unconsciously unaware of their limitations. Consciously and unconsciously, you are measured by your ability to make good decisions. If you can demonstrate strength in these areas, you'll be perceived as a leader, and you will carry credibility with you. Common sense and judgment are talents that have to do with being presented with a choice and making the right decision.

How do you improve your ability to make good decisions? You gut can tell you the right thing to do. Your peers and friends can do it. For many people, a difficult situation can be resolved by talking about it. The more you talk, the better the chance a solution will precipitate and present itself to you. We all have a method of contemplation that works best for us. Do you know yours? Some people get ideas in the shower, others while they exercise. When do your ideas arrive? These vehicles for resolving issues clear away the confusing chaff so you can make a good choice. Mastering your ability to quickly make good choices hones your ability to have common sense about decisions. Look around you. I bet there are people you have respect for who demonstrate strong common sense. Associate with them. Learn how they think.

Common sense is learned, but we all have the ability to do it. Like riding a bike, once we get the hang of it, it becomes second nature. The more people you interact with who have strong common sense, the better you will become. All it takes is you learning how to cut through all the crap and see what makes sense. Sometimes it's easy, sometimes it's very difficult. You will make mistakes, and that is good. Learn from them. As long as you're open to growing, you will be making good choices in no time.

Nothing can be further from good judgment than getting in an argument where you lose control or completely miss the point. Arguing and disagreement are all part of a normal interaction when differing opinions collide. Why people argue can be complicated. Sometimes, it's not in anybody's interest to pursue a discussion where the cost may be far greater than any real benefit. Using common sense when arguing is a discipline that every salesperson has to master.

How to Disagree and Argue

When you're arguing with a fool, make sure he isn't doing the same thing.—Old proverb

Discourse with conflicting opinions can be a very healthy thing. It's good to be challenged, as long as it's done with respect and courtesy. If you work with a team of people, you might argue about things. You have to admit, sometimes people are more right than you. In sales, we are most concerned about results, not how good we look or how a path to a goal is achieved. We might discover a better idea from someone else, and sometimes that involves an argument over how to do something. If we can suppress our ego, we might find a better solution to a problem. Arguing can do that.

You might not argue much or you might argue a lot. It all depends on the corporate culture, the kind of person you are, and how much pressure you are under. Arguing isn't a bad thing in and of itself. In fact, it can quickly resolve issues that have been festering. When it becomes personal is when it can get destructive. Some companies encourage people to challenge ideas. They want a low level of steady conflict to always be working among their employees. Things get sorted out faster and bad ideas don't live as long.

Arguments can get testy. That isn't a good thing, but sometimes it's unavoidable, especially if the other person is a hothead. If you find yourself suddenly in an argument with someone and you are in public or have other employees around you, go to a private room where (potentially) louder voices won't distract others. Arguing in public is rude. Also, if the company leadership has heated arguments in front of the employees, it can be very demoralizing and people will lose respect. If the individual you are arguing with refuses to talk privately, reply that you won't discuss anything until you do. This is very important.

Arguing can get out of control, and it is partly your job to keep it constructive. Manage your anger and keep it from making you emotional. You'll never win or gain anything from getting emotional. People don't like hotheads, and in sales, that's a really bad rap to carry around with you. Don't let it get personal either. Though you may be cool, don't insult the person. That is called baiting, and its only purpose is to hurt and foster anger. If the other person is getting emotional, he or she may not respond to reason very well and will just be using it as an excuse to pound on you.

Sometimes people argue because they are upset with themselves. They may be out of touch and having some kind of conflict that has them edgy and ripe to give it a go. Try to keep the argument on the subject and to the point. Focus on coming to a final decision. If you are being rational and the other person is not, consider backing out of the argument. If you want to cool it down, stop talking. Keep your voice very calm but not too calm. Try to point out that you would like the other person to tone it down. If he or she continues there may be no way for you to make headway. Don't walk away unless there is nothing else you can do. Walking away from an argument is immature and signifies an inability to communicate. Only do this as a last resort.

In some cases, you may find yourself moderating a disagreement. You will have two sides presenting their case to each other. The job of the moderator will be to not take sides and to make sure both sides get a chance to present their case. The moderator steers the discussion, keeps track of time, and hopefully can bring it all to a graceful close. Moderators can get baited to join one side or the other, but you have to resist that. As soon as you take a side, you're no longer impartial. This pretty much defeats the whole point of having a moderator.

There will be times when you suddenly find yourself moderating a disagreement between a customer and one of your people. This can happen when you bring a factory person to visit your customer, and during the meeting someone says something inappropriate. Your factory person is insulted or thinks the customer has no idea what he or she is talking about. Tempers can flare, and the dialogue gets intense. Your job is to take a neutral position and cool things down as fast as possible before too much damage is done. You can avoid these situations by doing a good job setting the expectation with your factory people before you bring them to the meeting. But if a factory person has a reputation for being a hothead or behaving inappropriately in meetings with customers, it might not be a good idea to bring that individual anywhere with you.

When the argument is over, win or lose, you have to be able to get over it and move on with your life. If you resent the other person for arguing better than you, you won't get very far. Resentment is a bad thing for you to bring to work every day. Just like when you argue with a friend, when you're done and you're still mad, you have to realize that either you get over it and forgive the other person (in your head) or never see him or her again. You can't live in some middle world after an argument. This is hard for some people to live with. In your mind, you have to tell yourself that when it's done, you live with the decision and move on.

Arguments are a way to learn about yourself and your limitations. They are opportunities to grow and become a better person. When you are witness to other people arguing, take mental notes on how they make their case. If you find someone who is very good at arguing, figure out how he or she does it so well. I am not saying to do this so you win every argument. It is important because many people don't know how to argue. This makes it frustrating when you argue with people who present their case in a confused, emotional way. You end up trying to keep them on track while you present your own case. If you can make your case in an objective way, you have a better chance at winning. Also, senior management will respect a person who can argue without getting sidetracked or presenting points in a confused way.

Like fire, arguing can be good or terribly destructive. Be mature and control yourself with other people. Disagreement can lead to a new idea or understanding. Just don't cross the line and become irritated and belligerent. You are better than that, right?

When in a discussion, whether a disagreement or just plain conversation, sometimes we talk more than is necessary. While relating information to customer or factory person, never give out more than you have to. Exposing more information than necessary risks creating a distracting situation that derails the purpose of the conversation. Talking too much is one way a salesperson exposes too much information. Most salespeople like to talk and are very engaging. Some talk incessantly without clearly understanding where the conversation is taking the receiving party. When you talk, you should know what you will say before you say it—nothing more and nothing less.

Talking Too Much

When you are on the phone with someone who wants to get off the phone with you, get off right away. Don't keep on talking even if you think it's important. If the other person wants to get off, you can be sure what you are talking about is not important to that person. He or she may tell you in a subtle way, but you have the keen sense of perception, right? Don't ignore it. This is very important. Nothing is more irritating than telling people you have to go and they keep on talking. Holding someone on the line can be very bad for you, as it tells that person's unconscious self you think you're more important. If people have the perception you talk too much on the phone, it may keep them from calling you another time because you're too much trouble to talk to. I had a manager who used to hang up on subordinates if they didn't get it. I know several salespeople who I avoid calling unless I have to because a phone call with them is at least twenty minutes of chat.

By the way, if you fall into the too-chatty category, you might be doing this when you're face-to-face too. The same rule holds true when you are with someone in person. Be sensitive to cues that people want to go. There can be direct or indirect cues. Body language may be closing their notebook as you're talking or getting up to leave. They may stop giving you active listening feedback, or they may just say, "Hey, I have to go." Don't think keeping them hostage is a good thing for you. Whatever you're talking about is finished if they indicate they want to end the meeting. If you continue to hold them in the meeting, you'll only do yourself a disservice. They won't want to see you again if they can avoid it.

This can be very destructive to your career if you do this with senior managers. It's probably a safe bet a senior manager will write you off as a chatterbox if you talk too much on the phone or in person. Senior managers don't suffer people with diarrhea-mouth, and if they categorize you as such, getting back on the good list is just about impossible. Don't blow it. Many people who talk too much about themselves are not good listeners and usually get limited time with people. If you think you have this problem, fix it. Have a brief conversation, get to the point, and hang up or leave. If you're buddies with someone and chat with that person, okay, do it. If the person chats back, you can continue. But if you're the one putting all the energy into the conversation, there is a problem. You'd be amazed how much people appreciate brevity.

This principle is so easy to follow, yet many people just don't get it. A windbag will eventually earn a reputation, making it more difficult to do business. Most of these people get weeded out anyway. Don't let this happen to you. If you are engaged in conversation with someone, are you paying attention to "I have to go" cues? As soon as you see one, find a way to quickly wind down your conversation and end it. If you need to ask for something, do it quickly and let the person go. Being sensitive to other people's needs is a sign of solid character.

Seeing those cues is much harder when you are on the phone rather than in person. (Remember 67 percent of all communication is nonverbal.) The more you talk with people, the more tuned you will be in noticing subtle cues that the conversation is over. Always be aware that what you want to do may not be what the person you are talking to wants. The more adept you are at listening perceptively and ending a conversation, the better off you'll be as a salesperson.

When talking, asking questions is one way we learn. Some people are excessively sensitive to what other people think of them. As a confident salesperson, you shouldn't worry about what other people think of you because you know what you are doing is right and your job performance demonstrates that. Comparing yourself to other people and doubting yourself too much leads to insecurity. When people are insecure, they hold themselves back. Insecure people are deathly afraid of asking questions. They are very worried it will expose some weakness that will make them look stupid.

Don't Ever Be Embarrassed to Ask Questions

It is better to remain silent and be thought a fool, than open one's mouth and remove all doubt.—Mark Twain (Samuel Clemens), humorist and author

When you ask a question, you want an answer so you can learn something. But the process of asking a question also exposes your ignorance in that subject. What people fear is that everyone who is in earshot of the question already knows the answer, and it's so obvious even someone who's stupid knows. By asking the question, you publicly expose your lack of intelligence. This can be very humiliating. At least that is the fear. Most times, that perception is unrealistic and based on a lack of confidence.

Your questions are important. Holding back will hamper your ability to understand a topic and learn something. One of the primary reasons people hold back a question is worry over how others will judge the quality of the question. People get scared over what people think of them. People are very worried about how they look to others. But there can be a large cost to not asking, which is why when people really want to ask a question, they get very nervous.

Worrying about how you look to other people all the time means that you are insecure and have a problem that needs to be fixed. You should have enough confidence in yourself to not care what other people think and understand that getting an answer is more important. People will end up respecting you more for having the guts to ask a question, especially when they are too scared to ask themselves.

Of course, there are times when it is inappropriate to ask questions. Most of the time, though, we inhibit ourselves because of the fear of looking stupid. Why do you care what other people think? In sales, performance is how you are judged, not the type of questions you ask. In meetings with customers, you are expected to ask "dumb" questions to get the customer to talk about an issue that needs clarification.

I know some sales guys who ask the dumbest questions, but they are great salespeople and are respected for that, not the questions. Also, simple questions can be asked by salespeople who are dumb like a fox. Life is too important to let things slip because of inhibitions. Have you ever regretted it when you withheld asking a question and someone else asked it instead?

In a public setting, the motivations of people asking questions are complex. Judging someone by the quality of a question is the foolish act here, because you have no idea how this person is learning or why he or she is asking the question. Assuming a question is dumb could mean you're the one having a problem understanding the complexities of the situation you are in.

I have been in sales meetings when an associate asked what I thought were the dumbest questions I had ever heard come out of the mouth of a salesperson. All during the meeting, I was cringing as each question came out, thinking the customer would write us off as loonies. After the meeting was over, I noticed the customer's attitude and body language was great. No evidence of damage. As we walked to the car, I asked the sales guy why he was asking those questions. He explained a detailed strategy he had worked out beforehand to get a specific piece of information from the customer. He did that to get the customer to not feel threatened. It was obvious who the dummy was. Me. His strategy was so sublime it went right by the customer and me. He got his information and nobody even knew what happened. You can't assume you know why a question is being asked. Because of that, you can't judge quality of questions asked in public.

Try not to ask questions you already know the answer to unless you have a strategy behind it. People can unconsciously detect you already know the answer, which could cause them to wonder if you have some agenda, creating a lack of trust. Another reason people ask questions they already know the answer to is that they are insecure and want to look smart in front of people. This also can be perceived by others, so don't do it.

Composing a good question is a learned skill. The more questions you ask, the better you get at it. So if you don't keep asking questions, you'll never be good at it. If you fear asking questions or feel regret for not asking when you had the chance to, try to work on that. Listen carefully to how other people ask questions. That can help you pick up things you may not have realized. Get more experience at it. Really try to ask more questions. Ask a close friend or associate for advice. Don't be afraid. You have to just break out and start asking. You may flub up, but everyone does, so don't sweat it. I would bet that 99 percent of the questions you ask are just fine. So don't be afraid to ask questions, and remember, many people will admire you for having the guts to bring up the question they were too scared to ask.

Speaking of asking the right question, you can look at this from the other side as well, and learn how to answer a question without looking like an idiot. While this may seem a simple task, many people just can't answer a question without giving a long-winded answer. They get so sidetracked by their incessant rambling that they forget what the original question was.

Can You Answer a Question?

When you work up the courage to ask a question, the last thing you want is a long, drawn-out, rambling diatribe that has little if anything to do with answering your query. Some people are just incapable of answering a question directly because they lack the skills to see their way clearly to an answer. This is a complex problem, and it can involve personality issues. Even some salespeople find answering questions succinctly hard to do. I am amazed at the number of people who cannot come up with simple answers, or who write up reports that are needlessly complex and rambling. If someone asks you a question, he or she expects an answer, not a tirade that careens around the answer like a car driven by a drunk driver. This is very frustrating. Some people can't stand it. If you have a customer or manager who doesn't have much patience, you could be in a position to lose your credibility and be written off as someone to avoid.

A long time ago, I built a house. I was the primary contractor—a much bigger job than I expected. I was responsible for hiring subcontractors and managing their activities, including paying them. I was working at my regular job at the time, so I couldn't be at the site all the time. I did the best I could maintaining daily contact by phone with the subcontractors. (It turns out this was not a good thing to do, as it distracted me from my work.) Finally, the house was finished and I moved in. About three months later, I got a bill in the mail from a trucking company I had never heard of. The bill was for over $3,000 for hauling expenses incurred in work done on my property. Since I had never heard of this company, I refused to pay the bill, and they took me to small claims court. It is here I learned a very important lesson.

While I was waiting for my case to be called before the judge, I watched and listened to all the people's cases that came before me. I noticed when these people were called up to plead and defend their case against each other, they spent a lot of time talking and not really getting to the point. They were more interested in hearing themselves talk or telling the judge how bad the other person was, which wasn't really what he wanted to hear. All the judge wanted to hear was the facts. Many of the people who went before the judge had a lot of trouble making their case. The judge would frequently become agitated with plaintiffs and defendants who deviated from the subject or didn't answer questions directly. In fact, I noticed that if you rambled on too much, the judge might even give favor to the other person even though that side's case might be weaker. Also, the plaintiff and defendant would interrupt each other, and that would make the judge mad too.

When on the rare occasion someone would answer the judge's question directly, he seemed to relax and listen more closely. His body language was definitely telegraphing his feelings and the indication was very clear to me: be concise and to the point with this guy. I could do that.

When my case got called, I went up to the bench with the plaintiff. The judge asked the plaintiff what the problem was. She went on and on about how good their company was and how they do great work for people. The judge had to keep asking her to answer the question. She seemed to not hear the judge and insisted on talking endlessly about the plight of her company. She even became irritated with the judge for stopping her all the time. When she finished, the judge turned to me and asked me for my side of the story. I simply said, "Your honor, I had no verbal or written agreement with these people." He turned to her and asked her if that was true. She became flustered and started saying again what a good a company they were. The judge interrupted her, asking again if this was true. She finally said yes, and then admitted that another contractor had told them to do the work at my house without my consent. The judge said she needed to be paid by the other contractor and closed the case.

In meetings, some people want to look intelligent. This can lead to talking too much and not answering questions directly. They think extensively elaborating after getting a question makes them look smart. This can be unconscious behavior, so they don't even know they're doing it. This behavior can keep you from building a relationship with customers if they think you can't answer their questions.

Another problem in not answering questions directly is trust. If you always make it difficult to get an answer from you, this can elicit an unconscious inclination to not trust you. They believe you are avoiding answering their question for some reason. This is another reason to answer questions directly.

Another situation to be wary of is when you bring a factory person to visit a customer. It's amazing how many account calls I've been on where I've brought along people from my company and they can't answer a question directly. The factory person begins to answer it and then goes on a tangent he or she finds Interesting, or he or she may feel the customer should hear something else instead. The factory person needs to give the answer some good spin. There could be a good reason for this, because he or she thinks what the customer needs to hear is not what they asked directly. But customers are smarter than you think, always. Answer their questions first; then make your point second. Nothing can make you or your company lose credibility faster than frustrating a customer. Many times I've needed to interrupt a factory person at the height of his or her exuberance to note that he or she still needed to answer the customer's question. Sometimes the factory person doesn't take it very well. If an answer follows, then all is fine. If not, the factory person may begin to argue with you in front of the customer. Perhaps this kind of person shouldn't be in front of customers? You decide.

Answering questions directly without spin can help your credibility and create long-lasting consultive relationships. There are other ways to create an air of credibility for yourself. One is coupling your words to your actions. While saying what you do and doing what you say may seem simple, unconscious forces and other personality traits and desires can completely separate your actions and words.

Actions Speak Louder Than Words

Nothing demonstrates intent better than action. No matter what someone tells you, what that person actually does demonstrates clear intention. While this may seem rather simple, the interpretation can be cloudy. Because of unconscious or factors like denial, you or others may or may not see the action as a deliberate and clear communication of exactly what that person's intentions are.

When the unconscious person is driving the action, the conscious person is pretty much unaware of what's going on. The conscious person may say one thing, but the actions indicate another. Actions broadcast intent, and when the unconscious is in control, you can clearly read, by the actions, what is going on in the unconscious mind. This can be helpful in trying to read a very complex-behaving customer. People who are clever manipulators can make it look like they are unconsciously acting out. But salespeople can pretty much count on actions to communicate true intention despite what is said.

Talk is cheap, and there's a reason why. People want to believe what they're being told is true. If we as a society always stated untruths or misleading information, it would be difficult for anything to get done. Fortunately, most conversations have a foundation of truth or accuracy. But when personalities get involved, the message can get distorted. This can happen intentionally or unintentionally. Our unconscious and conscious selves are complicated entities. They motivate us to persuade or even manipulate behavior for many reasons. Some people say one thing and do another without even being conscious of it. People who are disconnected from their unconscious are literally behaving one way and talking about something completely different. Sometimes it is done consciously with the intent to throw you off track.

People can fall into the trap of wanting to believe what is said so strongly, they ignore the signals that the actions are in conflict with it. This happens when both people are engaged in a sort of codependence. You tell me what you wish, and I'll pretend it's true even though you don't deliver.

As a salesperson, you have to be perceptive. Actions are a form of communication, and they indicate exactly what is on a person's mind. How a person behaves tells you exactly what he or she *really* wants to do. We all experience this in life. To be good at what you do, you need to step back and objectively ask yourself if the behavior matches the talk. If you are close to someone, this may be hard to do. At some point, you have to say if it walks like a duck, quacks like a duck, and looks like a duck, it must be a duck.

There will be situations where you can't believe a person is actually behaving contrary to what he or she told you. It can be so stunning it shakes your belief structure. This could happen with your best customer or even your manager. One day, it could suddenly strike you that everything you believed about this person was wrong. This is why you have to trust in only actions as the real truth.

If you are a careful observer of behavior, you can figure many situations out that others may not. When commitments are made in business is when the real story comes out. Watching for the follow-up and how it is completed will tell you much about your relationship. Being perceptive about this will help you be an effective salesperson who doesn't get taken advantage of.

A BASIC LIST OF GOOD ADVICE

- Take responsibility for your behavior.
- In searching for a career, do something you really like, and the money will follow.
- If you stop making yourself better, you stop growing.
- Not everybody you know will like you making yourself better.
- Everyone has unique strengths—know what yours are.
- Be a good listener.
- Know body language.
- Always be discreet—especially if you are told something in confidence.
- When you are talking with someone and he or she has to go, let him or her, quickly.
- Don't talk about yourself.
- It's not about you all the time.
- Read as much as you can.
- There is no substitute for experience.
- If it seems stupid, it probably is.
- If something seemed too easy, you could be missing something.
- Follow your gut—it doesn't lie.
- Know when you've gotten a good kick in the pants and grow from it.
- If you can't teach it, you don't know it.
- Teaching it will help you learn it.
- If you have an idea you really think is unique and powerful, make it a reality. Will you fight for it? Because if you don't, someone else will do it.
- If there is something great to invent, eventually someone will invent it. It's just a matter of who is first.
- If you think it can't be done, you will never be the one who does it.
- How often do you hear, "Hey, I thought of that years ago!" This is the difference between those who dream and those who make dreams reality.

- Of all the people who have wonderful ideas and dreams, less than 5 percent make them happen. What is holding you back?
- For some reason, many organizations fall victim to the Catch-22 syndrome. They get to a size where the organization takes on a life and direction of its own, which has nothing to do with the original mission.
- If you need to get something done, don't hesitate.
- Don't try to answer questions you don't know the answer to.
- Say you don't know when you don't.
- Don't ask questions you can answer yourself.
- If you think you know all the answers, you are a fool.
- Whenever you speak with someone, try to understand how he or she feels about what you're saying.
- There is always someone who does things better than you.
- There is always someone who does things worse than you.
- Know when you need help and don't be ashamed to ask for it.
- Develop friends, family, and mentors. Cherish them.
- If you have a family, love them always.
- Keep a good network fresh and vibrant.
- You have to take risks, but don't be stupid.
- Peer pressure is done by the insecure who are worried about what they are doing, with no regard to your well-being.
- People who intentionally make a person feel bad have deep problems and shouldn't be trusted.
- There is no good ending to the use of drugs.
- Begin with the end in sight.—Steven Covey
- Know your limits and push them.
- If you stay in your comfort zone without leaving it, you are a zombie.
- Fear is a good signal but also will limit you if you let it.
- If you commit to something, stay committed. Otherwise, why are you committing?
- Admit your mistakes. Making mistakes is how we learn.
- People who make fun of people who are bold enough to ask questions are too scared to ask themselves and are ashamed of themselves.
- If you are in a group and feel you should ask a question but are too embarrassed, know there are probably several others who want to ask the same question and feel the same way.
- Life isn't fair or unfair, it just is.
- Life is about choice.

- Don't be self-conscious about yourself. Other people probably feel the same way you do.
- If you don't like someone, that person probably doesn't like you either.
- If you like someone, that person probably likes you too.
- Always ask yourself, what would the other person do? But don't feel compelled to do it because he or she does.
- Don't care what others think about you. If you do, you will have no identity and hate yourself.
- If you hurt others, make amends. If others hurt you, forgive them and move on.
- Treat people as you would like to be treated.
- If you died today, what would be the eulogy said for you? Who would say it?
- Having money doesn't mean you're smart or good.
- People are smarter than you think.
- Managers know more than you think they do.
- People who work for you know more about what is going on than you think.
- Actions speak louder than words.
- Talk is cheap.
- Just because someone says something doesn't make it right or true.
- If you are successful, give back to society your gifts.
- Get yourself spiritually centered.
- Always question authority.
- Never believe everything you read.
- Everybody has an opinion.
- Don't criticize without offering a constructive solution.
- Try to be a good communicator.
- Learn to speak in public.
- Know what you know and know what you don't know.
- When asked a question, try to answer it clearly and simply. Don't ramble.
- Get to the point quickly.
- When writing e-mails or other documents, keep it short as possible. Always ask yourself if it could be shorter.
- Assume all e-mails/chat sessions that you send will be read by people you never intended to receive them at the worst possible time.

- Expressing overt anger and insulting people in e-mails makes you look like an idiot.
- Anything you send electronically—whether videos, pictures, e-mails, or other types of documents—will have a good chance of showing up at any time in the future at the most inconvenient time.
- When being told something, no matter who is telling you or what your relationship to that person is, remember there is always another side to the story.
- When making decisions, evaluate as much data as you can and get input from others, but always know that in the end, it is you who has to make the decision, so don't delay.
- Be aware of the contingencies of your behavior.—B. F. Skinner
- If you want to make yourself better, practice, practice, practice.
- Be true to your friends and yourself.
- If enough friends or family are telling you something about yourself, it is probably true.
- Pursue self-actualization, and if you don't know what that means, it doesn't mean you aren't self-actualized.
- Don't cheat.
- Be a person of good character.
- It's not always about you.
- Be courteous.
- Have good manners.
- Know etiquette.
- Be polite.
- Feel good about yourself and what you do.
- If you worry a lot and it bothers you, get help with it. If you worry a lot but overall it doesn't bother you, you're just that way.
- Asking for help is not a sign of weakness. On the contrary, it is a sign that you have the strength to make yourself better.
- Exercise.
- Get over it.
- Try to keep your boss happy. If you can't, leave your job.
- If you are unhappy in your job or relationship, it's better to try to resolve it as soon as possible. If you can't resolve it, you probably should leave.
- Look around you and enjoy the world you're living in. Your stay is shorter than you think.
- Have strong role models with good character.

- Be a leader. Remember, if you're not the lead dog, the scene never changes.
- What is important to you may not be important to others.
- What is important to others may not be important to you.
- How you perceive the world may be very different from the way other people do. That doesn't make it wrong.
- If you really believe in something, don't let it go easily. Fight for it.
- Be passionate about something you strongly believe in.
- Know when to fight battles and when to lose battles to win wars.
- Eventually you will be betrayed. Spend your time and energy getting over it. Look ahead rather than backward at getting revenge.
- Forgiveness is about releasing your negativity, feeling sorry for the other person, and moving on. It doesn't mean you have to repeat the situation again.
- Don't be an idiot. Make good decisions.
- Be ready to seize opportunity. Know it when it presents itself. Also, know you may be forced to give something up to get it.
- Compromise is not a bad word.
- In choosing and leaving jobs, you always have to do what is right for yourself first.
- When selling, you always have to sell yourself first.
- People who demean others are insecure and not to be trusted.
- Don't destroy other people's ideas. Recognize their ideas may be better than yours.
- People who don't know how to listen will never learn.
- People who think very highly of themselves will tell you so.
- People who lie to you think they're smarter than you—a strategic weakness.
- If you believe the world is screwing you, it is you who are screwing yourself.
- Life is what you make it.
- Nothing ventured, nothing gained.
- Time will heal all.